CONTENTS

Collins World Atlas, first published 1986 by
William Collins Sons & Co. Ltd., P.O. Box, Glasgow G4 0NB
Reprinted 1987

Collins World Atlas
© William Collins Sons & Co. Ltd. 1986
Maps © William Collins Sons & Co. Ltd. 1983, 1984,
1985, 1986 and © Collins-Longman Atlases 1969-1983,
1984, 1985 and 1986

Prepared and designed by Collins Cartographic under
the direction of Andrew M Currie, M.A., Managing
Editor.

Printed and bound in Scotland
by William Collins Sons & Co. Ltd.

ISBN 0 00 447 634 4

COLLINS

LONDON · GLASGOW · SYDNEY · AUCKLAND · TORONTO · JOHANNESBURG

Earth's Dimensions

Superficial area	510 066 000 km²
Land surface	148 326 000 km²
Water surface	361 740 000 km²
Equatorial circumference	40 075 km
Meridional circumference	40 007 km
Volume	$1 083 230 \times 10^6$ km³
Mass	5.976×10^{21} tonnes

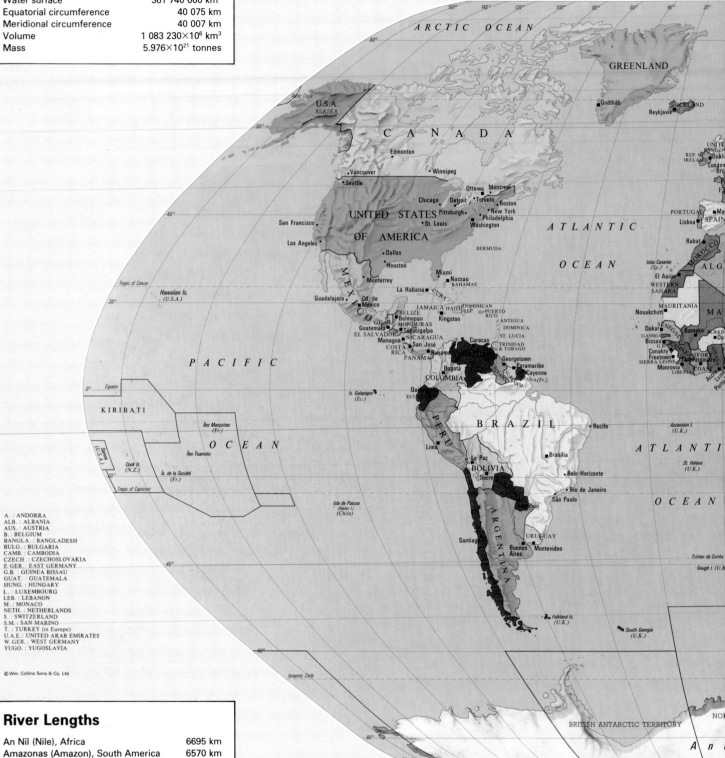

A. : ANDORRA
ALB. : ALBANIA
AUS. : AUSTRIA
B. : BELGIUM
BANGLA. : BANGLADESH
BULG. : BULGARIA
CAMB. : CAMBODIA
CZECH. : CZECHOSLOVAKIA
E. GER. : EAST GERMANY
G.B. : GUINEA BISSAU
GUAT. : GUATEMALA
HUNG. : HUNGARY
L. : LUXEMBOURG
LEB. : LEBANON
M. : MONACO
NETH. : NETHERLANDS
S. : SWITZERLAND
S.M. : SAN MARINO
T. : TURKEY (in Europe)
U.A.E. : UNITED ARAB EMIRATES
W. GER. : WEST GERMANY
YUGO. : YUGOSLAVIA

© Wm. Collins Sons & Co. Ltd.

River Lengths

An Nīl (Nile), Africa	6695 km
Amazonas (Amazon), South America	6570 km
Mississippi-Missouri, North America	6020 km
Chang Jiang (Yangtze), Asia	5471 km
Ob-Irtysh, Asia	5410 km
Huang He (Hwang Ho), Asia	4840 km
Zaïre, Africa	4630 km
Amur, Asia	4416 km
Lena, Asia	4269 km
Mackenzie, North America	4240 km
Niger, Africa	4183 km
Mekong, Asia	4180 km
Yenisey, Asia	4090 km
Murray-Darling, Oceania	3717 km
Volga, Europe	3688 km

Lake and Inland Sea Areas

Some areas are subject to seasonal variations

Caspian Sea, U.S.S.R./Iran	371 795 km²	Lake Tanganyika, East Africa	32 893 km²
Lake Superior, U.S.A./Canada	82 413 km²	Great Bear Lake, Canada	31 792 km²
Lake Victoria, East Africa	69 485 km²	Ozero Baykal (Lake Baikal), U.S.S.R.	30 510 km²
Aralskoye More (Aral Sea), U.S.S.R.	66 457 km²	Great Slave Lake, Canada	28 930 km²
Lake Huron, U.S.A./Canada	59 596 km²	Lake Malaŵi, Malaŵi/Mozambique	28 490 km²
Lake Michigan, U.S.A.	58 016 km²	Lake Erie, U.S.A./Canada	25 667 km²

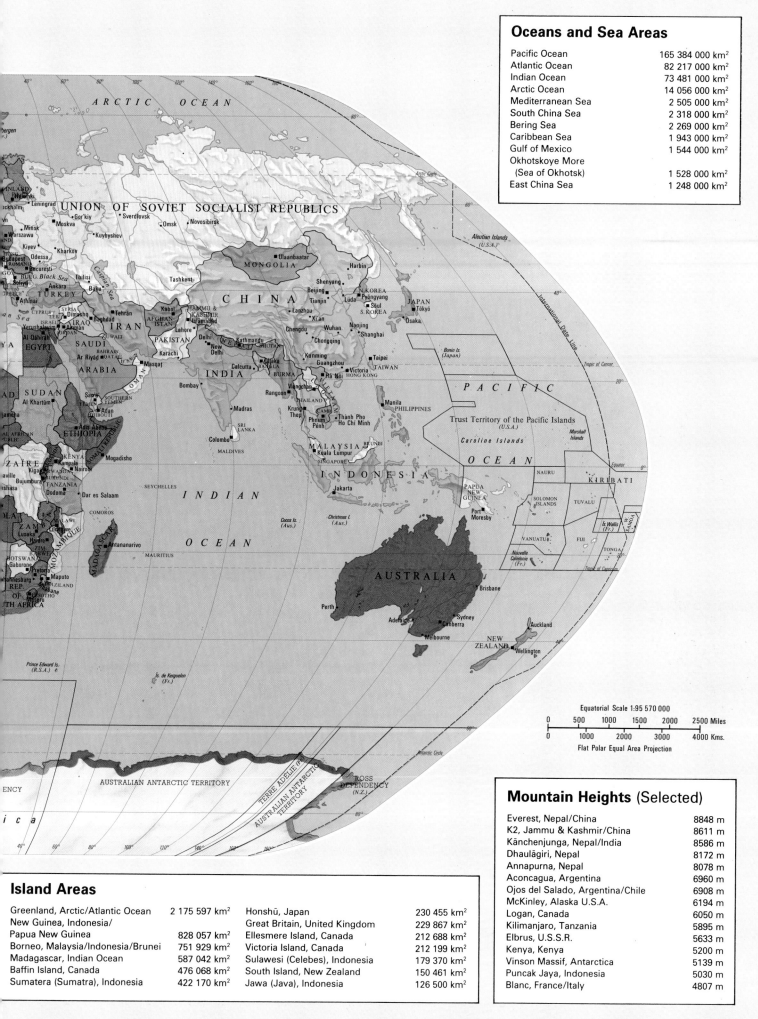

Oceans and Sea Areas

Pacific Ocean	165 384 000 km²
Atlantic Ocean	82 217 000 km²
Indian Ocean	73 481 000 km²
Arctic Ocean	14 056 000 km²
Mediterranean Sea	2 505 000 km²
South China Sea	2 318 000 km²
Bering Sea	2 269 000 km²
Caribbean Sea	1 943 000 km²
Gulf of Mexico	1 544 000 km²
Okhotskoye More (Sea of Okhotsk)	1 528 000 km²
East China Sea	1 248 000 km²

Mountain Heights (Selected)

Everest, Nepal/China	8848 m
K2, Jammu & Kashmir/China	8611 m
Kānchenjunga, Nepal/India	8586 m
Dhaulāgiri, Nepal	8172 m
Annapurna, Nepal	8078 m
Aconcagua, Argentina	6960 m
Ojos del Salado, Argentina/Chile	6908 m
McKinley, Alaska U.S.A.	6194 m
Logan, Canada	6050 m
Kilimanjaro, Tanzania	5895 m
Elbrus, U.S.S.R.	5633 m
Kenya, Kenya	5200 m
Vinson Massif, Antarctica	5139 m
Puncak Jaya, Indonesia	5030 m
Blanc, France/Italy	4807 m

Island Areas

Greenland, Arctic/Atlantic Ocean	2 175 597 km²	Honshū, Japan	230 455 km²
New Guinea, Indonesia/ Papua New Guinea	828 057 km²	Great Britain, United Kingdom	229 867 km²
Borneo, Malaysia/Indonesia/Brunei	751 929 km²	Ellesmere Island, Canada	212 688 km²
Madagascar, Indian Ocean	587 042 km²	Victoria Island, Canada	212 199 km²
Baffin Island, Canada	476 068 km²	Sulawesi (Celebes), Indonesia	179 370 km²
Sumatera (Sumatra), Indonesia	422 170 km²	South Island, New Zealand	150 461 km²
		Jawa (Java), Indonesia	126 500 km²

Equatorial Scale 1:95 570 000

0 500 1000 1500 2000 2500 Miles

0 1000 2000 3000 4000 Kms.

Flat Polar Equal Area Projection

ASIA

COUNTRY	POPULATION	AREA sq. km.	CAPITAL
AFGHANISTAN	16 786 000	647 497	Kābol (Kabul)
BAHRAIN	371 000	622	Al Manāmah
BANGLADESH	92 619 000	143 998	Dhaka
BHUTAN	1 355 000	47 000	Thimbu
BRUNEI	193 000	5 765	Bandar Seri Begawan
BURMA	33 640 000	676 552	Rangoon
CAMBODIA	6 981 000	181 035	Phnum Pénh (Phnom Penh)
CHINA	1 031 883 000	9 596 961	Beijing (Peking)
CYPRUS	645 000	9 251	Levkosia (Nicosia)
HONG KONG	5 233 000	1 045	
INDIA	711 664 000	3 287 590	New Delhi
INDONESIA	151 720 000	1 904 345	Jakarta
IRAN	40 240 000	1 648 000	Tehrān
IRAQ	13 997 000	434 924	Baghdād
ISRAEL	4 022 000	20 770	Yerushalayim (Jerusalem)
JAPAN	118 449 000	372 313	Tōkyō
JORDAN	2 779 000	97 740	'Ammān
KUWAIT	1 562 000	17 818	Al Kuwayt (Kuwait)
LAOS	3 902 000	236 800	Viangchan (Vientiane)
LEBANON	2 739 000	10 400	Bayrūt (Beirut)
MALAYSIA	14 765 000	329 749	Kuala Lumpur
MALDIVES	150 000	298	Malé
MONGOLIA	1 764 000	1 565 000	Ulaanbaatar (Ulan Bator)
NEPAL	15 020 000	140 797	Kathmandu
NORTH KOREA	18 747 000	120 538	Pyŏngyang
OMAN	948 000	212 457	Masqaṭ (Muscat)
PAKISTAN	87 125 000	803 943	Islāmābād
PHILIPPINES	50 740 000	300 000	Manila
QATAR	258 000	11 000	Ad Dawḥah (Doha)
SAUDI ARABIA	9 684 000	2 149 690	Ar Riyāḍ (Riyadh)
SINGAPORE	2 472 000	620	Singapore
SOUTH KOREA	39 331 000	98 484	Sŏul (Seoul)
SOUTHERN YEMEN	2 093 000	332 968	'Adan (Aden)
SRI LANKA	15 189 000	65 610	Colombo
SYRIA	9 660 000	185 180	Dimashq (Damascus)
TAIWAN	18 458 000	35 961	Taipei
THAILAND	48 450 000	514 000	Krung Thep (Bangkok)
TURKEY	46 312 000	780 576	Ankara
UNITED ARAB EMIRATES	1 043 000	83 600	
VIETNAM	56 205 000	333 000	Hà Nôi (Hanoi)
YEMEN	6 077 000	195 000	Şan 'ā'

AFRICA

COUNTRY	POPULATION	AREA sq. km.	CAPITAL
ALGERIA	20 293 000	2 381 741	Alger (Algiers)
ANGOLA	7 452 000	1 246 700	Luanda
BENIN	3 618 000	112 622	Porto-Novo
BOTSWANA	937 000	600 372	Gaborone
BURKINA	6 360 000	274 200	Ouagadougou
BURUNDI	4 460 000	27 834	Bujumbura
CAMEROON	8 865 000	475 442	Yaoundé
CAPE VERDE	329 000	4 033	Praia
CENTRAL AFRICAN REPUBLIC	2 456 000	622 984	Bangui
CHAD	4 643 000	1 284 000	N'Djamena
COMOROS	370 000	2 171	Moroni
CONGO	1 621 000	342 000	Brazzaville
DJIBOUTI	332 000	22 000	Djibouti
EGYPT	44 673 000	1 001 449	Al Qāhirah (Cairo)
EQUATORIAL GUINEA	381 000	28 051	Malabo
ETHIOPIA	32 775 000	1 221 900	Ādis Ābeba (Addis Ababa)
GABON	563 000	267 667	Libreville
GAMBIA	635 000	11 295	Banjul
GHANA	12 244 000	238 537	Accra
GUINEA	5 285 000	245 857	Conakry
GUINEA BISSAU	810 000	36 125	Bissau
IVORY COAST	8 568 000	322 462	Yamoussoukro
KENYA	17 864 000	582 646	Nairobi
LESOTHO	1 409 000	30 355	Maseru
LIBERIA	2 113 000	111 369	Monrovia
LIBYA	3 224 000	1 759 540	Ṭarābulus (Tripoli)
MADAGASCAR	9 233 000	587 041	Antananarivo
MALAŴI	6 267 000	118 484	Lilongwe
MALI	7 342 000	1 240 000	Bamako
MAURITANIA	1 730 000	1 030 700	Nouakchott
MAURITIUS	983 000	2 045	Port Louis
MOROCCO	21 667 000	446 550	Rabat
MOZAMBIQUE	12 615 000	783 000	Maputo
NAMIBIA	852 000	824 292	Windhoek
NIGER	5 686 000	1 267 000	Niamey
NIGERIA	82 392 000	923 768	Abuja
RWANDA	5 276 000	26 338	Kigali
SÃO TOMÉ AND PRÍNCIPE	86 000	964	São Tomé
SENEGAL	5 968 000	196 192	Dakar
SEYCHELLES	64 000	280	Victoria
SIERRA LEONE	3 672 000	71 740	Freetown
SOMALI REPUBLIC	5 116 000	637 657	Mogadisho
SOUTH AFRICA, REPUBLIC OF	31 008 000	1 221 037	Cape Town (Kaapstad)/ Pretoria
SUDAN	19 451 000	2 505 813	Al Kharṭūm (Khartoum)
SWAZILAND	585 000	17 363	Mbabane
TANZANIA	17 982 000	945 087	Dodoma
TOGO	2 747 000	56 000	Lomé
TUNISIA	6 672 000	163 610	Tunis
UGANDA	13 225 000	236 036	Kampala
WESTERN SAHARA	165 000	266 000	El Aaiún
ZAÏRE	26 377 000	2 345 409	Kinshasa
ZAMBIA	5 680 000	752 614	Lusaka
ZIMBABWE	7 540 000	390 580	Harare

CITY	COUNTRY	POPULATION
NEW YORK	United States	16 479 000
CIUDAD DE MÉXICO (MEXICO CITY)	Mexico	13 994 000
TŌKYŌ	Japan	11 695 000
SHANGHAI	China	10 820 000
LOS ANGELES	United States	10 607 000
PARIS	France	9 863 000
BUENOS AIRES	Argentina	8 436 000

CITY	COUNTRY	POPULATION
MOSKVA (MOSCOW)	U.S.S.R.	8 011 000
CHICAGO	United States	7 664 000
BEIJING (PEKING)	China	7 570 000
SÃO PAULO	Brazil	7 199 000
CALCUTTA	India	7 031 000
SŎUL (SEOUL)	South Korea	6 879 000
LONDON	United Kingdom	6 696 000
BOMBAY	India	5 971 000

NORTH AMERICA

COUNTRY	POPULATION	AREA sq. km.	CAPITAL
ANTIGUA AND BARBUDA	77 000	442	St John's
BAHAMAS	218 000	13 935	Nassau
BARBADOS	249 000	431	Bridgetown
BELIZE	145 000	22 965	Belmopan
BERMUDA	55 000	53	Hamilton
CANADA	24 625 000	9 976 139	Ottawa
COSTA RICA	2 324 000	50 700	San José
CUBA	9 782 000	114 524	La Habana (Havana)
DOMINICA	81 000	751	Roseau
DOMINICAN REPUBLIC	5 744 000	48 734	Santo Domingo
EL SALVADOR	4 999 000	21 041	San Salvador
GREENLAND	52 000	2 175 600	Godthâb/Nuuk
GRENADA	113 000	344	St George's
GUATEMALA	7 699 000	108 889	Guatemala
HAITI	5 201 000	27 750	Port-au-Prince
HONDURAS	3 955 000	112 088	Tegucigalpa
JAMAICA	2 253 000	10 991	Kingston
MEXICO	73 011 000	1 972 547	Ciudad de México (Mexico City)
NICARAGUA	2 918 000	130 000	Managua
PANAMA	2 043 000	75 650	Panamá
PUERTO RICO	3 242 000	8 897	San Juan
ST KITTS-NEVIS	44 000	266	Basseterre
ST LUCIA	122 000	616	Castries
ST VINCENT AND THE GRENADINES	124 000	389	Kingstown
UNITED STATES OF AMERICA	232 057 000	9 363 123	Washington

SOUTH AMERICA

COUNTRY	POPULATION	AREA sq. km.	CAPITAL
ARGENTINA	28 432 000	2 766 889	Buenos Aires
BOLIVIA	5 916 000	1 098 581	La Paz/Sucre
BRAZIL	126 806 000	8 511 965	Brasilia
CHILE	11 617 000	756 945	Santiago
COLOMBIA	28 776 000	1 138 914	Bogotá
ECUADOR	8 945 000	283 561	Quito
FALKLAND ISLANDS	2 000	12 173	Stanley
GUIANA	73 000	91 000	Cayenne
GUYANA	793 000	214 969	Georgetown
PARAGUAY	3 026 000	406 752	Asunción
PERU	18 790 000	1 285 216	Lima
SURINAM	352 000	163 265	Paramaribo
TRINIDAD AND TOBAGO	1 060 000	5 128	Port of Spain
URUGUAY	2 947 000	177 508	Montevideo
VENEZUELA	14 714 000	912 050	Caracas

EUROPE

COUNTRY	POPULATION	AREA sq. km.	CAPITAL
ALBANIA	2 858 000	28 748	Tiranë
ANDORRA	40 000	453	Andorra
AUSTRIA	7 571 000	83 849	Wien (Vienna)
BELGIUM	9 845 000	30 513	Bruxelles/ Brussel (Brussels)
BULGARIA	9 107 000	110 912	Sofiya (Sofia)
CZECHOSLOVAKIA	15 400 000	127 869	Praha (Prague)
DENMARK	5 119 000	43 069	Köbenhavn (Copenhagen)
EAST GERMANY	16 864 000	108 178	East Berlin
FINLAND	4 835 000	337 009	Helsinki
FRANCE	54 221 000	547 026	Paris
GREECE	9 793 000	131 944	Athinai (Athens)
HUNGARY	10 696 000	93 030	Budapest
ICELAND	236 000	103 000	Reykjavik
IRELAND, REPUBLIC OF	3 483 000	70 023	Dublin
ITALY	56 355 000	301 225	Roma (Rome)
LIECHTENSTEIN	26 000	157	Vaduz
LUXEMBOURG	366 000	2 586	Luxembourg
MALTA	360 000	316	Valletta
MONACO	27 000	1.5	Monaco
NETHERLANDS	14 342 000	40 844	Amsterdam
NORWAY	4 123 000	324 219	Oslo
POLAND	36 748 000	312 677	Warszawa (Warsaw)
PORTUGAL	10 056 000	92 082	Lisboa (Lisbon)
ROMANIA	22 638 000	237 500	Bucureşti (Bucharest)
SAN MARINO	21 000	61	San Marino
SPAIN	37 935 000	504 782	Madrid
SWEDEN	8 327 000	449 964	Stockholm
SWITZERLAND	6 384 000	41 288	Bern (Berne)
U.S.S.R.	269 994 000	22 402 200	Moskva (Moscow)
UNITED KINGDOM	56 459 000	244 046	London
WEST GERMANY	61 546 000	248 577	Bonn
YUGOSLAVIA	22 795 000	255 804	Beograd (Belgrade)

OCEANIA

COUNTRY	POPULATION	AREA sq. km.	CAPITAL
AUSTRALIA	15 226 000	7 686 848	Canberra
FIJI	658 000	18 272	Suva
KIRIBATI	60 000	886	Tarawa
NAURU	8 000	21	Nauru
NEW CALEDONIA	146 000	19 058	Nouméa
NEW ZEALAND	3 230 000	268 676	Wellington
PAPUA NEW GUINEA	3 094 000	461 691	Port Moresby
SOLOMON ISLANDS	246 000	28 446	Honiara
TONGA	101 000	699	Nuku'alofa
TUVALU	8 000	24	Funafuti
VANUATU	126 000	14 763	Vila
WESTERN SAMOA	159 000	2 842	Apia

Map coverage extends to every part of the world in a balanced scheme that avoids any individual country or regional bias. Map areas are chosen to reflect the social, economic, cultural or historical importance of a particular region. Each double spread or single page map has been planned deliberately to cover an entire physical or political unit. Generous map overlaps are included to maintain continuity. Each of the continents is treated systematically in a subsection of its own. As an aid to the reader in locating the required area, a postage stamp key map is incorporated into the title margin of each map page.

Map projections have been chosen to reflect the different requirements of particular areas. No map can be absolutely true on account of the impossibility of representing a spheroid accurately on a flat surface without some distortion in either area, distance, direction or shape. In a general world atlas it is the equal area property that is most important to retain for comparative map studies and feature size evaluation and this principle has been followed wherever possible in this map section.

Map scales, as expressions of the relationship which the distance between any two points of the map bears to the corresponding distance on the ground, are in the context of this atlas grouped into three distinct categories.

Large scales, of between 1 : 1 000 000 (1 centimetre to 10 kilometres or 1 inch to 16 miles) and 1 : 2 500 000 (1 centimetre to 25 kilometres or 1 inch to 40 miles), are used to cover particularly dense populated areas of Western Europe and Japan.

Medium scales, of between 1 : 2 500 000 and 1 : 7 500 000 are used for maps of important parts of Europe, North America, Australasia, etc.

Small scales, of less than 1 : 7 500 000 (e.g. 1 : 10 000 000, 1 : 15 000 000, 1 : 25 000 000 etc.), are selected for maps of the complete world, oceans and many of the larger countries.

The actual scale at which a particular area is mapped

therefore reflects its shape, size and density of detail, and as a basic principle the more detail required to be shown of an area, the greater its scale. However, throughout this atlas, map scales have been limited in number, as far as possible, in order to facilitate comparison between maps.

Map measurements give preference to the metric system which is now used in nearly every country throughout the world. All spot heights and ocean depths are shown in metres and the relief and submarine layer delineation is based on metric contour levels. However, all linear scalebar and height reference column figures are given in metric and imperial equivalents to facilitate conversion of measurements for the non-metric reader.

Map symbols used are fully explained in the legend below. Careful study and frequent reference to this legend will aid in the reader's ability to extract maximum information.

Topography is shown by the combined means of precise spot heights, contouring, layer tinting and three-dimensional hill shading.

Hydrographic features such as coastlines, rivers, lakes, swamps and canals are clearly differentiated.

Communications are particularly well represented with the contemporary importance of airports and road networks duly emphasized.

International boundaries and national capitals are fully documented and internal administrative divisions are shown with the maximum detail that the scale will allow. Boundary delineation reflects the 'de facto' rather than the 'de jure' political interpretation and where relevant an undefined or disputed boundary is distinguished. However there is no intended implication that the publishers necessarily endorse or accept the status of any political entity recorded on the maps.

Settlements are shown by a series of graded town stamps, each representing a population size category, based on the latest census figures.

Other features, such as notable ancient monuments, oases, national parks, oil and gas fields, are selectively included on particular maps that merit their identification.

Lettering styles used in the maps have been chosen with great care to ensure maximum legibility and clear distinction of named feature categories. The size and weight of the various typefaces reflect the relative importance of the features. Town names are graded to correspond with the appropriate town stamp.

Map place names have been selected in accordance with maintaining legibility at a given scale and at the same time striking an appropriate balance between natural and man-made features worthy of note. Name forms have been standardized according to the widely accepted principle, now well established in international reference atlases, of including place names and geographical terms in the local language of the country in question. In the case of non-Roman scripts (e.g. Arabic), transliteration and transcription have either been based on the rules recommended by the Permanent Committee on Geographical Names and the United States Board on Geographic Names, or as in the case of the adopted Pinyin transcription of Chinese names, a system officially proposed by the country concerned. The diacritical signs used in each language or transcription have been retained on all the maps and throughout the index. However the English language reader's requirements have also been recognised in that the names of all countries, oceans, major seas and land features as well as familiar alternative name versions of important towns are presented in English.

Map sources used in the compilation of this atlas were many and varied, but always of the latest available information. At each stage of their preparation the maps were submitted to a thorough process of research and continual revision to ensure that on publication all data would be as accurate as practicable. A well-documented data bank was created to ensure consistency and validity of all information represented on the maps.

SYMBOLS

Relief

		Feet	Relief	Metres
	Land contour	16404		5000
▲ 8848	Spot height (metres)	9843		3000
⋈	Pass	6562		2000
	Permanent ice cap	3281		1000
		1640		500
		656		200
		Land Dep. 0	Sea Level	Sea Level
		656		200
		13123		4000
		22966		7000

Hydrography

	Submarine contour
▼11034	Ocean depth (metres)
(217)	Lake level (metres)
	Reef
	River
	Intermittent river
	Falls
	Dam
	Gorge
	Canal
	Lake/Reservoir
	Intermittent lake
	Marsh/Swamp

© Wm. Collins Sons & Co. Ltd.

Administration

▬▬▬	International boundary
- - -	Undefined/Disputed international boundary
─·─·─	Internal division : First order
······	Internal division : Second order
▨ ◉ · / ◎ ▢ ·	National capitals

Settlement

Each settlement is given a town stamp according to its population size and scale category.

	1:1M-1:2½M	1:2½M-1:7½M	1:7½M or smaller
▨	over 1 000 000	over 1 000 000	over 1 000 000
◉	500 000-1 000 000	500 000-1 000 000	500 000-1 000 000
◎	100 000-500 000	100 000-500 000	100 000-500 000
⊙	25 000-100 000	25 000-100 000	under 100 000
○	10 000-25 000	under 25 000	—
·	under 10 000	—	—
	Major urban area (1:1M-1:2½M only)		

The size of type used for each settlement is graded to correspond with the appropriate town stamp.

Communications

Tunnel ━ ━	Main railway
⊕	Main airport
- - - -	Track

Road representation varies with the scale category.

═══	Principal road	} 1:1M-1:2½M
───	Other main road	
───	Principal road	} 1:2½M-1:7½M
───	Other main road	
───	Principal road	1:7½M or smaller

Other features

∴	Ancient monument
⌣	Oasis
⬭	National Park
▲	Oil field
△	Gas field
─·─	Oil/Gas pipeline

Lettering

Various styles of lettering are used - each one representing a different type of feature.

ALPS	Physical feature	KENYA	Country name
Red Sea	Hydrographic feature	IOWA	Internal division
Paris	Settlement name	(Fr.)	Territorial administration

ATLANTIC OCEAN

NORWAY

NORTH SEA

DENMARK

NETHERLANDS

WEST GERMANY

BELGIUM

LUXEMBOURG

REPUBLIC OF IRELAND

IRISH SEA

UNITED KINGDOM

SCOTLAND

ENGLAND

WALES

NORTHERN IRELAND

Celtic Sea

English Channel

FRANCE

Relief

Feet	Metres
16 404	5000
9843	3000
6562	2000
3281	1000
1640	500
656	200
0	Sea Level
Land Dep.	
656	200
13 123	4000
22 966	7000

Scale 1:6 500 000

0   50   100   150 Miles

0   50   100   150   200   250 Kms.

Conic Projection

© Collins · Longman Atlases Cbii

ENGLAND AND WALES

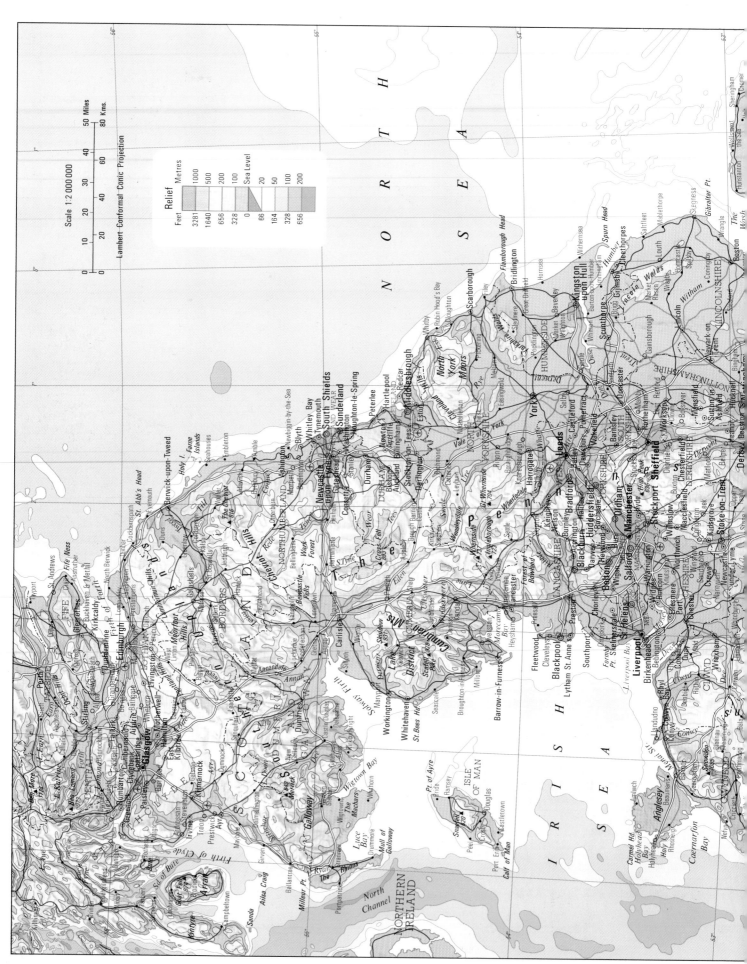

9

COTLAND

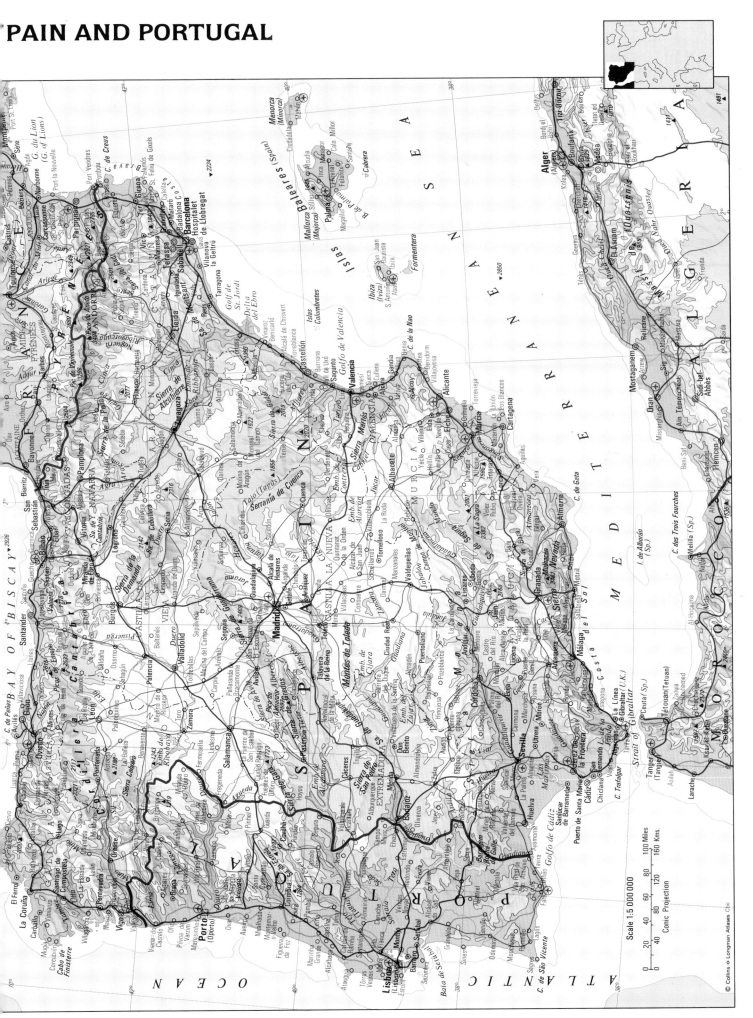

Scale 1:5 000 000

Conic Projection

© Collins ◇ Longman Atlases Cbri

ITALY AND THE BALKANS

CENTRAL EUROPE

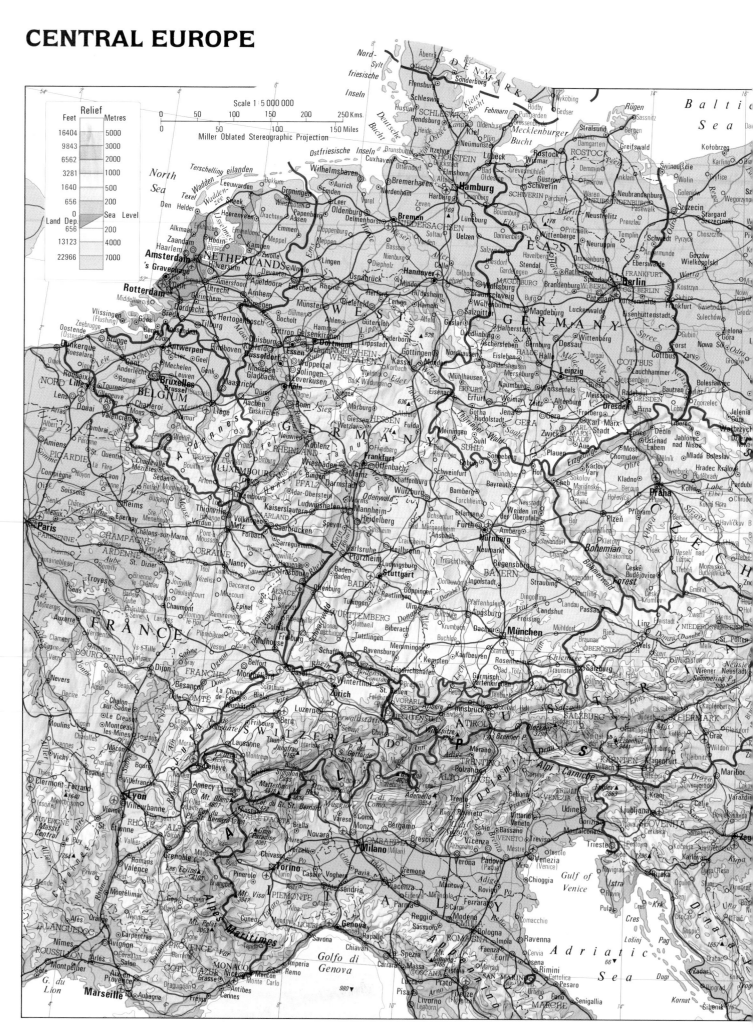

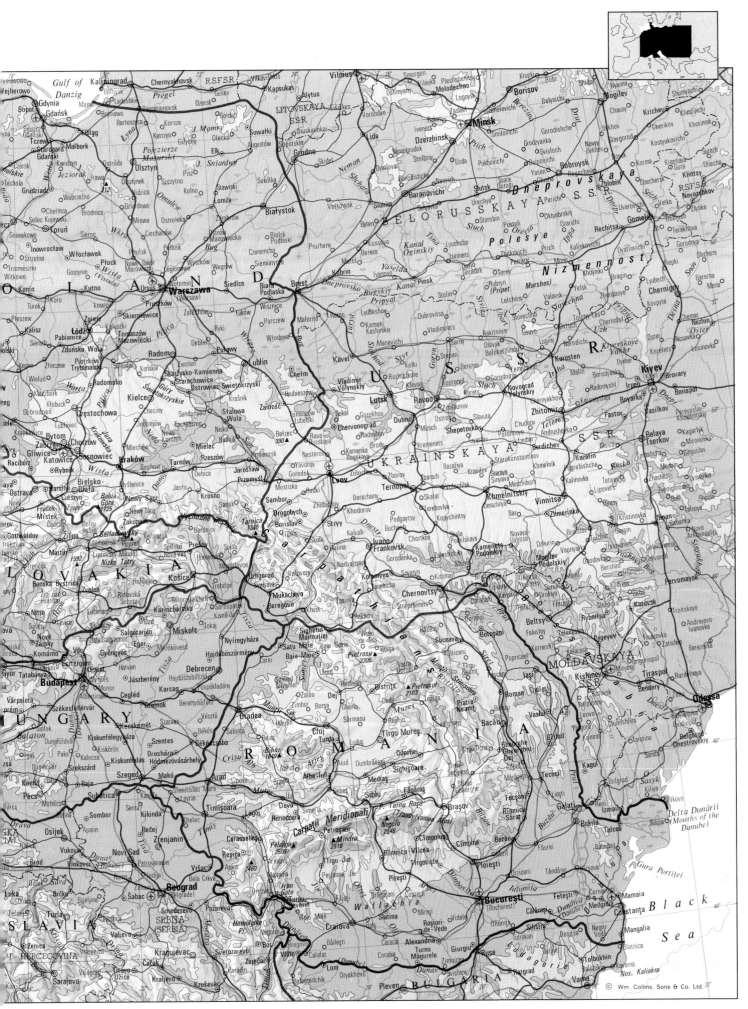

SCANDINAVIA AND BALTIC LANDS

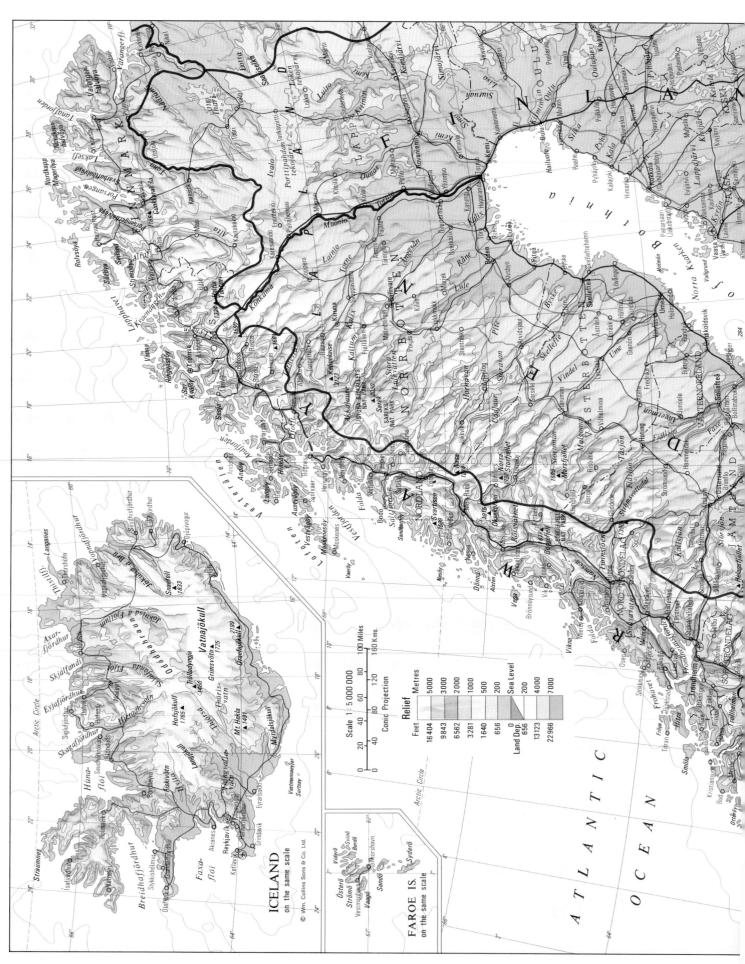

ICELAND
on the same scale

© Wm. Collins Sons & Co. Ltd.

FAROE IS.
on the same scale

Scale 1 : 5 000 000
Conic Projection

Relief

Feet	Metres
16 404	5000
9843	3000
6562	2000
3281	1000
1640	500
656	200
0	Sea Level
Land Dep.	200
656	
13123	4000
22966	7000

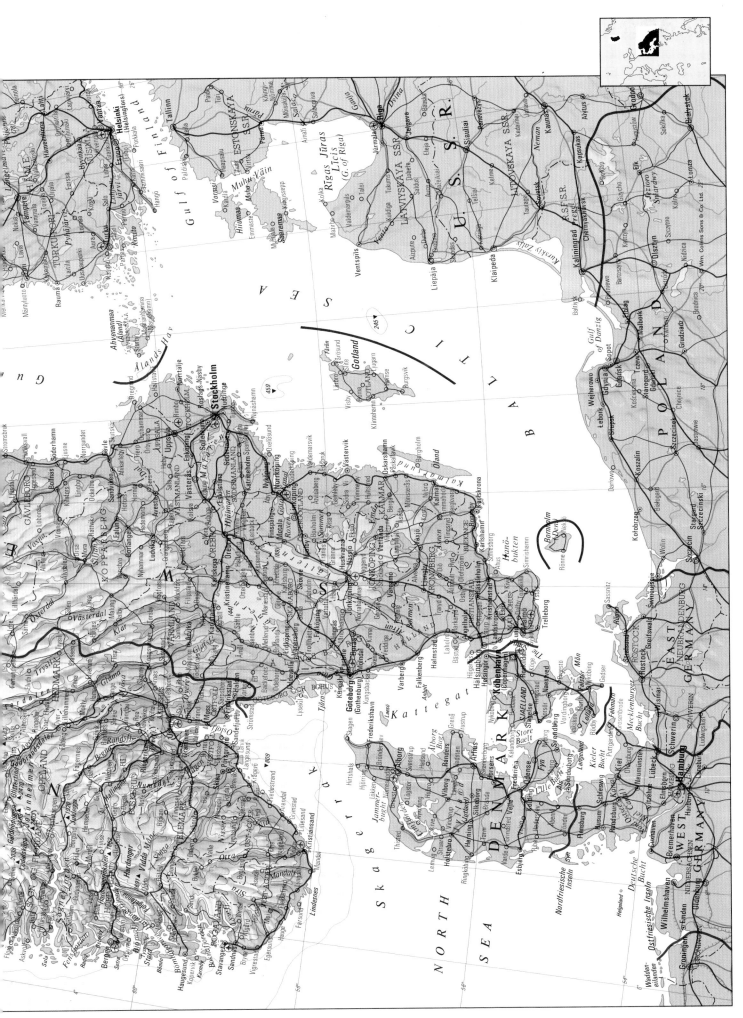

U.S.S.R. IN EUROPE

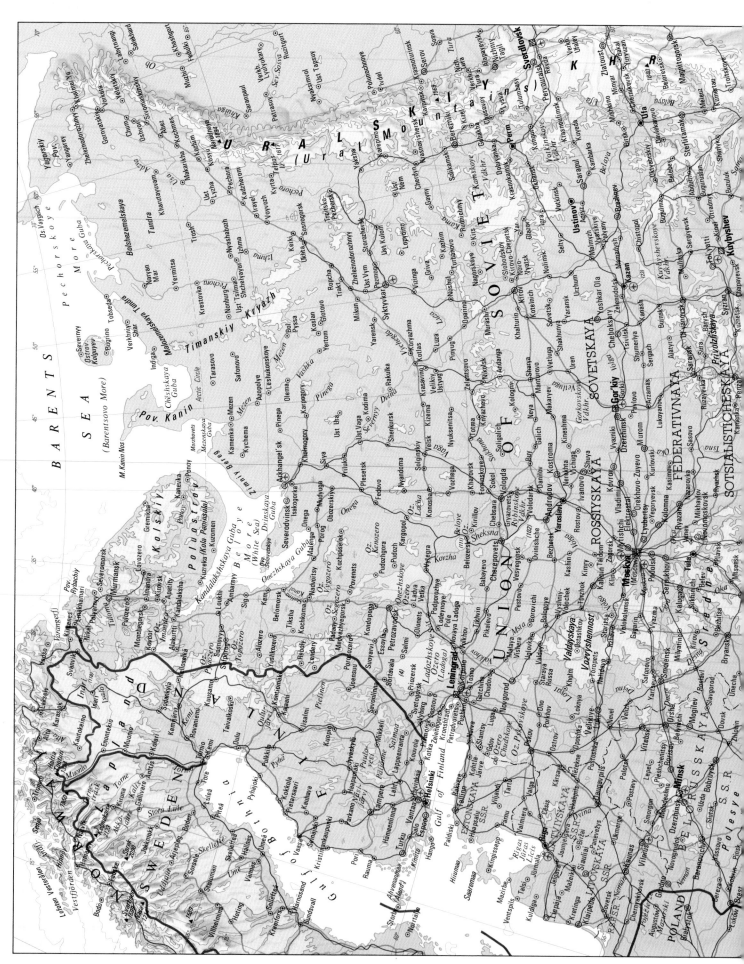

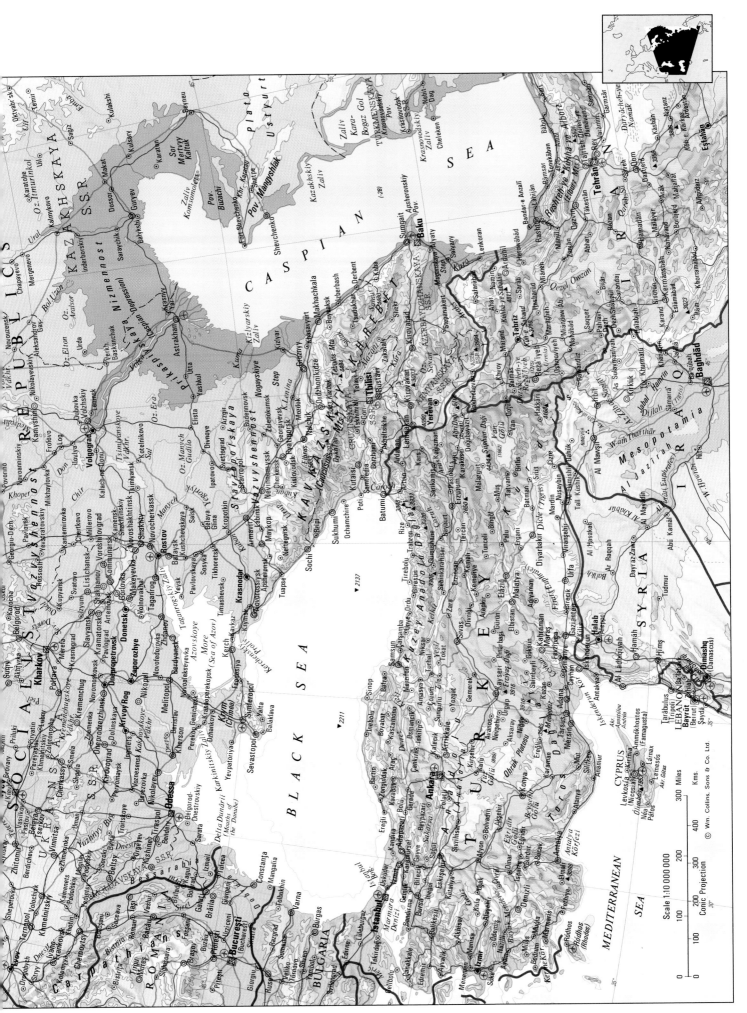

21

U.S.S.R.

MIDDLE EAST AND SOUTH ASIA

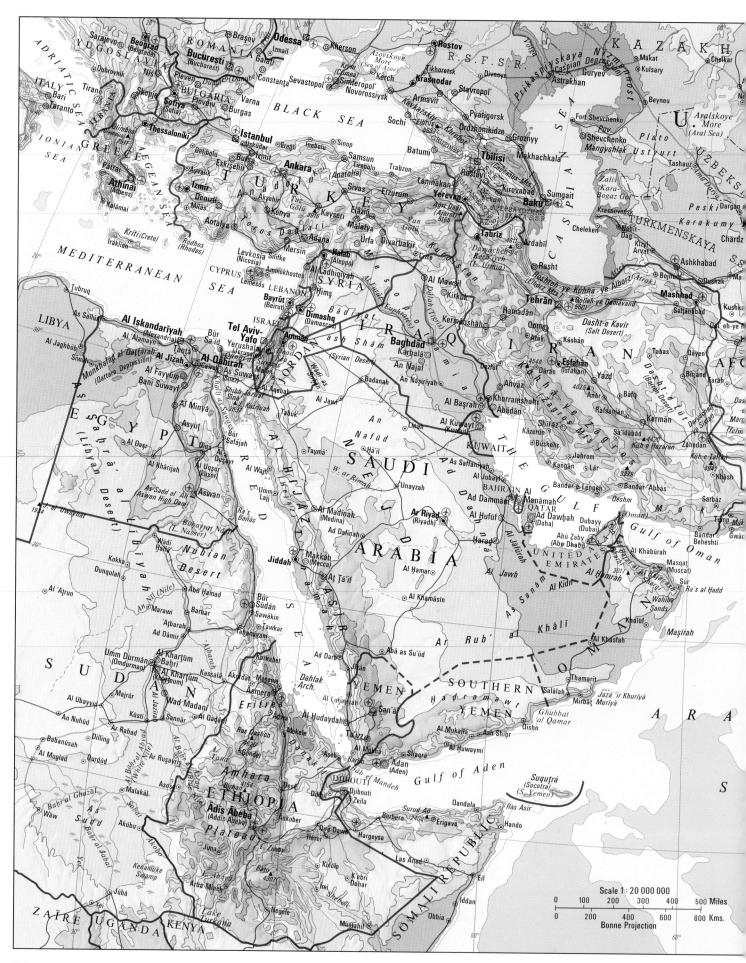

Scale 1 : 20 000 000

| 0 | 100 | 200 | 300 | 400 | 500 Miles |

| 0 | 200 | 400 | 600 | 800 Kms. |

Bonne Projection

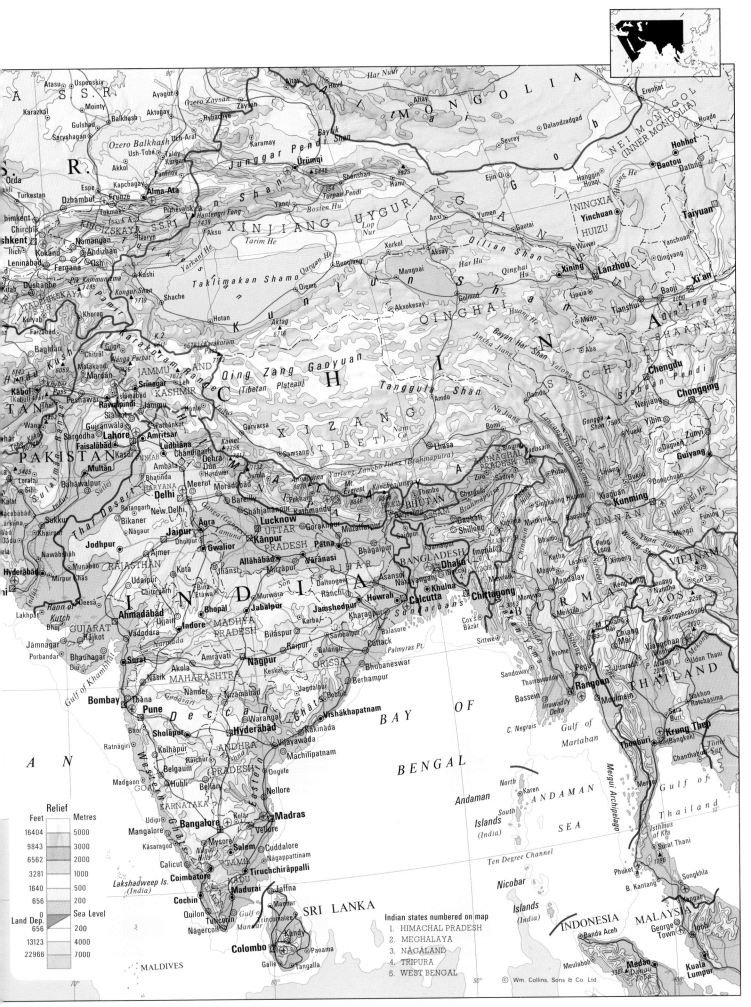

25

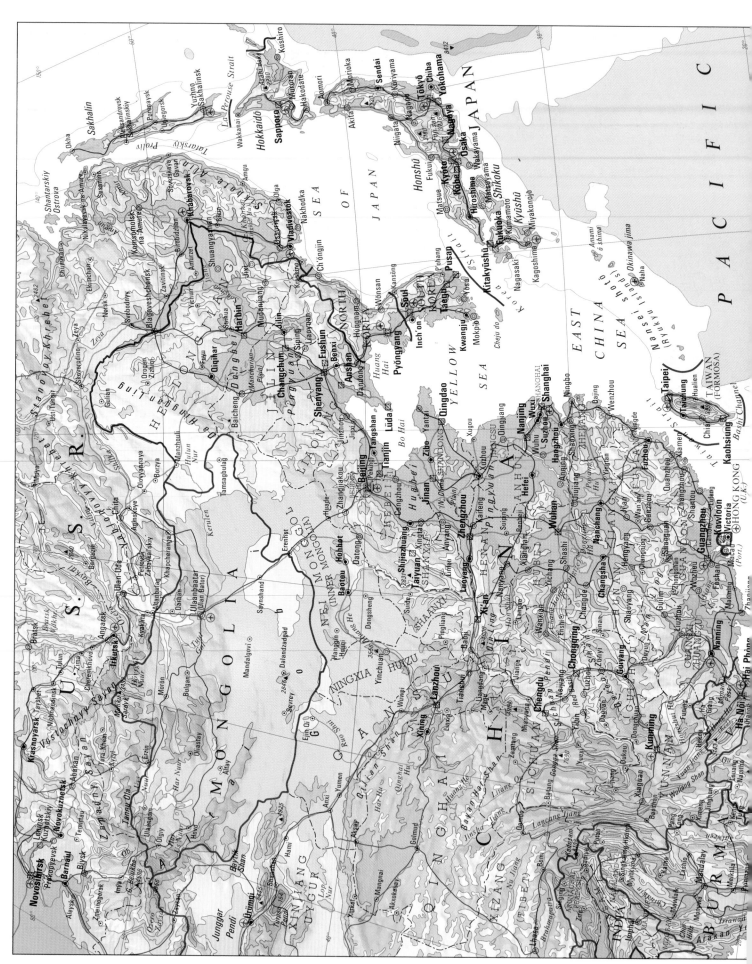

JAPAN

EW ZEALAND

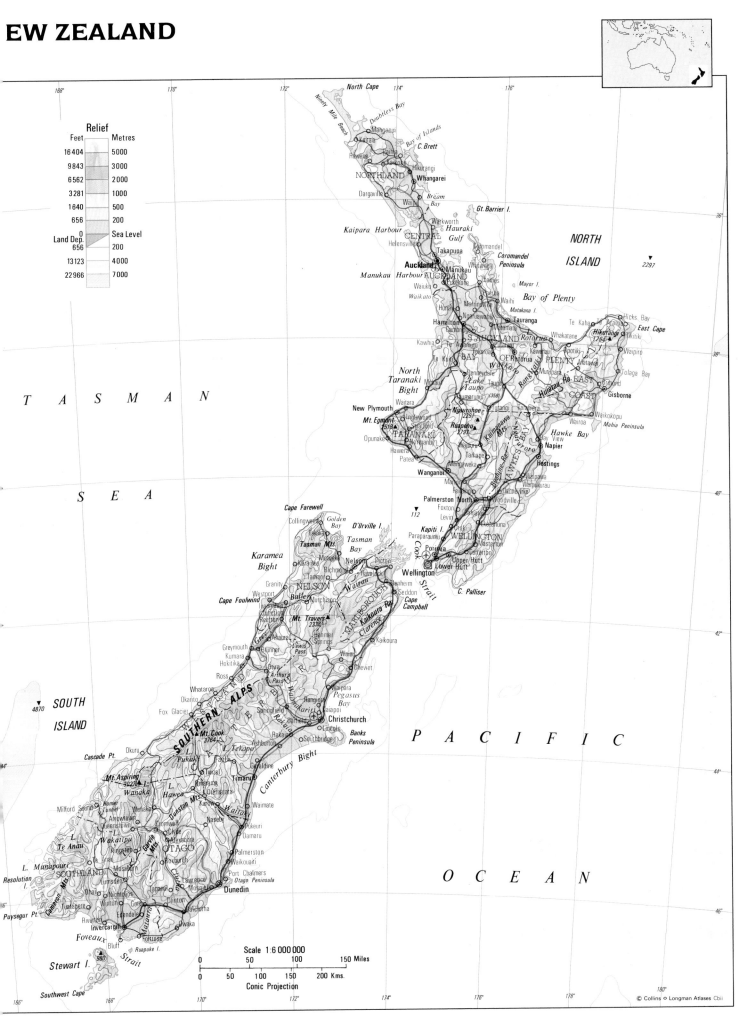

PACIFIC OCEAN

SAMOA ISLANDS
Scale 1:7 500 000

Faleälupo Apia Fagamalo
Salailua Puapua
Savai'i Balelologa
Matautu Upolu Tiavea
WESTERN Samoa
SAMOA (U.S.A.) Manua Is.
Ofu Olosega
Tau
Pago Pago C. Matatula
Tutuila Steps Pt.

FIJI
Gt. Sea Reef Undu C.
Lambasa Vanua Levu
Mbutha Yathata
Mbua Koro Taveuni
Lautoka Ngau Koro
Nandi Viti Sea
Singatoka Levu Lau
Kandavu Passage Suva Group
Kandavu
Scale 1:15 000 000

RAROTONGA
(N.Z.)
Pokoinu Avatiu Avarua
Aroa Matavera
Arorangi Te 653 Ngatangiia
Manga
Muri
Titikaveka
Scale 1:500 000

NIUE
(N.Z.)
Hikutavake Mutalau
Tuapa Toi
Maketu Lakepa
Alofi Alofi Mutalau Liku
Bay
Avatele 66 Hakupu
Avatele Pt. Naiea
Tepa Pt. Vaiea
Scale 1:1 000 000

GUAM
(U.S.A.)
Ritidian
Pt. Pati Pt.
Philippine Mt. Santa Rosa
Sea 267 Catalina
Agana Pt.
Orote Yona
Pen. Talofofo
Merizo Malolos
Inarajan
Scale 1:2 000 000

VANUATU AND NEW CALEDONIA
Banks Is.
C. Cumberland
C. Quiros
Espiritu
Santo I. Oba Maewo
Luganville Pentecost I.
Coral Malekula Ambrim
Sea Epi Shepherd
VANUATU Islands
Emae Tongoa
Vila Efate
Récifs
d'Entrecasteaux
Grand Passage
Grand Eromanga
Récif
de Tana
Cook Lenakel
Aneityum
Koumac
Voh Île Ouvéa
Kone Île Loyauté
Houailou Lifou (Loyalty Is.)
Boulari Île Maré
Nouvelle
Calédonie Île des
(New Caledonia) Yaté Pins
(Fr.) Nouméa
Scale 1:15 000 000
© Wm. Collins Sons & Co. Ltd.

30

HAWAIIAN ISLANDS
(U.S.A.)

Haena · Kauai
Mana · Kapaa
Nihau · Lihue
Wahiawa · Oahu Kailua
Honolulu · Kaiwi Channel · Molokai
Maunaloa · Honokahua
Lanai · Lanai City · *Maui* Hana
Kahoolawe · Alenuihaha Channel
Upolu Pt. · Honokaa
Waimea · 3508 · Hilo
Hawaii · Mauna Loa · 4171
Papa · Pahala
Naalehu

Scale 1:10 000 000

KIRITIMATI (CHRISTMAS I.)
(Kiribati)

North West Pt. · Main Camp
London · Paris · North East Pt.
South West Pt. · Bay of Wrecks
South East Pt.

Scale 1:2 500 000

TONGA
Scale 1:7 500 000

Vava'u Group · Uta Vava'u
Late · Kao · Ha'apai Group
Tofua · Fonuafo'ou · Nomuka Group
Nuku'alofa · Tongatapu Group
Tongatapu · Eua

MARQUESAS ISLANDS
(France)

Hatutu · Eiao
Nuku Hiva · Ua Huka · Tai-o-haé
Ua Pu · Hiva Oa · Atuona
Îles Marquises (Marquesas Is.) · Fatu Hiva

Scale 1:10 000 000

EASTER ISLAND
(Chile)

Cabo Norte · Bahia la Pérouse
Tereyaka · Cabo O'Higgins
601 · Cabo Roggeveen
Isla de Pascua (Easter I.) · Pta. Cuidado
Hanga Roa · Vaihu
Rano Kao · 410 · Cabo Sur

Scale 1:1 000 000

SOCIETY ISLANDS
(France)

Motu Iti · Îles sous le Vent
Bora Bora · Tahaa
Uturoa · Huahine
Raiatea · Tetiaroa
Moorea · Papeete
Papetoai · Tahiti
Maiao · Tautira · Presqu'île de Taiarapu
Îles du Vent
Îles de la Société (Society Islands)

Scale 1:7 500 000

TAHITI
(France)

Papeete · Papenoo · Tiarei
Tataa · Faaone
Punaauia · Orohena · 2237 · Isthme de Taravao
· Taravao · Tautira
Maraa · Tahiaa · Vairaa
Atimaono · Bora Pt.
Toanoanu · Fareara

Scale 1:2 500 000

Gulf of Alaska · Kodiak I.
Prince Rupert · **Edmonton** · **CANADA**
Queen Charlotte Is. · **Calgary**
Rocky Mountains
Vancouver · **Winnipeg** · Winnipeg · Québec · **Montréal**
Vancouver I. · **Seattle** · **Ottawa** · **Boston**
Columbia · Superior · **Detroit** · **New York**
Portland · Michigan · **Chicago** · **Philadelphia**
UNITED STATES · **Washington**
2140 · **Kansas City** · **Atlanta**
San Francisco · **Denver** · Mt. Elbert 4399 · **OF AMERICA**
Colorado · Arkansas · Mississippi
Los Angeles · **Dallas** · **Jacksonville**
San Diego · El Paso · **Houston** · **New Orleans**
I. de Guadalupe (Mex.) · Rio Grande · **Miami** · BAHAMAS
Tropic of Cancer · **Gulf of Mexico** · **La Habana** (Havana) · DOMINICAN REP.
Golfo de California · **M E X I C O** · Yucatan Peninsula · Yucatan Basin · HAITI · Greater Antilles
Guadalajara · **Cd. de México** · JAMAICA
Is. de Revilla Gigedo (Mex.) · (Mexico City) · BELIZE
GUATEMALA · **CARIBBEAN SEA** · Curaçao (Neth.)
EL SALVADOR · HONDURAS · **Tegucigalpa** · Venezuelan Basin
Guatemala Trench · NICARAGUA · **Managua** · Colombian Basin · Curaçao
Clipperton (Fr.) · Guatemala Basin · COSTA RICA · **Caracas** · **VENEZUELA**
Isla del Coco · **Bogotá**
COLOMBIA
Is. Galapagos (Ecuador) · **Cali**
Quito · **ECUADOR**
Guayaquil
Equator · Peru Basin
Lima · **PERU**
Malden I. · Caroline I. · Îles Marquises (Marquesas Is.) (Hiva Oa)
Flint I. · Nuku Hiva · (France) · Arequipa
5275 · Îles du Désappointement · **La Paz**
Rangiroa · Îles Tuamotu
Is. sous le Vent · Tahiti · East Pacific Ridge
(Société (Society Is.) · Papeete
Rurutu · Tubuai · 5298
Austral Tropic of Capricorn · Mangareva · Oeno I. · Henderson I. (U.K.)
Raivavae · Is. Gambier · Pitcairn I. · Ducie I.
Îles Tubuai · Rapa · South West Peru Ridge
Isla de Pascua (Easter I.) (Chile) · Sala y Gomez (Chile) · San Félix (Chile)
2994 · 2423 · San Ambrosio
S O U T H   P A C I F I C   O C E A N
Eastern Pacific Basin · 1604 · 2743 · Islas Juan Fernández (Chile) · Chile Basin
878 · 1615 · N.W. Chile Ridge · **Santiago** · Puerto Montt
Antarctic Ridge · **ARGENTINA**
Pacific-Antarctic Basin · **PERU-CHILE TRENCH**
Antarctic Circle · Cabo de Hornos

Scale 1:60 000 000
0 200 400 600 800 1000 Miles
0 400 800 1200 1600 Kms.
Modified Zenithal Equidistant Projection

WESTERN AUSTRALIA

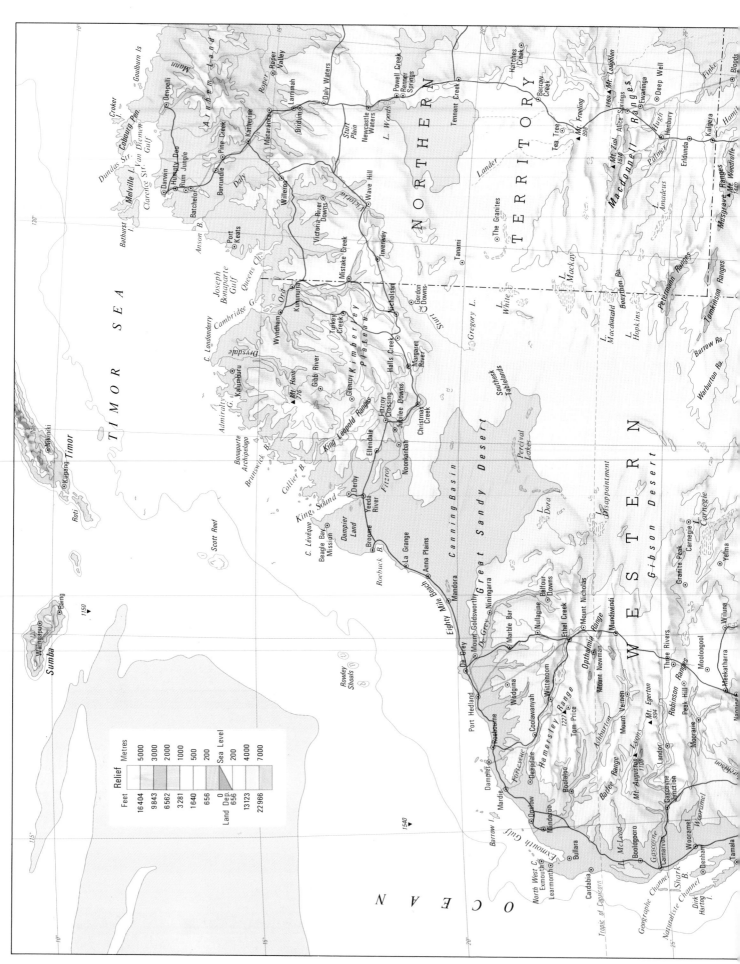

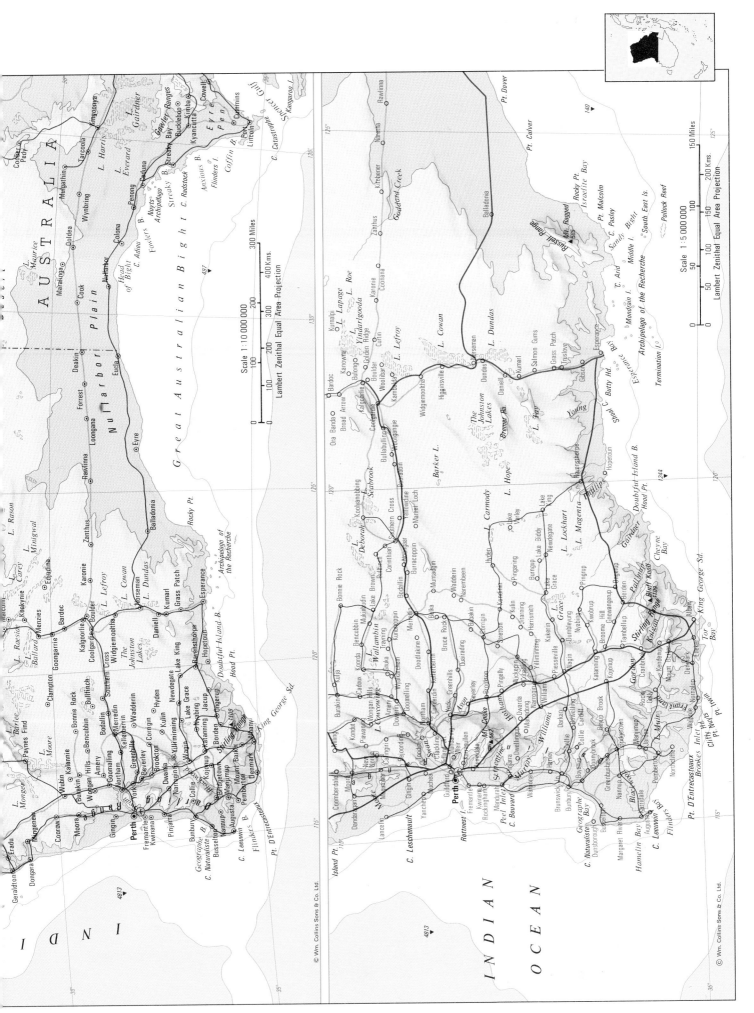

AUSTRALIA

Great Australian Bight

Nullarbor Plain

Scale 1:10 000 000
Lambert Zenithal Equal Area Projection

INDIAN

OCEAN

Perth

INDIAN OCEAN

Scale 1:5 000 000
Lambert Zenithal Equal Area Projection

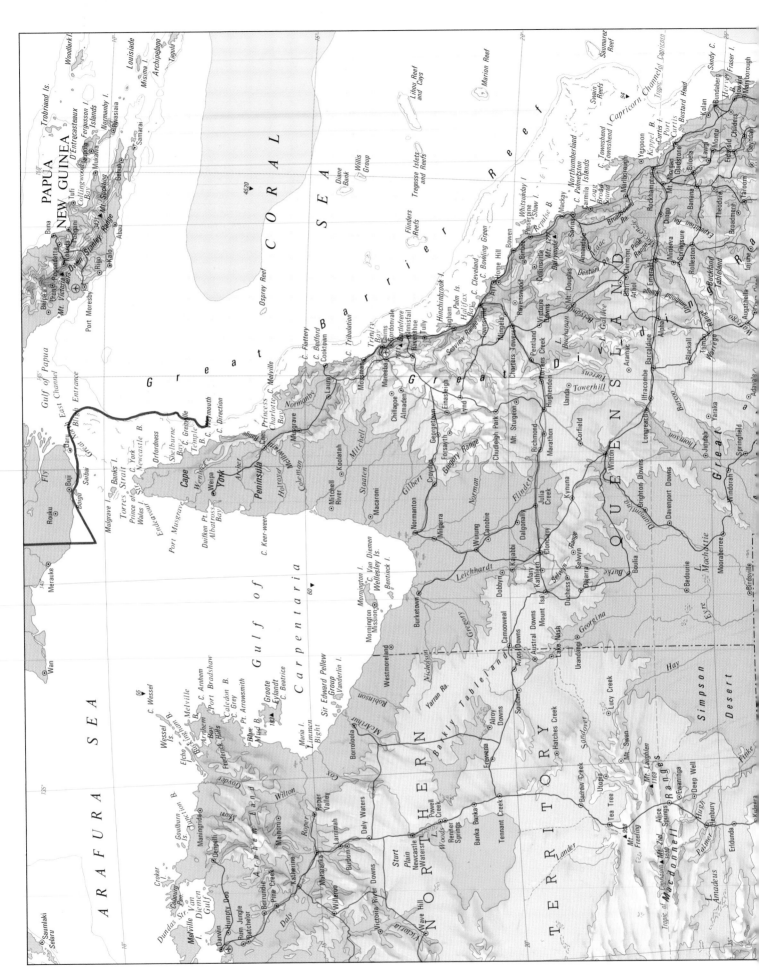

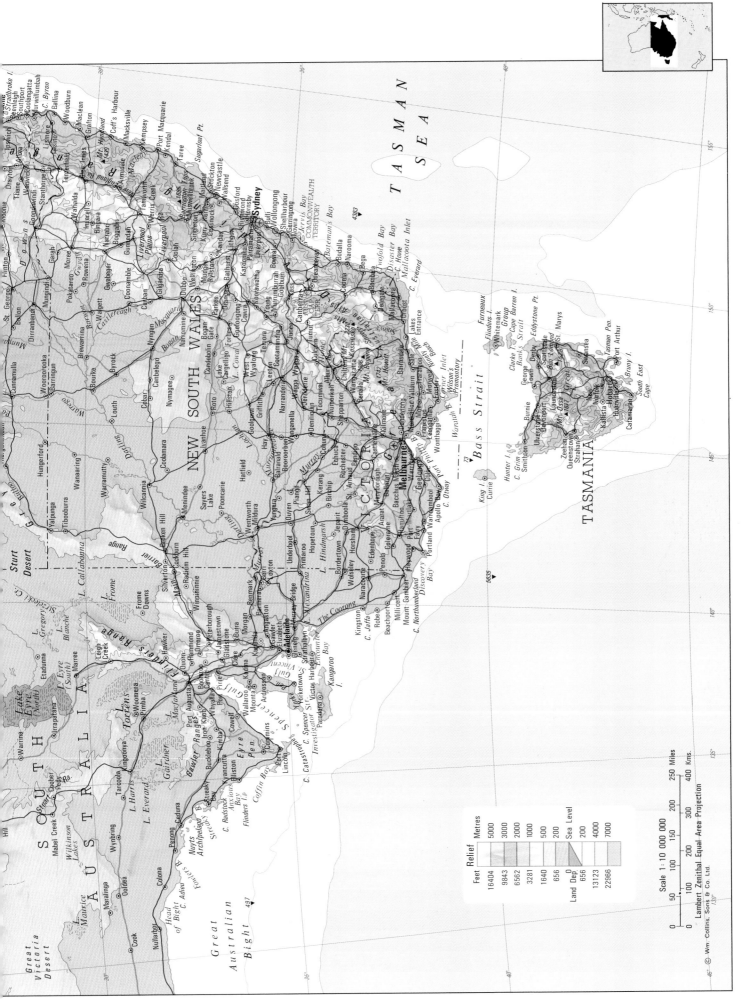

SOUTHEAST AUSTRALIA

CANADA AND ALASKA

UNITED STATES

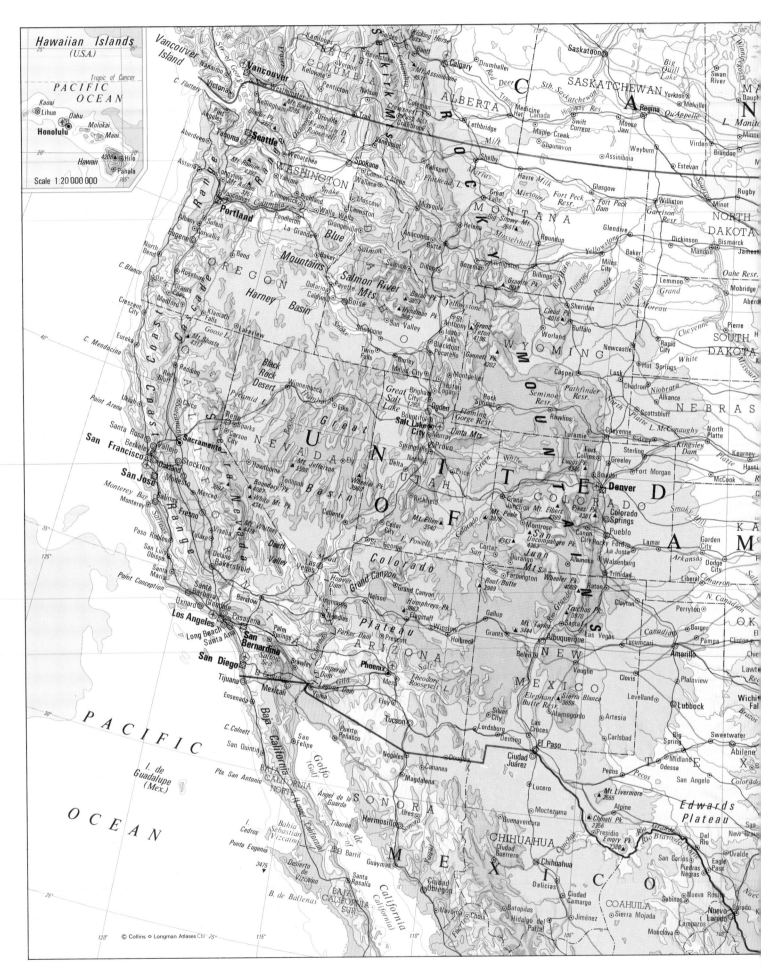

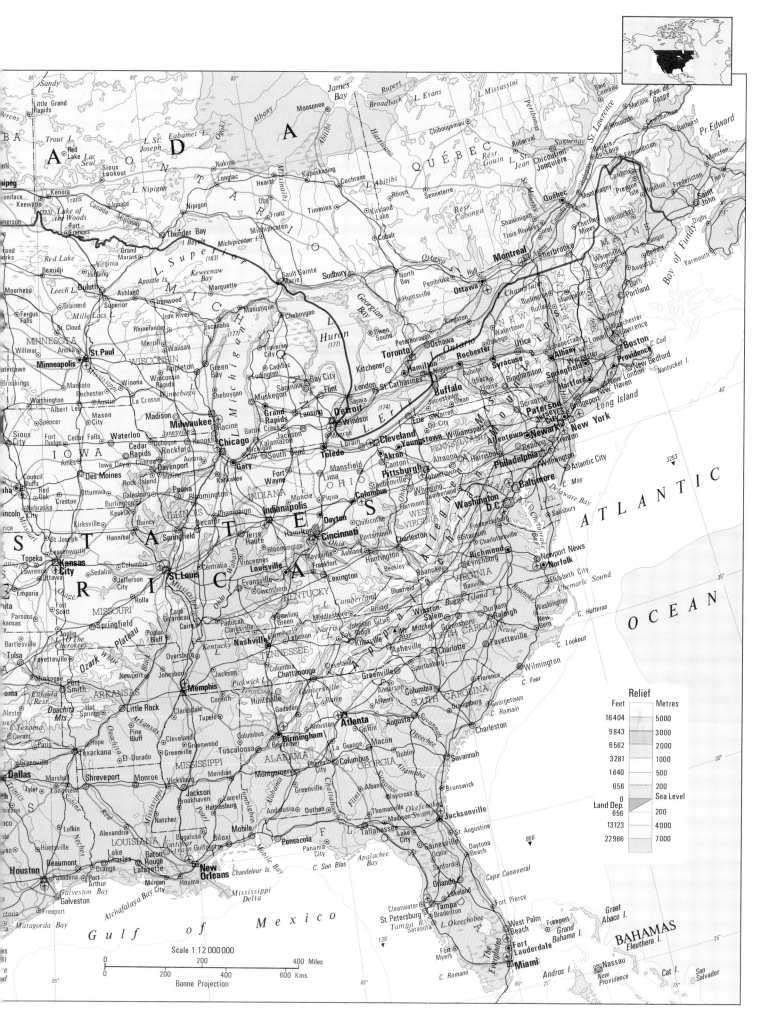

CENTRAL AMERICA AND THE CARIBBEAN

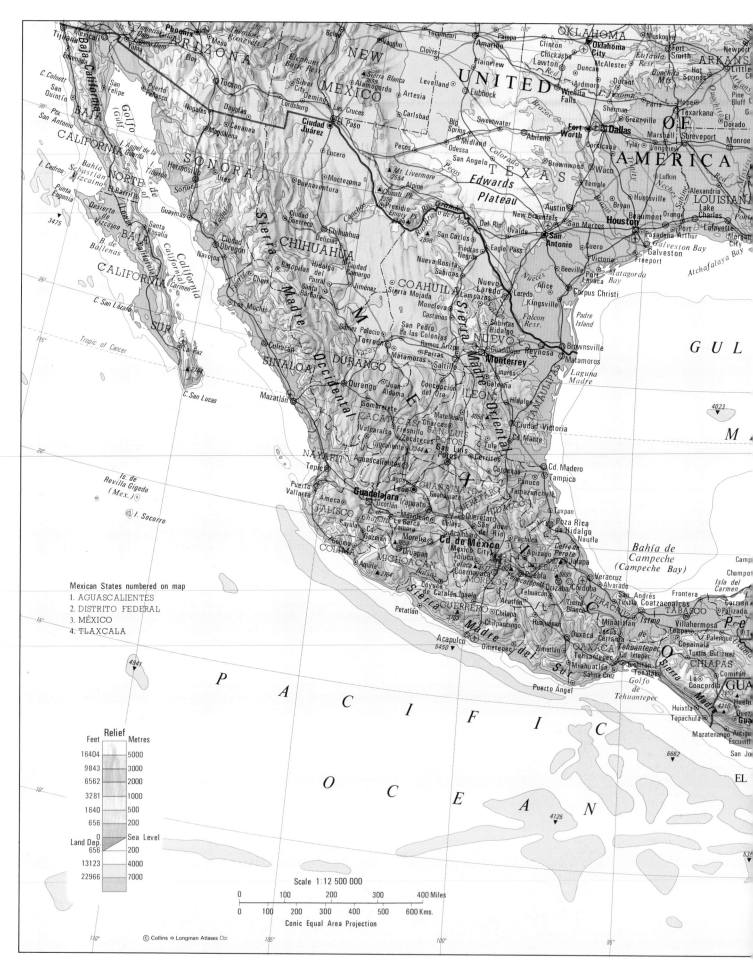

Mexican States numbered on map
1. AGUASCALIENTES
2. DISTRITO FEDERAL
3. MÉXICO
4. TLAXCALA

Relief

Feet	Metres
16404	5000
9843	3000
6562	2000
3281	1000
1640	500
656	200
0	Sea Level
Land Dep.	
656	200
13123	4000
22966	7000

Scale 1:12 500 000

0   100   200   300   400 Miles

0   100   200   300   400   500   600 Kms.

Conic Equal Area Projection

© Collins ◇ Longman Atlases Cbi

TENNESSEE
Columbia
Chattanooga
Cleveland
Asheville
NORTH
Charlotte
Fayetteville
New Bern
C. Lookout
Huntsville
Pickwick
Guntersville
Greenville
Spartanburg
CAROLINA
enn
Rome
Anderson
SOUTH
Wilmington
ATES
Birmingham
Atlanta
Columbia
CAROLINA
C. Fear
Bessemer
La Grange
Griffin
Augusta
Orangeburg
C. Romain
aloosa
ALABAMA
Columbus
Macon
Dublin
Charleston
Phenix City
Montgomery
Georgetown
GEORGIA
Greenville
Savannah
Mobile
Andalusia
Dothan
Albany
Ogeechee
Brunswick
C. San Blas
Thomasville
Okefenokee
Swamp
ATLANTIC
deleur
Mobile Bay
Apalachee
Bay
Gainesville
Jacksonville
OCEAN
ississippi
elta
C. San Blas
Lake City
St. Augustine
30°
Ocala
Daytona Beach
866
Sanford
Orlando
Cape Canaveral
1137
Clearwater
Lakeland
Fort Pierce
St. Petersburg
Tampa
West
Sarasota
Bradenton
Lake
Palm
Tampa B.
Okeechobee
Beach
Freeport
Great
Fort Myers
The
Grand
Abaco I.
Everglades
Fort
Bahama I.
C. Romano
Lauderdale
New
Eleuthera I.
25°
Miami
Providence
Rock Sound
C. Sable
Nicolls
Nassau
Cat I.
Key West
Town
Andros
San
Florida Keys
Andros I.
Town
The Bight
Salvador
Straits
of Florida
Rolleville
Rum Cay
Samana Cay
Gt.
Exuma
Long I.
Plana Cays
Mayaguana I.
Cárdenas
Archo. de Sabana
Crooked I.
Turks and Caicos Is.
20°
La Habana
Matanzas
Archo. de Camaguey
Acklin's I.
Caicos Is.
(U.K.)
(Havana)
Sagua
la Grande
Caibarién
Turks Is.
Marianao
Güines
Santa Clara
Morón
Pinar del Rio
Sancti
Great
Matthew
Guane
Golfo de
Cienfuegos
Spíritus
Ciego de Avila
Inagua
Town
Île de
Puerto Plata
8528
Puerto Rico Trench
Batabanó
Trinidad
Nuevitas
la Tortue
San Francisco
Nueva
CUBA
Camagüey
Holguín
Banes
la Macorís
Samaná
San Juan
Gerona
Archo. de los
Victoria
Baracoa
Cap-Haitien
Puerto
Bayamón
Arecibo
Isla de Pinos
Canarreos
Jardines de la
de las Tunas
Bayamo
S. Luis
Gonâve
L. de
Valverde
Santiago
1338
Reina
Manzanillo
Guantánamo
la Tortue
La Vega
DOMINICAN
Mayagüez
Ponce
Caguas
Little
Sa. Maestra
Port-de-Paix
St. Marc
REP.
La Romana
Cayman
Turquino
Santiago
Cap-Haitien
San Juan
Santo
S. Pedro
Mona
PUERTO
Cayman Brac
1971
de Cuba
HAITI
Azua
Domingo
Saona
RICO
4647
C. Cruz
Île de la
S. Cristóbal
Barahona
(U.S.A.)
Grand Cayman
Gonâve
Port-au-
2680
Hispaniola
Georgetown
Montego Bay
St. Ann's Bay
2414
Prince
Antilles
Cayman Is.
Port
Les
(U.K.)
Black River
Antonio
Cayes
4297
May Pen
JAMAICA
Kingston

BAHAMAS

Netherlands
Antilles
Aruba
Curaçao
Bonaire
Willemstad
Pta. Gallinas
Pen. de la
4242
Guajira
Golfo de
Santa
Ríohacha
Uribia
Paraguaná
Pto. Fijo
Marta
Sa. Nevada de
Concepción
La Vela
Maracaibo
Labinas
Barranquilla
Sta. Marta
Ciudad Ojeda
Barquisimeto
Valencia
Cartagena
Baranoa
Sabanalarga
Valledupar
L. de
Carora
Turbaco
Arjona
Maracaibo
San Carlos
Mene Grande
Acarigua
Magangué
del Zulia
Trujillo
Carmen
Entonrados
Mérida
VENEZUELA
Cereté
Guanare
Montería
Ocaña
Barinas
COLOMBIA

NORTHEAST U.S.A. – SOUTH CENTRAL CANADA

Relief

Metres							
5000	3000	2000	1000	500	200	Sea Level	

Feet							Land Dep.		
16 404	9843	6562	3281	1640	656	0	656	13 123	22 966
							200	4000	7000

Scale 1:7 500 000

Conic Equidistant Projection

200 Miles
300 Kms.

© Wm. Collins Sons & Co. Ltd.

SOUTH AMERICA – EAST

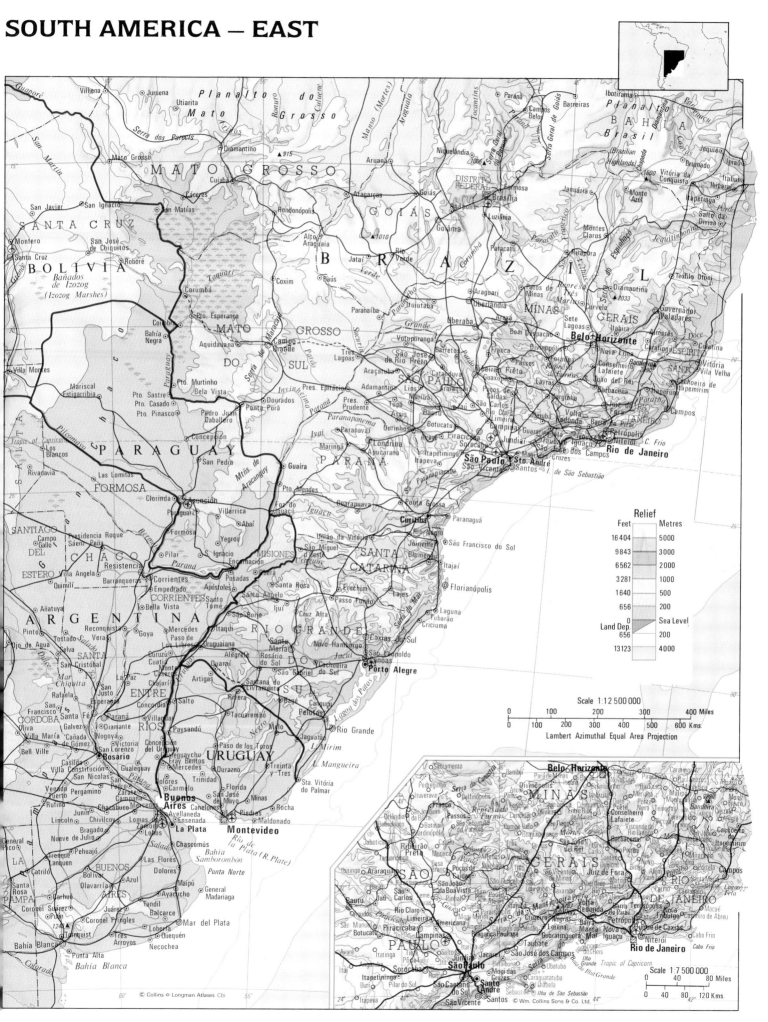

Relief

Feet	Metres
16 404	5000
9843	3000
6562	2000
3281	1000
1640	500
656	200
0	Sea Level
Land Dep.	
656	200
13 123	4000

Scale 1:12 500 000

0   100   200   300   400 Miles
0   100 200 300 400 500 600 Kms.
Lambert Azimuthal Equal Area Projection

Scale 1:7 500 000
0   40   80 Miles
0   40   80   120 Kms.

© Wm. Collins Sons & Co. Ltd.

© Collins ◇ Longman Atlases Cbi

45

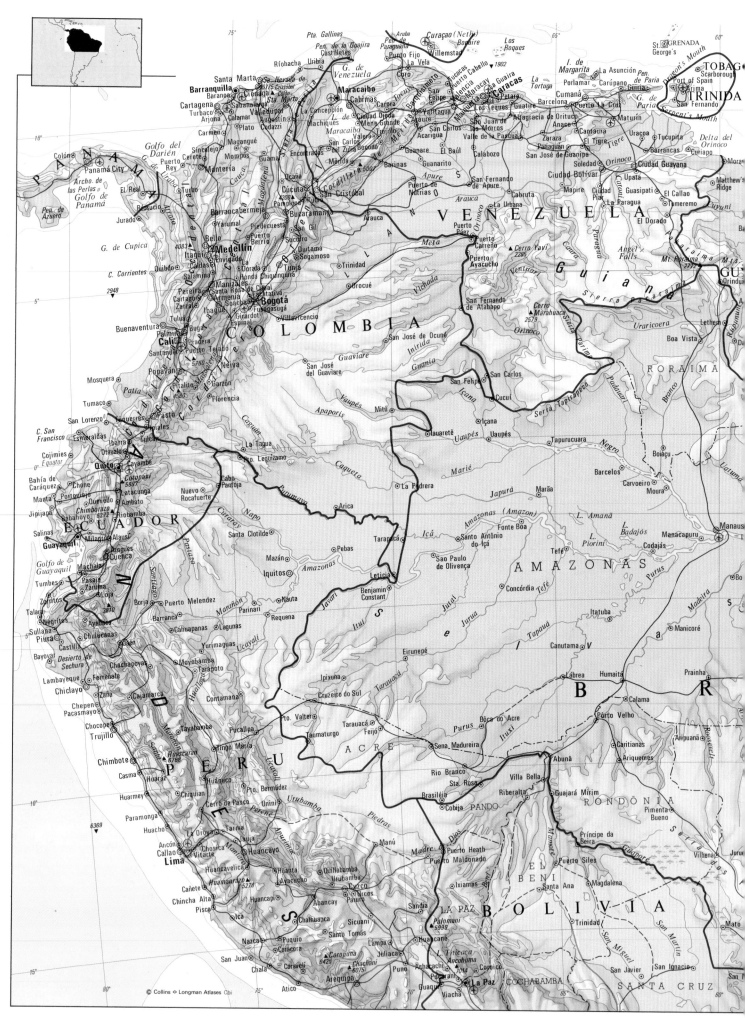

46

Relief

Feet		Metres
16 404		5000
9843		3000
6562		2000
3281		1000
1640		500
656		200
0		Sea Level
Land Dep.		
656		200
13 123		4000

Scale 1:12 500 000

Lambert Azimuthal Equal Area Projection

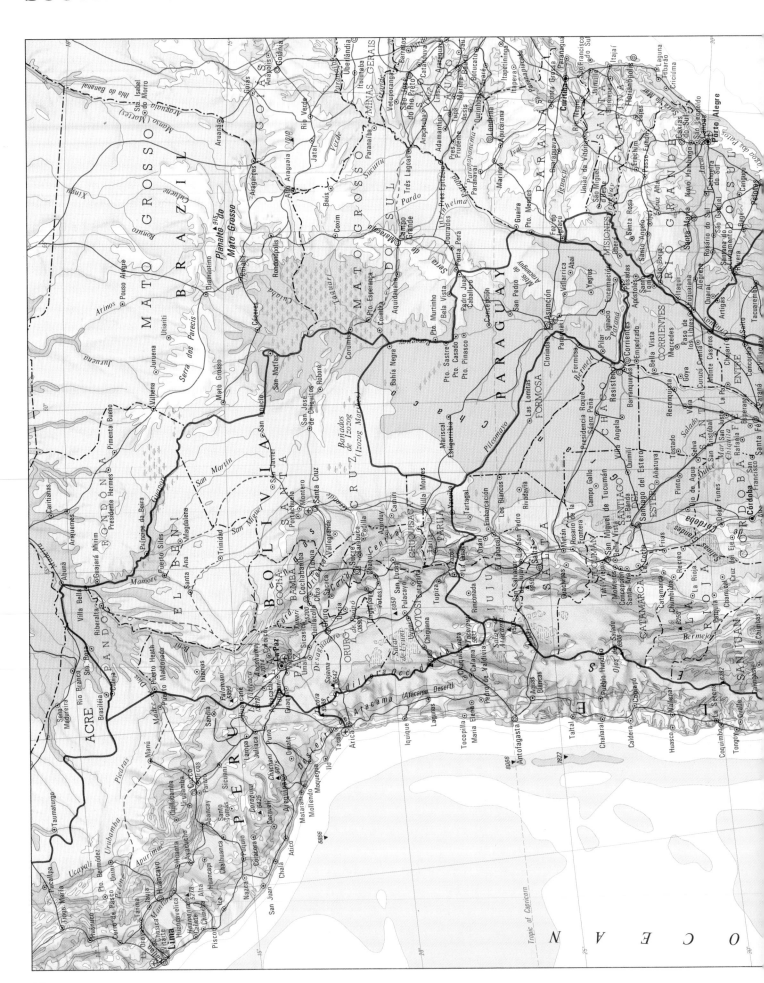

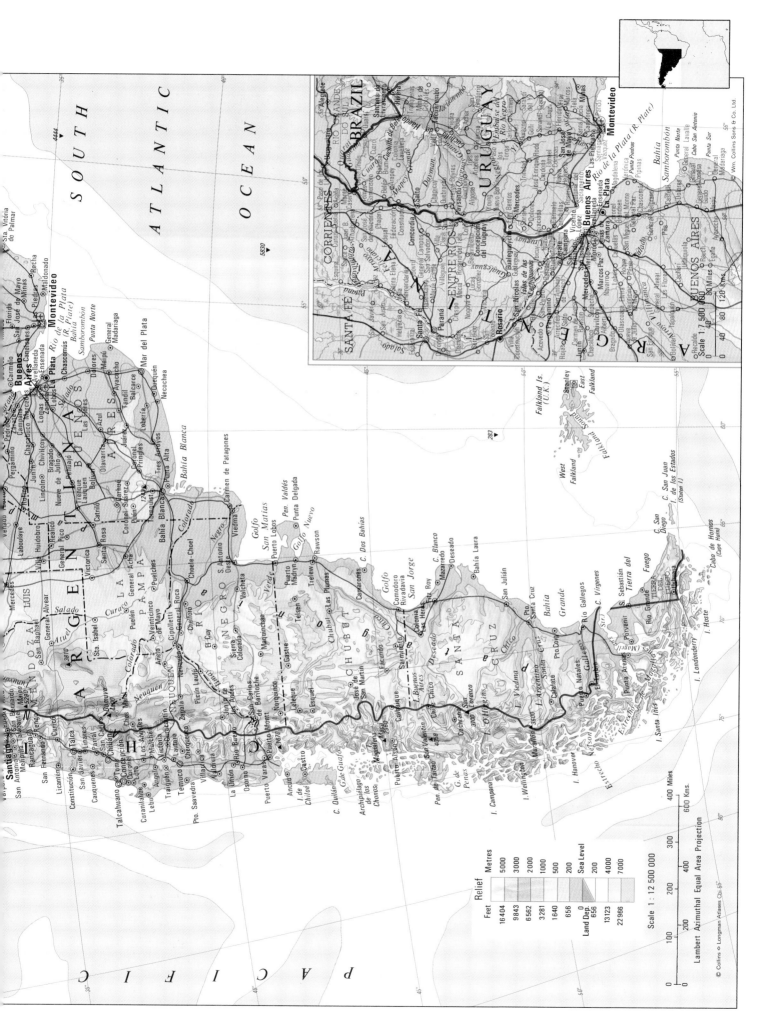

NORTHERN AFRICA

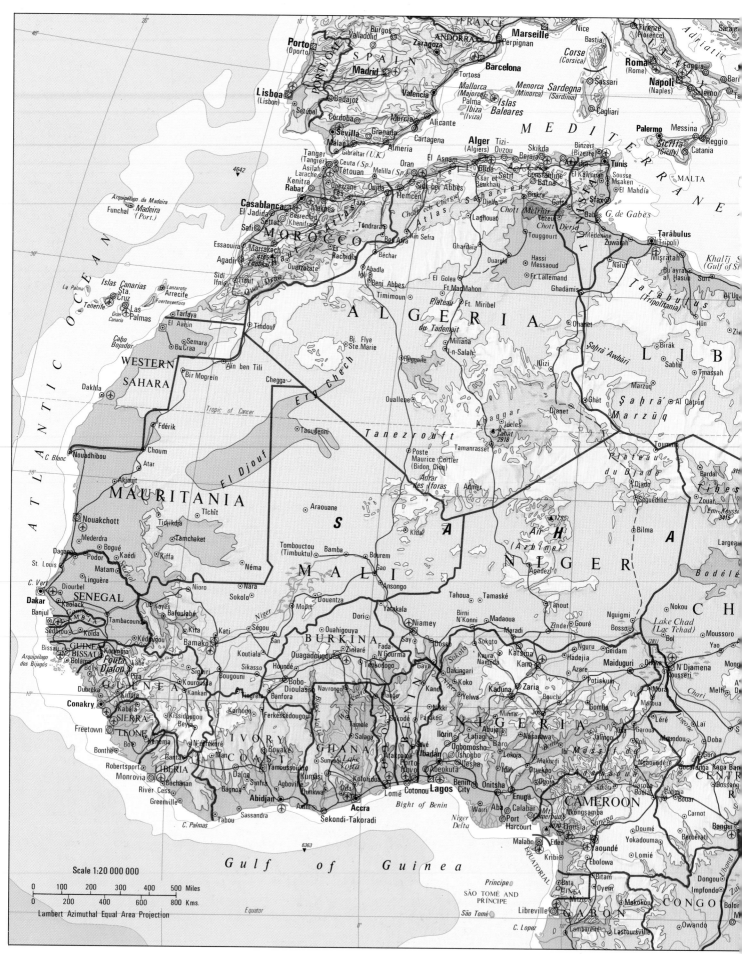

Scale 1:20 000 000

| 0 | 100 | 200 | 300 | 400 | 500 Miles |

| 0 | 200 | 400 | 600 | 800 Kms. |

Lambert Azimuthal Equal Area Projection

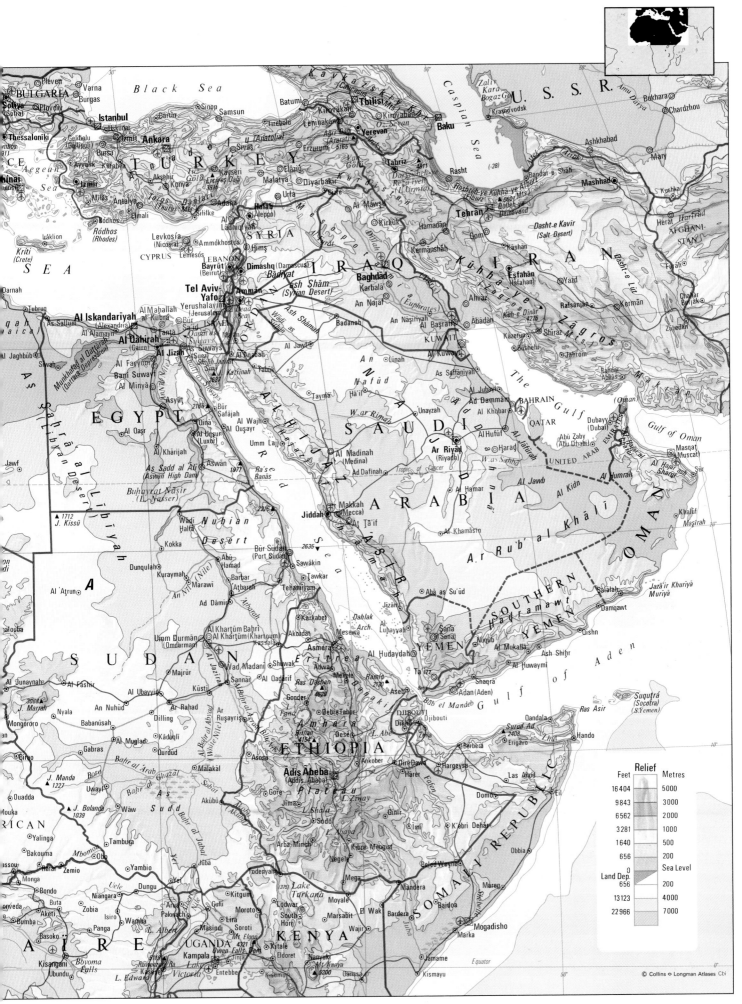

Black Sea

BULGARIA
Pleven
Varna
Burgas
Sofiya
(Sofia)
Plovdiv
Sinop
Samsun

Istanbul
Üsküdar
İzmit   Ankara
Bursa
Thessaloniki
Gelibolu
(Gallipoli)
İzmir
Kütahya

CE
Aegean
Sea
Ayvalık
Manisa
Afyon
Konya
Eskişehir
Kayseri
Sivas
Erzurum

Batumi
Kirovakan
Leninakan
Tbilisi
Kirovabad
Baku

Caspian
Sea

U.S.S.R.
Zaliv
Kara-
Bogaz
Krasnovodsk
Amu Darya
Bukhara
Chardzhou

Ashkhabad
Mary
Kushka

TURKEY
Elmalı
Antalya
Taurus Dağları
(Taurus Mts.)
Silifke
Adana
Halab
(Aleppo)

Erciyes Dağı
3916

Malatya
Diyarbakır
Urfa
Elazığ
Van
Van Gölü
Ağrı Dağı
(Ararat)
5165

Yerevan
Oz. Sevan

Tabriz
4811

Rasht
Bandar-e Shāh
(-28)

Herāt
Harīrūd
AFGHANI-
STAN

Kriti
(Crete)
Ródhos
(Rhodes)

SEA
Iráklion

Levkosía
(Nicosia)
CYPRUS
Lemesós
Ammókhostos

SYRIA
Ḩimṣ

Dimashq (Damascus)
Bādiyat
Ash Shām
(Syrian Desert)

Badaneh

Kirkūk
Hamadān

Tehrān
Dasht-e Kavir
(Salt Desert)

Qom
Kāshān

Mashhad
Kushka

Ḩamā

LEBANON
Bayrūt
(Beirut)

Tel Aviv
Yafo
ISRAEL
Yerushalayim
(Jerusalem)
Dead Sea

Amman
JORDAN

IRAQ
Baghdad
Karbalā'
An Najaf

Al Mawṣil

An Nāṣirīyah
Al Baṣrah

Eşfahān
(Isfahan)

Ahvāz

Kermānshāh

IRAN
Kūhhā-ye Zāgros
Zāgros Mts.

Yazd

Kāshān
Kermān
Chahār
Borjak

Darnah
Ṭubruq
As Sallūm

Al Iskandarīyah
(Alexandria)
Al 'Alamayn

Al Qāhirah
(Cairo)
Al Jīzah
(Giza)

Al Maḩallah
al Kubrā
Būr Sa'īd
Ṭanṭā
As Suways
(Suez)

Qanāt as
Suways

Kuwait
Al Kuwayt

An
Nafūd
Linah

As Saffānīyah

Ad Dammām
BAHRAIN

Rafsanjān
Shīrāz
Jahrom

Kāzerūn
Būshehr

Ābādān
Ā_bādān

Bandar 'Abbās

Makrān

Gulf of Oman

Shibh Jazīrat
Sīnā'
(Sinai)
Kāṭrīnah
2637
Ṭābah

As
Sallūm
Al Jaghbūb
Sīwah
Mukhfaḑ al Qaṭṭārah
(Qattara Depression)

Al Fayyūm
Banī Suwayf
Al Minyā

Asyūṭ
2186
Būr Safājah

Al Wajh
Umm Lajj

Tabūk
Ḩā'il
Taymā'

Unayzah
Al Jubayl
Al Khubar
QATAR
Al Hufūf
Harad

Abū Ẓaby
(Abu Dhabi)
Dubayy
(Dubai)

UNITED ARAB EMIRATES

Masqaṭ
Muscat

EGYPT
Al Qaṣr
Al K.hārijah

Qinā
Al Uqṣur
(Luxor)
Al Ousayr

Ra's Banās
1977

Jawf

Ar Riyāḑ
(Riyadh)
SAUDI
Al Jafūrah

Al 'Aṭrun
J. Kissū
1712

As Sadd al 'Ālī
(Aswan High Dam)
Aswān

Buḩayrat Nāṣir
(L. Nasser)

2216

AL HIJAZ
Al Madīnah
(Medina)

Ad Dafīnah
Tropic of Cancer
W. as Sahbā
Al Khamāsīn
Al Hamar
Al Jawb
Al Kidn
Al Ḩumrah

Ar Rub' al Khālī
Khalīf
Maṣīrah

OMAN
Al Hajar ash
Sharqī
Ṣūr

Wadi
Nubian
Desert
Ḩalfā
Kokka

Makkah
(Mecca)
Jiddah

At Ṭā'if

ARABIA
'ASĪR

SOUTHERN

Jazā'ir Khurīyā
Muriya
Ṣalālah
Ḩaḑramawt
Damqawt

Dunqulah
Kuraymah
Marawi
Abū
Ḩamad
Barbar
Atbarah

Būr Sūdān
(Port Sudan)
Sawākin
2635
Tawkar

Akordat
Dahlak
Arch.

Al Luḩayyah
Nuqūb
Al Mukallā
Ash Shiḩr
Al Ḩuwaymī
YEMEN

Ad Dāmir
Karkabet
Ţahāmīyam

Gulf of Aden

Al 'Aṭrun
SUDAN
Al Junaynah
Al Fāshir

Nyala
J. Marrah
3088

Mongororo
Babanūsah

Ar Rahad
Kūstī
Ar Ruṣayriṣ

An Nuḩūd
Dilling
Kāduqli

Al Ubayyiḑ

Al Khartūm Baḥri
Al Khartūm
(Khartoum)
Umm Durmān
(Omdurman)
Wad Madani
Al Jazīrah
Kassalā
Sannār
Al Qaḑārif
Shuwak

Eritrea
Atbara
Asmera
Mesewa
Keren

Mekele
Ras Dashen
4620
Gonder

Dahlak
Arch.

Ramlo
2130

Aseb
Danakil

DJIBOUTI
Djibouti
Dikhil
Zeila

Sana'
(Sanaa)

Dhamar
YEMEN
Ta'izz

Adan (Aden)
Shaqra

Berbera
Erigavo
Las Anod
Surud Ad
2408

Ras Asir
Qandala

Suquṭrā
(Socotra)
(S.Yemen)

Hando
Zhu

Al Muglad
Gabras

Umm Ruwābah

Tambura

Nyala
Birao

Ouadda
J. Manda
1227

Mouka
Yalinga

Bakouma

RICAN
asso
Monga

Bondo
Buta
Aketi
Bumba
Basoko

AIRE
Kisangani
Ubundu

Boyoma
Falls

Kisangani

Mbomou
Obo

Yambio
Uele
Niangara
Dungu
Panga
Wamba
Isiro
Zobia

Bahr al 'Arab
Boro

As
Sudd

Bahr al Ghazāl
Ākūbū
Sobat

Waw
Juba
Yei

J. Bolanda
1039

Mandera
Mareg

Baidoa
Bardera
Jilib

Juba
Lugh

SOMALI
REPUBLIC
Mogadisho
Marka
Obbia
Boled Weyne
Domo
Eil

ETHIOPIA
Debre Tabor
Amhara
4154
Dese
Ankober

Adis Abeba
(Addis Ababa)
Plateau
L. Tana
Fänd

Debre Markos

Gore
L. Shala
Jima
Sodo
Awasa
Arba Minch
Kibre Mengist
Negele

L. Ziway
L. Abaya

Dire Dawa
Harer
Jijiga

Hargeysa

Ogaden
Ginir
K'ebri Deḩar
Imī

Kitgum
Gulu
Lira
Soroti
Lake
Turkana
(375)
Moroto
Lodwar
South
Horr

Marsabit

Moyale
El Wak

Wajir

CENTRAL
Juba
Nairobi

KENYA
UGANDA
Kampala
Masindi
Mt Elgon
4321
Kitale
Eldoret
Mt Kenya
5200
Nanyuki
Garissa

Kasese
Entebbe
Lake Victoria
Kisumu
Kismayu

L. Albert
L. Edward

Ruwenzori
Ra

Owen Falls Dam

Equator

© Collins ○ Longman Atlases Cbi

Relief		
Feet		**Metres**
16 404		5000
9843		3000
6562		2000
3281		1000
1640		500
656		200
0		Sea Level
Land Dep.		
656		200
13 123		4000
22 966		7000

51

CENTRAL AND EAST AFRICA

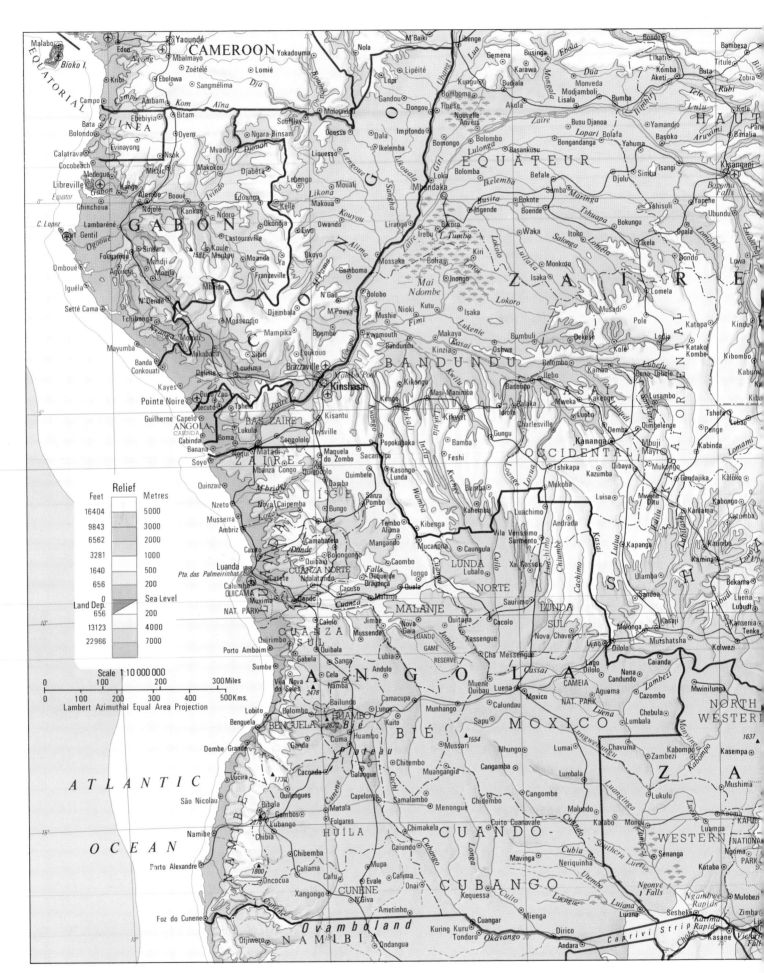

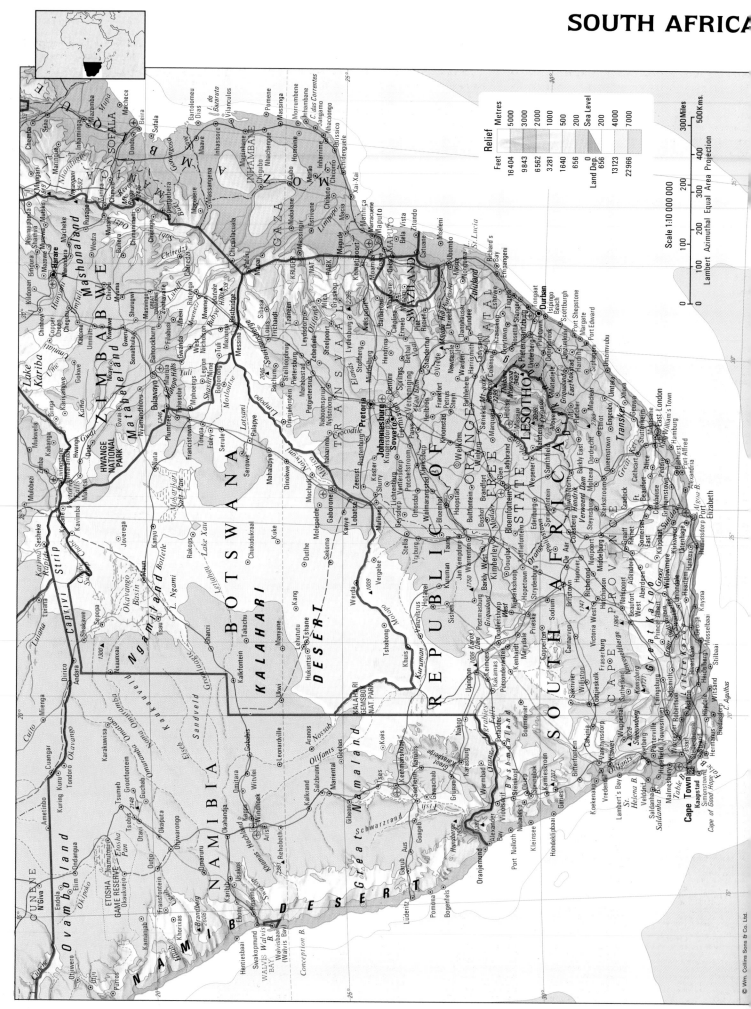

SOUTH AFRICA

Relief

Feet	Metres
16404	5000
9843	3000
6562	2000
3281	1000
1640	500
656	200
0	Sea Level
656	200
13123	4000
22966	7000

Land Dep.

Scale 1:10 000 000

300 Miles
500 Kms.

Lambert Azimuthal Equal Area Projection

© Wm. Collins Sons & Co. Ltd.

Introduction

The Index includes an alphabetical list of selected names appearing on the maps. Each entry consists of the name followed by a page reference and the name's location on the map, given by latitude and longitude co-ordinates. Most features are indexed to the largest scale map on which they appear, however when the name applies to countries or other extensive features it is generally indexed to the map on which it appears in its entirety. Aerial features are generally indexed using co-ordinates which indicate the centre of the feature. The latitude and longitude indicated for a point feature gives the location of the point on the map. In the case of rivers the mouth or confluence is always taken as the point of reference.

Names in the Index are generally in the local language and where a conventional English version exists, this is cross referenced to the entry in the local language. Names of features which extend across the boundaries of more than one country are usually named in English if no single official name exists. Names in languages not written in the Roman alphabet have been transliterated using the official system of the country if one exists, e.g. Pinyin system for China, otherwise the systems recognised by the United States Board on Geographical Names have been used.

Names abbreviated on the maps are given in full in the Index.

Abbreviations of Geographical Terms

b., B.	bay, Bay
c., C.	cape, Cape
d.	internal division e.g. county, region, state.
des.	desert
est.	estuary
f.	physical feature e.g. valley, plain, geographic district or region
g., G.	gulf, Gulf
i., I., is., Is.	island, Island, islands, Islands
l., L.	lake, Lake
mtn., Mtn.	mountain, Mountain
mts., Mts.	mountains, Mountains
pen., Pen.	peninsula, Peninsula
Pt.	Point
r.	river
resr., Resr.	reservoir, Reservoir
Sd.	Sound
str., Str.	strait, Strait

A

Aachen 16 50.46N 6.06E
Aarau 16 47.24N 8.04E
Aare r. 16 47.37N 8.13E
Aba 50 5.06N 7.21E
Abā as Su'ūd 24 17.28N 44.06E
Ābādān 24 30.21N 48.15E
Abadla 50 31.01N 2.45W
Abakan 23 53.43N 91.25E
Abaya, L. 51 6.20N 38.00E
Abbeville 12 50.06N 1.51E
Abbotsbury 9 50.40N 2.36W
Abe, L. 51 11.06N 41.50E
Abéché 51 13.49N 20.49E
Åbenrå 19 55.02N 9.26E
Aberayron 9 52.15N 4.16W
Aberdare 9 51.43N 3.27W
Aberdare Range mts. 53 0.20S 36.40E
Aberdeen 11 57.08N 2.07W
Aberdovey 9 52.33N 4.03W
Aberfeldy 11 56.37N 3.54W
Abergavenny 9 51.49N 3.01W
Abersoch 8 52.50N 4.31W
Aberystwyth 9 52.25N 4.06W
Abidjan 50 5.19N 4.01W
Abilene Tex. 40 32.27N 99.45W
Abingdon 9 51.40N 1.17W
Abitibi r. 44 51.03N 80.55W
Abitibi, L. 44 48.42N 79.45W
Abou Deïa 50 11.20N 19.20E
Aboyne 11 57.05N 2.48W
Abrantes 13 39.28N 8.12W
Abruzzi d. 14 42.05N 13.45E
Abu Dhabi see Abū Ẓaby 24
Abū Ḩamad 51 19.32N 33.20E
Abuja 50 9.12N 7.11E
Abunã 46 9.41S 65.20W
Abū Ẓaby 24 24.27N 54.23E
Åby 19 58.40N 16.11E
Abyaḑ, Al Baḩr al r. 24 15.38N 32.31E
Acámbaro 42 20.01N101.42W
Acapulco 42 16.51N 99.56W
Acatlán 42 18.12N 98.02W
Accra 50 5.33N 0.15W
Accrington 8 53.46N 2.22W
Achill I. 10 53.57N 10.00W
Achinsk 22 56.10N 90.10E
Aconcagua mtn. 48 32.39S 70.00W
Acqui 14 44.41N 8.28E
Acraman, L. 36 32.02S135.26E
Adamaoua, Massif de l' mts. 50 7.05N 12.00E
Adams N.Y. 44 43.49N 76.01W
Adams, Mt. 40 46.13N121.29W
'Adan 24 12.50N 45.00E
Adana 21 37.00N 35.19E
Adapazari 21 40.45N 30.23E
Adda r. 14 45.08N 9.55E
Ad Dafīnah 24 23.18N 41.58E
Ad Dāmir 51 17.37N 33.59E
Ad Dammām 24 26.23N 50.08E
Ad Darb 24 17.44N 42.15E
Ad Dawḩah 24 25.15N 51.34E
Addis Ababa see Ādīs Ābeba 51
Adelaide 36 34.56S138.36E
Aden see 'Adan 24
Aden, G. of 24 13.00N 50.00E
Adendorp 54 32.18S 24.31E
Adige r. 14 45.10N 12.20E
Adirondack Mts. 44 44.00N 74.00W
Ādīs Ābeba 51 9.03N 38.42E
Adiyaman 21 37.46N 38.15E
Admiralty Is. 30 2.10S147.00E
Adour r. 12 43.28N 1.35W
Adra 13 36.43N 3.03W
Adrano 14 37.39N 14.49E
Adriatic Sea 14 42.30N 16.00E
Ādwa 51 14.12N 38.56E
Aegean Sea 15 39.00N 25.00E
Afghanistan 25 32.45N 65.00E
Afmadu 53 0.27N 42.05E
Afyon 21 38.46N 30.32E
Agadez 50 17.00N 7.56E
Agadir 50 30.26N 9.36W
Agana 30 13.28N144.45E
Agboville 50 5.55N 4.15W
Agde 12 43.19N 3.28E
Agen 12 44.12N 0.38E
Aghada 10 51.50N 8.13W
Āgra 25 27.11N 78.01E
Agra r. 13 42.12N 1.43W
Agreda 13 41.51N 1.55W
Agri r. 15 40.13N 16.45E
Ağri 21 39.44N 43.03E
Ağri Daği mtn. 21 39.45N 44.15E
Agrigento 14 37.19N 13.36E
Aguascalientes 42 21.51N102.18W
Águeda r. 13 41.00N 6.56W
Aguilas 13 37.25N 1.35W
Agulhas, C. 54 34.50S 20.00E
Agulhas Negras mtn. 45 22.20S 44.43W
Ahaggar mts. 50 24.00N 5.50E
Ahaura 29 42.21S171.33E
Ahlen 16 51.46N 7.53E
Ahmadābād 25 23.02N 72.37E
Ahvāz 24 31.17N 48.44E
Aigues-Mortes 12 43.34N 4.11E
Ailsa Craig i. 11 55.15N 5.07W
Ain r. 12 45.47N 5.12E
Aïna r. 52 0.38N 12.47E
Aïn ben Tili 50 26.00N 9.32W
Aïn Sefra 50 32.45N 0.35W
Aïr mts. 50 18.30N 8.30E
Airdrie 11 55.52N 3.59W
Aire 12 43.39N 0.15W
Aire r. 8 53.42N 0.54W
Aisne r. 12 49.27N 2.55E
Aix-en-Provence 12 43.31N 5.27E
Aix-les-Bains 12 45.42N 5.55E
Aíyina i. 15 37.43N 23.30E
Aíyion 15 38.15N 22.05E
Ajaccio 12 41.55N 8.43E
Ajmer 25 26.27N 74.38E
Akashi 28 34.38N134.59E
Aketi 52 2.46N 23.51E
Akhḑar, Al Jabal al mts. 51 32.10N 22.00E
Akhelóös 15 38.20N 21.04E
Akhisar 15 38.54N 27.49E
Akita 26 39.44N140.05E
Akjoujt 50 19.45N 14.23W
Aklavik 38 68.12N135.00W
Ākobo r. 51 8.30N 33.15E
Akola 25 20.44N 77.00E
Akpatok I. 39 60.30N 68.30W
Akron Ohio 44 41.04N 81.31W
Aksaray 21 38.22N 34.02E
Akşehir 21 38.22N 31.24E
Aksu 25 42.10N 80.00E
Aktogay 22 46.57N 79.40E
Akūbū r. see Ākobo r. 51
Akxokesay 25 36.48N 91.06E
Alabama d. 41 33.00N 87.00W
Alabama r. 41 31.05N 87.55W
Alakurtti 20 67.00N 30.23E
Al 'Alamayn 51 30.50N 28.57E
Alamosa 40 37.28N105.54W
Alanya 21 36.32N 32.02E
Al' Aqabah 24 29.32N 35.00E
Alaşehir 15 38.22N 28.29E
Alaska d. 38 65.00N153.00W
Alaska, G. of 38 58.45N145.00W
Alaska Range mts. 38 62.10N152.00W
Al 'Aţrun 51 18.11N 26.36E
Alazani r. 21 41.06N 46.40E
Alba 14 44.42N 8.02E
Albacete 13 39.00N 1.52W
Alba-Iulia 17 46.04N 23.33E
Albania 15 41.00N 20.00E
Albany r. 39 52.10N 82.00W
Albany Ga. 41 31.37N 84.10W
Albany N.Y. 44 42.39N 73.45W
Albany Oreg. 40 44.38N123.07W
Al Başrah 24 30.33N 47.50E
Al Bayḑā' 51 32.50N 21.50E
Albemarle Sd. 41 36.10N 76.00W
Alberche r. 13 40.00N 4.45W
Albert, L. 53 1.45N 31.00E
Alberta d. 38 55.00N115.00W
Albert Nile r. 53 3.30N 32.00E
Albi 12 43.56N 2.08E
Ålborg 19 57.03N 9.56E
Alborz, Reshteh-ye Kūhhā-ye mts. 24 36.00N 52.30E
Albuquerque 40 35.05N106.38W
Alburquerque 13 39.13N 6.59W
Albury 37 36.03S146.53E
Alcácer do Sal 13 38.22N 8.30W
Alcamo 14 37.59N 12.58E
Alcañiz 13 41.03N 0.09W
Alcaudete 13 37.35N 4.05W
Alcázar de San Juan 13 39.24N 3.12W
Alcira 13 39.10N 0.27W
Alcoy 13 38.42N 0.29W
Alcudia 13 39.51N 3.09E
Aldan 23 58.44N125.22E
Aldan r. 23 63.30N130.00E
Aldeburgh 9 52.09N 1.35E
Alderney i. 9 49.42N 2.11W
Aldershot 9 51.15N 0.47W
Aldridge 9 52.36N 1.55W
Alegrete 49 29.46S 55.46W
Aleksandrovsk Sakhalinskiy 23 50.55N142.12E
Alençon 12 48.25N 0.05E
Aleppo see Ḩalab 24
Alès 12 44.08N 4.05E
Alessandria 14 44.54N 8.37E
Ålesund 18 62.28N 6.11E
Aleutian Is 30 52.00N176.00W
Aleutian Range mts. 38 58.00N156.00W
Alexander Archipelago is. 38 56.30N134.30W
Alexander Bay town 54 28.36S 16.26E
Alexandria B.C. 38 52.38N122.27W
Alexandria Ont. 44 45.18N 74.39W
Alexandria see Al Iskandarīyah 51
Alexandria Va. 44 38.48N 77.03W
Alexandroúpolis 15 40.50N 25.53E
Al Fāshir 51 13.37N 25.22E
Al Fayyūm 51 29.19N 30.50E
Alfiós r. 15 37.37N 21.27E
Alford 11 57.14N 2.42W
Al Furāt r. 24 31.00N 47.27E
Algeciras 13 36.08N 5.27W
Alger 50 36.50N 3.00E
Algeria 50 28.00N 2.00E
Alghero 14 40.33N 8.20E
Algiers see Alger 50
Algoa B. 54 33.50S 26.00E
Al Ḩajar ash Sharqī mts. 51 23.00N 59.00E
Al Ḩamar 24 22.26N 46.12E
Al Ḩudaydah 24 14.50N 42.58E
Al Hufūf 24 25.20N 49.34E
Al Ḩuwaymī 24 14.05N 47.44E
Aliákmon r. 15 40.30N 22.38E
Alicante 13 38.21N 0.29W
Alice Springs town 34 23.42S133.52E
Alima r. 52 1.36S 16.35E
Alingsås 19 57.56N 12.31E
Al Iskandarīyah 51 31.13N 29.55E
Aliwal North 54 30.41S 26.41E
Al Jaghbūb 51 29.42N 24.38E
Al Jawb f. 24 23.00N 50.00E
Al Jawf 24 29.49N 39.52E
Al Jazīrah f. 51 14.30N 33.00E
Al Jīzah 51 30.01N 31.12E
Al Jubayl 24 27.59N 49.40E
Al Junaynah 51 13.27N 22.30E
Al Khābūrah 24 23.58N 57.10E
Al Khamāsīn 24 20.29N 44.49E
Al Khārijah 51 25.27N 30.32E
Al Kharţūm 51 15.33N 32.35E
Al Kharţūm Baḩrī 51 15.39N 32.34E
Al Khubar 51 26.18N 50.06E
Al Kidn des. 24 22.20N 54.20E
Alkmaar 16 52.37N 4.44E
Al Kuwayt 24 29.20N 48.00E
Allāhābād 25 25.27N 81.51E
Allakaket 38 66.30N152.45W
Allegheny r. 44 40.27N 80.00W
Allegheny Mts. 41 38.30N 80.00W
Allen, Lough 10 54.07N 8.04W
Allentown 44 40.37N 75.30W
Aller r. 16 52.57N 9.11E
Alliance Nebr. 40 42.08N103.00W
Allier r. 12 46.58N 3.04E
Alloa 11 56.07N 3.49W
Al Luḩayyah 51 15.43N 42.42E
Alma-Ata 22 43.19N 76.55E
Almaden 34 17.20S144.41E
Almadén 13 38.47N 4.50W
Al Madīnah 24 24.30N 39.35E
Al Manāmah 24 26.12N 50.36E
Almansa 13 38.52N 1.06W
Almanzora r. 13 37.16N 1.49W
Al Mawşil 24 36.21N 43.08E
Almazán 13 41.29N 2.31W
Almeirim 13 39.12N 8.37W
Almelo 16 52.21N 6.40E
Almería 13 36.50N 2.26W
Älmhult 19 56.33N 14.08E
Al Minyā 51 28.06N 30.45E
Al Muglad 51 11.01N 27.50E
Al Mukallā 24 14.34N 49.09E
Al Mukhā 24 13.19N 43.15E
Almuñécar 13 36.44N 3.41W
Alnwick 8 55.25N 1.41W
Alofi 30 19.03S169.55W
Alónnisos i. 15 39.08N 23.50E
Alpes Maritimes mts. 12 44.07N 7.08E
Alpine 40 30.22N103.40W
Alps mts. 12 46.00N 7.30E
Al Qaḑārif 51 14.02N 35.24E
Al Qāhirah 51 30.03N 31.15E
Al Qaşr 51 25.42N 28.53E
Al Qaţrūn 50 24.55N 14.38E
Al Quşayr 51 26.04N 34.15E
Als i. 19 54.59N 9.55E
Alsace d. 12 48.25N 7.40E
Alsasua 13 42.54N 2.10W
Alston 11 54.48N 2.26W
Alta 18 70.00N 23.15E
Alta r. 18 69.50N 23.30E
Altai mts. 26 46.30N 93.30E
Altamura 15 40.50N 16.32E
Altanbulag 26 50.18N106.30E
Altea 13 38.37N 0.03W
Altenburg 16 50.59N 12.27E
Altnaharra 11 58.16N 4.26W
Alto Araguaia 47 17.19S 53.10W
Alton 9 51.08N 0.59W
Altoona 44 40.30N 78.24W
Al Ubayyiḑ 51 13.11N 30.10E
Al' Uqaylah 50 30.15N 19.12E
Al Uqşur 51 25.41N 32.24E
Alva 40 36.48N 98.40W
Alvarado 42 18.49N 95.46W
Älvdalen 19 61.14N 14.02E
Älvsbyn 18 65.39N 20.59E
Al Wajh 24 26.16N 36.28E
Alyaty 21 39.59N 49.20E
Amadeus, L. 32 24.50S130.45E
Amadjuak L. 39 65.00N 71.00W
Amagasaki 28 34.43N135.25E
Åmål 19 59.03N 12.42E
Amaliás 15 37.48N 21.21E
Amamula 53 0.17S 27.49E
Amares 13 41.38N 8.21W
Amarillo 40 35.14N101.50W
Amasya 21 40.37N 35.50E
Amazon r. see Amazonas r. 47
Amazonas r. 47 2.00S 52.00W
Ambāla 25 30.23N 76.46E
Ambarchik 23 69.39N162.27E
Amberg 16 49.27N 11.52E
Amble 8 55.20N 1.34W
Ambleside 8 54.26N 2.58W
Amboise 12 47.25N 1.00E
Ambriz 52 7.54S 13.12E
Amdo 25 32.22N 91.07E
Amersfoort 16 52.10N 5.23E
Amga 23 60.51N131.59E
Amga r. 23 62.40N135.20E
Amgu 26 45.48N137.36E
Amgun r. 23 53.10N139.47E
Amhara Plateau f. 51 10.00N 37.00E
Amiata mtn. 14 42.53N 11.37E
Amiens 12 49.54N 2.18E
Amlwch 8 53.24N 4.21W
'Ammān 24 31.57N 35.56E
Ammanford 9 51.48N 4.00W
Ammassalik 39 65.40N 38.00W
Ammókhostos 24 35.07N 33.57E
Amorgós i. 15 36.50N 25.55E
Ampala 43 13.16N 87.39W
Amrāvati 25 20.56N 77.45E
Amritsar 25 31.38N 74.53E
Amsterdam 16 52.22N 4.54E
Amu Darya r. 22 43.50N 59.00E
Amundsen G. 38 70.30N122.00W
Amur r. 23 53.17N140.00E
Anabar r. 23 72.40N113.30E
Anaconda 40 46.09N112.56W
Anadolu f. 21 38.00N 33.00E
Anadyr r. 23 65.00N176.00E
Anáfi i. 15 36.21N 25.50E
Anambas, Kepulauan is. 27 3.00N106.10E
Anápolis 47 16.19S 48.58W
Anār 24 30.54N 55.18E
Anatolia f. see Anadolu f. 21
Añatuya 48 28.26S 62.48W
Anchorage 38 61.10N150.00W
Ancón 46 11.50S 77.10W
Ancona 14 43.37N 13.33E
Andalusia 41 31.20N 86.30W
Andaman Islands 25 12.00N 92.45E
Andaman Sea 25 10.00N 95.00E
Andara 54 18.04S 21.26E
Andelot 12 48.15N 5.18E
Andenes 18 69.18N 16.10E
Anderson r. 38 69.45N129.00W
Andes mts. 49 32.40S 70.00W
Andhra Pradesh d. 25 17.00N 79.00E
Andizhan 22 40.48N 72.23E
Andorra town 12 42.30N 1.31E
Andorra 12 42.30N 1.32E
Andover 9 51.13N 1.29W
Andria 14 41.13N 16.18E
Andropov 20 58.01N 38.52E
Ándros i. 15 37.50N 24.50E
Andros I. 43 24.30N 78.00W
Andújar 13 38.02N 4.03W
Andulo 52 11.28S 16.43E
Aneto, Pico de mtn. 13 42.40N 0.19E
Angara r. 23 58.00N 93.00E
Angarsk 23 52.31N103.55E
Angaston 36 34.30S139.03E
Ånge 18 62.31N 15.40E
Ängelholm 19 56.15N 12.50E
Ångerman r. 18 63.00N 17.43E
Angers 12 47.29N 0.32W
Ångesån r. 18 66.22N 22.58E
Anglesey i. 8 53.16N 4.25W
Angoche 53 16.10S 39.57E
Angola 52 11.00S 18.00E
Angoulême 12 45.40N 0.10E
Anguilla i. 43 18.14N 63.05W
Angumu 53 0.10S 27.38E
Anholt i. 19 56.42N 11.34E
Aniak 38 61.32N159.40W
Anjouan i. 53 12.12S 44.28E
Ankara 21 39.55N 32.50E
Ānkober 51 9.32N 39.43E
Annaba 50 36.55N 7.47E
An Najaf 24 31.59N 44.19E
Annam Highlands see Annamitique, Chaîne mts. 27
Annamitique, Chaîne mts. 27 17.00N106.00E
Annan 11 54.59N 3.16W
Annan r. 11 54.58N 3.16W
Annandale f. 11 55.12N 3.25W
Anna Plains 32 19.18S121.34E
Annapurna mtn. 25 28.34N 83.50E
Ann Arbor 44 42.18N 83.43W
Annecy 12 45.54N 6.07E
Anniston 41 33.58N 85.50W
Annonay 12 45.15N 4.40E
An Nuhūd 51 12.41N 28.28E
Anoka 41 45.11N 93.20W
Anqing 26 30.40N117.03E
Ansbach 16 49.18N 10.36E
Anshan 26 41.06N122.58E
Anstruther 11 56.14N 2.42W
Antakya 21 36.12N 36.10E
Antalya 21 36.53N 39.42E
Antananarivo 3 18.55S 47.31E
Antequera 13 37.01N 4.34W
Antibes 12 43.35N 7.07E
Anticosti, Île d' i. 39 49.20N 63.00W
Antigua 42 14.33N 90.42W
Antigua i. 43 17.09N 61.49W
Antipodes Is. 30 49.42S178.50E
Antofagasta 48 23.39S 70.24W
Antrain 12 48.28N 1.30W
Antrim 10 54.43N 6.14W
Antrim d. 10 54.58N 6.20W
Antrim, Mts. of 10 55.00N 6.10W
Antwerpen 16 51.13N 4.25E
Anvik 38 62.38N160.20W
Anxi Gansu 26 40.32N 95.57E
Anyang 26 36.05N114.20E
Anzio 14 41.27N 12.37E
Aomori 26 40.50N140.43E
Aosta 14 45.43N 7.19E
Apalachee B. 41 29.30N 84.00W
Aparri 27 18.22N121.40E
Apeldoorn 16 52.13N 5.57E
Apia 30 13.48S171.45W
Apostle Is. 41 47.00N 90.30W
Apóstoles 48 27.55S 55.45W
Appalachian Mts. 41 39.30N 78.00W
Appennino mts. 14 42.00N 13.30E
Appleby 8 54.35N 2.29W
Appleton 41 44.17N 88.24W
Apucarana 45 23.34S 51.28W
Apure r. 46 7.40N 66.30W
Aquidauana 48 20.27S 55.45W
Aquila 42 18.30N103.50W
Aquitaine d. 12 44.40N 0.00
'Arab, Baḩr al r. 51 9.02N 29.28E
Arabian Sea 24 15.00N 64.00E
Aracaju 47 10.54S 37.07W
Araçatuba 45 21.12S 50.24W
Arafura Sea 27 9.00S133.00E
Aragarças 47 15.55S 52.12W
Aragón r. 13 42.20N 1.45W
Araguaia r. 47 5.20S 48.30W
Araguari r. 47 1.15N 50.05W
Arāk 24 34.06N 49.44E
Arakan Yoma mts. 25 19.30N 94.30E
Araks r. 21 40.00N 48.28E
Aral Sea see Aralskoye More sea 22
Aralsk 22 46.56N 61.43E
Aralskoye More sea 22 45.00N 60.00E
Aramac 34 22.59S145.14E
Aranda de Duero 13 41.40N 3.41W
Aran I. 10 53.07N 9.38W
Aran Is. 10 53.07N 9.38W
Aranjuez 13 40.02N 3.37W
Araouane 50 18.53N 3.31W
Araraquara 45 21.46S 48.08W
Ararat 36 37.20S143.00E
Ararat mtn. see Ağri Daği mtn. 21
Aras r. Turkey see Araks r. 21
Araxá 45 19.37S 46.50W
Arbatax 14 39.56N 9.41E
Arbroath 11 56.34N 2.35W
Arcachon 12 44.40N 1.11W
Arctic Bay town 39 73.05N 85.20W
Arctic Red r. 38 67.26N133.48W
Arctic Red River town 38 67.27N133.46W
Arda r. 15 41.39N 26.30E
Ardabīl 24 38.15N 48.18E
Ardara 10 54.46N 8.25W
Ardèche r. 12 44.31N 4.40E
Ardennes mts. 16 50.10N 5.30E
Ardila r. 13 38.10N 7.30W
Ardmore 10 51.58N 7.43W
Ardnamurchan, Pt. of 11 56.44N 6.14W
Ardrossan 11 55.38N 4.49W
Ards Pen. 10 54.30N 5.30W
Åre 18 63.25N 13.05E
Arecibo 43 18.29N 66.44W
Arena, Pt. 40 38.58N123.44W
Arendal 19 58.27N 8.48E
Arequipa 46 16.25S 71.32W
Arès 12 44.47N 1.08W
Arévalo 13 41.03N 4.43W
Arezzo 14 43.27N 11.52E
Arganda 13 40.19N 3.26W
Argelès-sur-Mer 12 42.33N 3.01E
Argens r. 12 43.10N 6.45E
Argentan 12 48.45N 0.01W
Argentina 49 36.00S 63.00W
Argentino, L. 49 50.15S 72.25W
Argenton 12 46.36N 1.30E
Argeş r. 15 44.13N 26.22E
Árgos 15 37.37N 22.45E
Argostólion 15 38.10N 20.30E
Århus 19 56.09N 10.13E
Ariano 14 41.04N 15.00E
Arica 48 18.29S 70.20W
Arima 46 10.38N 61.17W
Arinos r. 47 10.20S 57.35W
Aris 54 22.48S 17.10E
Arisaig 11 56.55N 5.51W
Ariza 13 41.19N 2.03W
Arizona d. 40 34.00N112.00W
Arkaig, Loch 11 56.58N 5.08W
Arkansas d. 41 35.00N 92.00W
Arkansas r. 41 33.50N 91.00W
Arkansas City 41 37.03N 97.02W
Arkhangel'sk 20 64.32N 41.10E
Árki i. 15 37.22N 26.45E
Arklow 10 52.47N 6.10W
Arlberg Pass 16 47.00N 10.05E
Arles 12 43.41N 4.38E
Arlington Va. 44 38.52N 77.05W
Arlon 16 49.41N 5.49E
Armadale 33 32.10S115.57E
Armagh 10 54.21N 6.41W
Armagh d. 10 54.16N 6.35W
Armavir 21 44.59N 41.10E
Armenia 46 4.32N 75.40W
Armidale 37 30.32S151.40E
Arnaud r. 39 60.00N 69.45W
Årnes 19 60.09N 11.28E
Arnhem 16 52.00N 5.55E
Arnhem, C. 34 12.10S137.00E
Arnhem B. 34 12.20S136.12E
Arnhem Land f. 34 13.10S134.30E
Arno r. 14 43.43N 10.17E
Ar Rahad 51 12.42N 30.33E
Arran i. 11 55.35N 5.14W
Arras 12 50.17N 2.46E
Arrecife 50 28.57N 13.32W
Ar Riyāḑ 24 24.39N 46.44E
Arrochar 11 56.12N 4.44W
Arrow, Lough 10 54.03N 8.20W
Ar Rub' al Khālī des. 24 19.00N 50.30E
Ar Ruşayriş 51 11.52N 34.23E
Árta 15 39.10N 20.57E
Artesia 40 32.51N104.24W
Arthur's Pass 29 42.50S171.45E
Artillery L. 38 63.09N107.52W
Artvin 21 41.12N 41.48E
Aru, Kepulauan is. 27 6.00S134.30E
Arua 53 3.02N 30.56E
Aruanã 47 14.54S 51.05W
Aruba i. 43 12.30N 70.00W
Arunachal Pradesh d. 25 28.40N 94.60E
Aruwimi r. 52 1.20N 23.36E
Arvagh 10 53.56N 7.35W
Arvidsjaur 18 65.35N 19.07E
Arzignano 14 45.31N 11.20E
Asahi dake mtn. 26 43.42N142.54E
Asansol 25 23.41N 86.59E
Aschaffenburg 16 49.58N 9.10E
Aschersleben 16 51.46N 11.28E
Ascoli Piceno 14 42.52N 13.36E
Aseb 51 13.01N 42.47E
Åseda 19 57.10N 15.20E
Ashbourne 10 53.31N 6.25W
Ashburton r. 32 21.15S115.00E
Ashburton 29 43.54S171.46E
Ashby de la Zouch 9 52.45N 1.29W
Ashcroft 38 50.43N121.17W
Asheville 41 35.35N 82.35W
Ashford Kent 9 51.08N 0.53E
Ashington 8 55.11N 1.34W
Ash Shiḩr 24 14.45N 49.36E
Ashton 54 33.49S 20.04E
Asinara i. 14 41.04N 8.18E
'Asīr f. 24 19.00N 42.00E
Askeaton 10 52.36N 9.00W
Askersund 19 58.53N 14.54E
Askim 19 59.35N 11.10E
Āsmera 51 15.20N 38.58E
Aspiring, Mt. 29 44.20S168.45E
As Saffānīyah 24 28.00N 48.48E
As Sallūm 51 31.31N 25.09E
Assam d. 25 26.30N 93.00E
Assen 16 53.00N 6.34E
Assiniboia 38 49.38N105.59W
Assis 45 22.37S 50.25W
As Suways 51 29.59N 32.33E
Asti 14 44.54N 8.13E
Astipálaia i. 15 36.35N 26.25E
Astorga 13 42.30N 6.02W
Astoria 40 46.12N123.50W
Astrakhan 21 46.22N 48.00E
Asunción 45 25.15S 57.40W
Aswān 51 24.05N 32.56E
Aswan High Dam see As Sadd al 'Ālī 51
Asyūţ 51 27.14N 31.07E
Atacama, Desierto des. 48 20.00S 69.00W
Atacama Desert see Atacama, Desierto des. 48
Atar 50 20.32N 13.08W
Atasu 22 48.42N 71.38E
'Aţbarah 51 17.42N 34.00E
'Aţbarah r. 51 17.47N 34.00E
Athabasca 38 54.44N113.15W
Athabasca r. 38 58.30N111.00W
Athabasca, L. 38 59.30N109.00W
Athenry 10 53.18N 8.45W
Athens see Athínai 15
Athens Ga. 41 33.57N 83.24W
Athínai 15 37.59N 23.42E
Athlone 10 53.26N 7.57W
Atholl, Forest of 11 56.50N 3.55W
Áthos mtn. 15 40.09N 24.19E
Atlanta Ga. 41 33.45N 84.23W
Atlantic City 44 39.22N 74.26W
Atlas Saharien mts. 50 34.20N 2.00E
Atlin 38 59.35N133.42W
Atrak r. Iran see Atrek r. 24
Ätran r. 19 56.53N 12.30E
Atrek r. 24 37.23N 54.00E
Aţ Ţā'if 24 21.15N 40.21E
Aubagne 12 43.17N 5.35E
Aube r. 12 48.30N 3.37E
Aubin 12 44.32N 2.14E
Aubusson 12 45.57N 2.11E
Auch 12 43.40N 0.36E
Auchterarder 11 56.18N 3.43W
Auckland 29 36.55S174.45E
Auckland Is. 30 50.35S166.00E
Aude r. 12 43.13N 2.20E
Augrabies Falls f. 54 28.33S 20.27E
Augsburg 16 48.21N 10.54E
Augusta Ga. 41 33.29N 82.00W
Aulnay 12 46.02N 0.22W
Aulne r. 12 48.30N 4.11W
Aumale 12 49.46N 1.45E
Aurich 16 53.28N 7.29E
Aurillac 12 44.56N 2.26E
Aus 54 26.41S 16.14E
Austin Minn. 41 43.40N 92.58W

Austin Tex. 40 30.18N 97.47W
Australia 27
Australian Alps mts. 37 36.30S148.30E
Australian Capital Territory d. 37 35.30S149.00E
Austria 16 47.30N 14.00E
Autun 12 46.58N 4.18E
Auxerre 12 47.48N 3.35E
Aux Sables r. 44 46.13N 82.04W
Avallon 12 47.30N 3.54E
Avanos 21 38.44N 34.51E
Avarua Rarotonga 30 21.12S159.46W
Aveiro 13 40.40N 8.35W
Avellaneda 49 34.40S 58.20W
Avellino 14 40.55N 14.46E
Aversa 14 40.58N 14.12E
Avesta 19 60.09N 16.12E
Aveyron r. 12 44.09N 1.10E
Avezzano 14 42.03N 13.26E
Aviemore 11 57.12N 3.50W
Avignon 12 43.56N 4.48E
Ávila 13 40.39N 4.42W
Avilés 13 43.35N 5.57W
Avon r. Australia 33 31.40S116.07E
Avon d. 9 51.35N 2.40W
Avon r. Dorset 9 50.43N 1.45W
Avon r. Glos. 9 52.00N 2.10W
Avonmouth 9 51.30N 2.42W
Avranches 12 48.42N 1.21W
Awe, Loch 11 56.18N 5.24W
Axel Heiberg I. 39 79.30N 90.00W
Axim 50 4.53N 2.14W
Axiós r. 15 40.31N 22.43E
Axminster 9 50.47N 3.01W
Ayaguz 22 47.59N 80.27E
Aydin 15 37.52N 27.50E
Áyios Evstrátios i. 15 39.30N 25.00E
Aylesbury 9 51.48N 0.49W
Aylsham 8 52.48N 1.16E
Ayr 11 55.28N 4.37W
Ayr r. 11 55.28N 4.38W
Ayre, Pt. of 8 54.25N 4.22W
Ayvalik 15 39.19N 26.42E
Azbine mts. see Aïr mts. 50
Azov, Sea of see Azovskoye More 21
Azovskoye More sea 21 46.00N 36.30E
Azraq, Al Baḥr al r. 51 15.45N 32.25E
Azuaga 13 38.16N 5.40W
Azul 49 36.46S 59.50W

B

Babanūsah 51 11.20N 27.48E
Babar, Kepulauan is. 27 8.00S129.30E
Bab el Mandeb str. 51 13.00N 43.10E
Bacan i. 27 0.73S127.63E
Bacău 17 46.32N 26.59E
Baccarat 12 48.27N 6.45E
Badajoz 13 38.53N 6.58W
Badalona 13 41.27N 2.15E
Badanah 24 30.59N 41.02E
Baden 16 48.01N 16.14E
Baden-Baden 16 48.45N 8.15E
Badgastein 16 47.07N 13.09E
Bādiyat ash Shām des. 24 32.00N 39.00E
Baffin d. 39 66.00N 72.00W
Baffin B. 39 74.00N 70.00W
Baffin I. 39 68.50N 70.00W
Bāfq 24 31.35N 55.21E
Bafra 21 41.34N 35.56E
Bagamoyo 53 6.26S 38.55E
Bagé 45 31.22S 54.06W
Baghdād 24 33.20N 44.26E
Bagheria 14 38.05N 13.30E
Baghlān 25 36.11N 68.44E
Bahamas 43 23.30N 75.00W
Bahāwalpur 25 29.24N 71.41E
Bahi 53 5.59S 35.15E
Bahía, Islas de la is. 43 16.10N 86.30W
Bahía Blanca 45 38.45S 62.15W
Bahrain 24 26.00N 50.35E
Baião 47 2.41S 49.41W
Bailundo 52 12.13S 15.46E
Baing 27 10.15S120.34E
Baird Mts. 38 67.35N161.30W
Baja 17 46.12N 18.58E
Baja California pen. 42 30.00N115.00W
Bakali r. 52 3.58S 17.10E
Baker Mont. 40 46.23N104.16W
Baker Oreg. 40 44.46N117.50W
Baker, Mt. 40 48.48N121.10W
Bakersfield 40 35.25N119.00W
Bakouma 51 5.42N 22.47E
Baku 21 40.22N 49.53E
Bala 8 52.54N 3.36W
Balaklava 21 44.31N 33.35E
Balakovo 20 52.04N 47.46E
Balama 53 13.19S 38.35E
Balashov 21 51.30N 43.10E
Balasore 25 21.30N 86.56E
Balboa 43 8.37N 79.33W
Balbriggan 10 53.36N 6.12W
Balcarce 49 37.52S 58.15W
Balclutha 29 46.16S169.46E
Baleares, Islas is. 13 39.30N 2.30E
Bali i. 27 8.20S115.07E
Balikesir 15 39.38N 27.51E
Balkan Mts. see Stara Planina mts. 15
Balkhash 22 46.51N 75.00E
Ballachulish 11 56.40N 5.08W
Ballantrae 11 55.06N 5.01W
Ballarat 36 37.36S143.58E
Ballater 11 57.03N 3.03W
Ballenas, Bahía de b. 42 26.40N113.30W
Ballina 10 54.08N 9.10W
Ballinasloe 10 53.20N 8.15W
Ballycastle 10 55.12N 6.15W
Ballyclare 10 54.45N 6.00W
Ballyconnell 10 54.06N 7.37W
Ballydehob 10 51.34N 9.28W
Ballygar 10 53.32N 8.20W
Ballygawley 10 54.28N 7.03W
Ballykelly 10 55.03N 7.00W
Ballymena 10 54.52N 6.17W
Ballymoney 10 55.04N 6.31W
Ballyshannon 10 54.30N 8.11W
Ballyvaughan 10 53.06N 9.09W
Ballyvourney 10 51.57N 9.10W
Balombo 52 12.20S 14.45E
Balsas r. 42 18.10N102.05W
Baltic Sea 19 57.00N 20.00E
Baltimore Md. 44 39.17N 76.37W
Baluchistan f. 25 28.00N 66.00E
Bamako 50 12.40N 7.59W
Bamberg 16 49.54N 10.53E
Bambesa 52 3.27N 25.43E
Bampton Devon 9 51.00N 3.29W
Banaba i. 30 0.52S169.35E
Banagher 10 53.12N 8.00W
Banalia 52 1.33N 25.23E
Banās, Ra's c. 24 23.54N 35.48E
Banbridge 10 54.21N 6.17W
Banbury 9 52.04N 1.21W
Banchory 11 57.03N 2.30W
Banda 52 3.47S 11.04E
Banda, Laut sea 27 5.00S128.00E
Banda Aceh 27 5.35N 95.20E
Bandar 'Abbās 24 27.10N 56.15E
Bandar-e Torkeman 51 36.55N 54.05E
Bandar Seri Begawan 27 4.56N114.58E
Banda Sea see Banda, Laut sea 27
Bandawe 53 11.57S 34.11E
Bandeira mtn. 45 20.25S 41.45W
Bandirma 15 40.22N 28.00E
Bandon 10 51.45N 8.45W
Bandon r. 10 51.43N 8.38W
Bandundu 52 3.20S 17.24E
Bandung 27 6.57S107.34E
Banff 11 57.40N 2.31W
Bangalore 25 12.58N 77.35E
Banghāzī 50 32.07N 20.05E
Bangka i. 27 2.20S106.10E
Bangkok see Krung Thep 27
Bangladesh 25 24.30N 90.00E
Bangor U.K. 10 54.40N 5.41W
Bangor U.K. 8 53.13N 4.09W
Bangor Maine 44 44.49N 68.47W
Bangui 50 4.23N 18.37E
Bangweulu, L. 53 11.15S 29.45E
Bani Suwayf 51 29.05N 31.05E
Banjarmasin 27 3.22S114.36E
Banjul 50 13.28N 16.39W
Ban Kantang 27 7.25N 99.35E
Banks I. N.W.T. 38 73.00N122.00W
Banks Pen. 29 43.45S173.10E
Banks Str. 35 40.37S148.07E
Bannockburn 11 56.06N 3.55W
Bantry 10 51.41N 9.27W
Bantry B. 10 51.40N 9.40W
Baoji 26 34.20N107.17E
Baoshan 26 25.07N 99.08E
Baotou 26 40.35N109.59E
Baradine r. 37 30.17S148.27E
Baranoa 46 10.50N 74.55W
Barbacena 45 21.13S 43.47W
Barbados 43 13.20N 59.40W
Barbastro 13 42.02N 0.07E
Barberton 54 25.46S 31.02E
Barbezieux 12 45.28N 0.09W
Barbuda i. 43 17.41N 61.48W
Barcaldine 34 23.31S145.15E
Barcellona 14 38.10N 15.13E
Barcelona 13 41.25N 2.10E
Bardai 50 21.21N 16.56E
Bardera 53 2.18N 42.18E
Bardsey i. 8 52.45N 4.48W
Bareilly 25 28.21N 79.25E
Barents Sea 20 73.00N 40.00E
Bari 15 41.08N 16.52E
Barito r. 27 3.35S114.35E
Barking 9 51.32N 0.05E
Barkly East 54 30.58S 27.33E
Barkly Tableland f. 34 19.00S136.40E
Barkly West 54 28.32S 24.29E
Bar-le-Duc 12 48.46N 5.10E
Barlee, L. 33 29.30S119.30E
Barlee Range mts. 32 23.40S116.00E
Barletta 14 41.20N 16.15E
Barmouth 8 52.44N 4.03W
Barnard Castle town 8 54.33N 1.55W
Barnaul 22 53.21N 83.15E
Barnet 9 51.39N 0.11W
Barnsley 8 53.33N 1.29W
Barnstaple 9 51.05N 4.03W
Baro 50 8.34N 6.26E
Barra i. 11 56.59N 7.28W
Barra Mansa 45 22.35S 44.12W
Barranca 46 4.50S 76.40W
Barrancas 46 8.45N 62.13W
Barranqueras 45 27.30S 58.55W
Barranquilla 46 11.10N 74.50W
Barreiras 47 12.09S 44.58W
Barreiro 13 38.40N 9.05W
Barreiros 47 8.49S 35.12W
Barrême 16 43.57N 6.22E
Barretos 45 20.37S 48.38W
Barrhead 11 55.47N 4.24W
Barrie 44 44.24N 79.40W
Barrington Tops mts. 37 32.30S151.28E
Barrow r. 10 52.17N 7.00W
Barrow 38 71.16N156.50W
Barrow Creek town 34 21.32S133.53E
Barrow I. 32 21.40S115.27E
Barrow-in-Furness 8 54.08N 3.15W
Barry 9 51.23N 3.19W
Barstow 40 34.55N117.01W
Bar-sur-Aube 12 48.14N 4.43E
Basel 16 47.33N 7.36E
Basilan i. 27 6.40N122.10E
Basildon 9 51.34N 0.25E
Basingstoke 9 51.15N 1.05W
Basoko 52 1.20N 23.36E
Basongo 52 4.23S 20.28E
Bassein 25 16.46N 94.45E
Basse-Terre 43 16.00N 61.43W
Bass Str. 35 39.45S146.00E
Bastia 12 42.41N 9.26E
Bastogne 16 50.00N 5.43E
Batang 26 30.02N 99.01E
Batangas 27 13.46N121.01E
Bath 9 51.22N 2.22W
Bathgate 11 55.44N 3.38W
Bathurst, C. 38 70.30N128.00W
Bathurst I. 39 76.00N100.00W
Bathurst Inlet town 38 66.48N108.00W
Batley 8 53.43N 1.38W
Baton Rouge 41 30.30N 91.10W
Battle 9 50.55N 0.30E
Battle Creek town 44 42.20N 85.11W
Batu mtn. 24 6.55N 39.46E
Batu, Kepulauan is. 27 0.30S 98.20E
Batumi 21 41.37N 41.36E
Baugé 12 47.33N 0.06W
Bauru 45 22.19S 49.07W
Bayan Har Shan mts. 26 34.00N 97.20E
Bayburt 21 40.15N 40.16E
Bay City Mich. 44 43.35N 83.52W
Bayern d. 16 48.30N 11.30E
Bayeux 12 49.16N 0.42W
Baykal, Ozero l. 23 53.30N108.00E
Bayonne 12 43.30N 1.28W
Bayreuth 16 49.56N 11.35E
Bayrūt 24 33.52N 35.30E
Baza 13 37.30N 2.45W
Bazas 12 44.26N 0.13W
Beachy Head 9 50.43N 0.15E
Beaufort Sea 38 72.00N141.00W
Beaufort West 54 32.20S 22.34E
Beauly 11 57.29N 4.29W
Beauly r. 11 57.29N 4.25W
Beaumont Tex. 41 30.04N 94.06W
Beaune 12 47.02N 4.50E
Beauvais 12 49.26N 2.05E
Beccles 9 52.27N 1.33E
Béchar 50 31.35N 2.17W
Bedford 9 52.08N 0.29W
Bedford, C. 34 15.14S145.21E
Bedford Levels f. 9 52.35N 0.08W
Bedfordshire d. 9 52.04N 0.28W
Bedlington 8 55.08N 1.34W
Beeston 8 52.55N 1.11W
Befale 52 0.27N 21.01E
Beg, Lough 10 54.47N 6.29W
Begna r. 19 60.32N 10.00E
Beijing 26 39.55N116.25E
Beira 54 19.49S 34.52E
Beirut see Bayrūt 24
Beitbridge 54 22.10S 30.01E
Beja 13 38.01N 7.52W
Béjar 13 40.24N 5.45W
Bela 25 26.14N 66.19E
Belalcázar 13 38.35N 5.10W
Belang 27 0.58N124.56E
Belau 30 7.30N134.30E
Belaya r. 22 55.40N 52.30E
Belcher Is. 39 56.00N 79.00W
Belcoo 10 54.18N 7.53W
Belém 47 1.27S 48.29W
Belen 40 34.39N106.48W
Belén, Cuchilla de mts. 49 30.49S 56.28W
Belfast 10 54.36N 5.57W
Belfast Lough 10 54.42N 5.45W
Belfort 12 47.38N 6.52E
Belgium 16 51.00N 4.30E
Belgorod 21 50.38N 36.36E
Belgrade see Beograd 17
Belitung i. 27 3.00S108.00E
Belize Belize 43 17.29N 88.20W
Belize C. America 43 17.00N 88.30W
Bellary 25 15.11N 76.54E
Belle Île 12 47.20N 3.10W
Belle Isle, Str. of 39 51.35N 56.30W
Belleville 44 44.10N 77.23W
Bell Ville 49 32.35S 62.41W
Belmopan 43 17.25N 88.46W
Belmullet 10 54.14N 10.00W
Belo Horizonte 45 19.45S 43.54W
Beloye More sea 20 65.30N 38.00E
Belozersk 20 60.00N 37.49E
Beltsy 17 47.45N 27.59E
Benalla 37 36.35S145.58E
Benavente 13 42.00N 5.40W
Benbecula i. 11 57.26N 7.18W
Ben Cruachan mtn. 11 56.26N 5.18W
Bend 40 44.04N121.20W
Bendigo 36 36.48S144.21E
Bengal, B. of 25 20.00N 90.00E
Benghazi see Banghāzī 50
Bengkulu 27 3.46S102.18E
Benguela 52 12.34S 13.24E
Ben Hope mtn. 11 58.24N 4.36W
Beni r. 48 10.23S 65.24W
Benidorm 13 38.33N 0.09W
Benin 50 9.30N 2.15E
Benin, Bight of 50 5.30N 3.00E
Benin City 50 6.19N 5.41E
Ben Lomond mtn. N.S.W. 37 30.04S151.43E
Ben Lomond mtn. U.K. 11 56.12N 4.38W
Ben Macdhui mtn. 11 57.04N 3.40W
Ben More mtn. Central 11 56.23N 4.31W
Ben More mtn. Strath. 11 56.26N 6.02W
Ben More Assynt mtn. 11 58.07N 4.52W
Ben Nevis mtn. 11 56.48N 5.00W
Benoni 54 26.12S 28.18E
Bentinck I. 34 17.04S139.30E
Benue r. 50 7.52N 6.45E
Ben Wyvis mtn. 11 57.40N 4.35W
Benxi 26 41.21N123.47E
Beograd 17 44.49N 20.28E
Berbera 51 10.28N 45.02E
Berbérati 50 4.19N 15.51E
Berdyansk 21 46.45N 36.47E
Bergama 15 39.08N 27.10E
Bergamo 14 45.42N 9.40E
Bergen 19 60.23N 5.20E
Bergen op Zoom 16 51.30N 4.17E
Bergerac 12 44.50N 0.29E
Bering Sea 38 65.00N170.00W
Bering Str. 38 65.00N170.00W
Berkshire d. 9 51.25N 1.03W
Berkshire Downs hills 9 51.32N 1.36W
Berlin 16 52.32N 13.25E
Bermejo r. Tucumán 48 26.47S 58.30W
Bern 16 46.57N 7.26E
Berne see Bern 12
Berwick-upon-Tweed 8 55.46N 2.00W
Besançon 12 47.14N 6.02E
Bessarabia f. 17 46.30N 28.40E
Betanzos 13 43.17N 8.13W
Bethal 54 26.26S 29.27E
Bethel Alas. 38 60.48N161.46W
Beverly Mass. 44 42.33N 70.53W
Bexhill 9 50.51N 0.29E
Bexley 9 51.26N 0.10E
Beyla 50 8.42N 8.39W
Bezhetsk 20 57.49N 36.40E
Bezhitsa 20 53.19N 34.17E
Béziers 12 43.21N 3.13E
Bhāgalpur 25 25.15N 87.00E
Bhamo 25 24.10N 97.30E
Bhopāl 25 23.16N 77.24E
Bhuj 25 23.16N 69.40E
Bhutan 25 27.15N 91.00E
Biarritz 12 43.29N 1.33W
Bicester 9 51.53N 1.09W
Biddeford 44 43.30N 70.26W
Bideford 9 51.01N 4.13W
Biel 12 47.09N 7.16E
Bié Plateau f. 52 13.00S 16.00E
Biggar 11 55.38N 3.31W
Bighorn r. 40 46.05N107.20W
Big Snowy Mtn. 40 46.46N109.31W
Bihać 14 44.49N 15.53E
Bihār 25 24.30N 86.00E
Bihor mtn. 17 46.26N 22.43E
Bijagós, Arquipélago dos is. 50 11.30N 16.00W
Bikaner 25 28.42N 73.25E
Bikin 23 46.52N134.15E
Bikoro 52 0.45S 18.09E
Bilāspur Madhya P. 25 22.05N 82.09E
Bilbao 13 43.15N 2.56W
Billingham 8 54.36N 1.18W
Billings 40 45.47N108.30W
Bill of Portland c. 9 50.32N 2.28W
Biloxi 41 30.30N 88.53W
Bima r. 52 3.24N 25.10E
Bindura 54 17.18S 31.20E
Binga 54 17.38S 27.19E
Bingen 16 49.58N 7.55E
Binghamton 44 42.08N 75.54W
Biograd 14 43.56N 15.27E
Birdum 32 15.38S133.12E
Birhan mtn. 51 11.00N 37.50E
Birkenhead 8 53.24N 3.01W
Birmingham U.K. 9 52.30N 1.55W
Birmingham Ala. 41 33.30N 86.55W
Birr 10 53.06N 7.56W
Biscay, B. of 12 45.30N 4.00W
Bishop Auckland 8 54.40N 1.40W
Bishop's Stortford 9 51.53N 0.09E
Biskra 50 34.48N 5.40E
Bismarck 40 46.50N100.48W
Bismarck Sea 30 4.00S147.00E
Bissau 50 11.52N 15.39W
Bitam 52 2.05N 11.30E
Bitburg 16 49.58N 6.31E
Bitlis 21 38.23N 42.04E
Bitola 15 41.02N 21.21E
Bitterfontein 54 31.02S 18.14E
Biumba 53 1.38S 30.02E
Biwa ko l. 28 35.10N136.00E
Biysk 22 52.35N 85.16E
Black r. Ark. 41 35.30N 91.20W
Blackall 34 24.25S145.28E
Blackburn 8 53.44N 2.30W
Black Mts. 9 51.52N 3.09W
Blackpool 8 53.48N 3.03W
Black Sea 24 43.00N 33.00E
Blacksod B. 10 54.04N 10.00W
Black Volta r. 50 8.14N 2.11W
Blackwater r. Waterford 10 51.58N 7.52W
Blaenau Ffestiniog 8 53.00N 3.57W
Blair Athol 34 22.42S147.33E
Blair Atholl 11 56.46N 3.51W
Blairgowrie 11 56.36N 3.21W
Blanc, Mont mtn. 12 45.50N 6.52E
Blanca, Bahía b. 49 39.20S 62.00W
Blanche, L. 36 29.15S139.40E
Blandford Forum 9 50.52N 2.10W
Blarney 10 51.56N 8.34W
Blavet r. 12 47.43N 3.18W
Blaye 12 45.08N 0.40W
Blenheim 29 41.32S173.58E
Bletchley 9 51.59N 0.45W
Bloemfontein 54 29.07S 26.14E
Blois 12 47.36N 1.20E
Bloody Foreland c. 10 55.09N 8.17W
Bloomington Ill. 41 40.29N 89.00W
Bloomington Ind. 44 39.10N 86.31W
Blue Mts. 40 45.00N118.00W
Blue Nile r. see Azraq, Al Baḥr al r. 51
Blue Stack Mts. 10 54.44N 8.09W
Blumenau 45 26.55S 49.07W
Blyth Northum. 8 55.07N 1.29W
Boa Vista 46 2.51N 60.43W
Bobo-Dioulasso 50 11.11N 4.18W
Bochum 16 51.28N 7.11E
Bodélé f. 50 16.50N 17.10E
Boden 18 65.50N 21.42E
Bodmin 9 50.28N 4.44W
Bodmin Moor 9 50.53N 4.35W
Bodø 18 67.18N 14.26E
Boende 52 0.15S 20.49E
Boggeragh Mts. 10 52.03N 8.53W
Bognor Regis 9 50.47N 0.40W
Bogor 27 6.34S106.45E
Bogotá 46 4.38N 74.05W
Bohol i. 27 9.45N124.10E
Boise 40 43.38N116.12W
Boké 50 10.57N 14.13W
Bokungu 52 0.44S 22.28E
Bolama 50 11.35N 15.30W
Bolbec 12 49.34N 0.28E
Bolivia 48 17.00S 65.00W
Bologna 14 44.30N 11.20E
Bolomba 52 0.30N 19.13E
Bolsover 8 53.14N 1.18W
Bolton 8 53.35N 2.26W
Bolu 21 40.45N 31.38E
Bolvadin 21 38.43N 31.02E
Bolzano 14 46.30N 11.20E
Boma 52 5.50S 13.03E
Bombay 25 18.58N 72.50E
Bombo 53 0.34N 32.32E
Bomi 26 29.50N 95.45E
Bomokandi r. 53 3.37N 26.09E
Bomongo 52 1.30N 18.21E
Bonar-Bridge town 11 57.53N 4.21W
Bonavista 39 48.38N 53.08W
Bo'ness 11 56.01N 3.36W
Bonin Is. 30 27.00N142.10E
Bonn 16 50.44N 7.06E
Bontang 27 0.05N117.31E
Boothia, G. of 39 70.00N 90.00W
Booué 52 0.00 11.58E
Borås 19 57.43N 12.55E
Bordeaux 12 44.50N 0.34W
Borden I. 38 78.30N111.00W
Borders d. 11 55.30N 2.53W
Bordertown 36 36.18S140.49E
Bordō i. 18 62.10N 7.13W
Borger 40 35.39N101.24W
Borisov 17 54.09N 28.30E
Borlänge 19 60.29N 15.25E
Borneo i. 27 1.00N114.00E
Bornholm i. 19 55.10N 15.00E
Borzya 23 50.24N116.35E
Boscastle 9 50.42N 4.42W
Bosna r. 15 45.04N 18.27E
Bosporus str. see Istanbul Boğazi str. 15
Bossangoa 50 6.29N 17.27E
Bosso 50 13.43N 13.19E
Boston Lincs. 8 52.59N 0.02W
Boston U.K. 8 52.59N 0.02W
Boston U.S.A. 44 42.21N 71.04W
Botany B. 37 34.04S151.08E
Bothnia, G. of 18 63.30N 20.30E
Botswana 54 22.00S 24.15E
Bouaflé 50 7.01N 5.47W
Bouaké 50 7.42N 5.00W
Bouar 50 5.58N 15.35E
Bougouni 50 11.25N 7.28W
Boulder 40 40.02N105.16W
Boulogne 12 50.43N 1.37E
Bourem 50 16.59N 0.20W
Bourg 12 46.12N 5.13E
Bourges 12 47.05N 2.23E
Bourgogne d. 12 47.10N 4.20E
Bournemouth 9 50.43N 1.53W
Boussac 12 46.22N 2.13E
Bouvard, C. 33 32.40S115.34E
Bowen 34 20.00S148.15E
Boyle 10 53.58N 8.19W
Boyne r. 10 53.43N 6.17W
Boyoma Falls f. 52 0.18N 25.32E
Bozeman 40 45.40N111.00W
Brač i. 15 43.20N 16.38E
Bracadale, Loch 11 57.22N 6.30W
Bräcke 18 62.44N 15.30E
Bradano r. 15 40.23N 16.52E
Bradford 8 53.47N 1.45W
Braemar 11 57.01N 3.24W
Braga 13 41.32N 8.26W
Brahmaputra r. 25 23.50N 89.45E
Braintree 9 51.53N 0.32E
Brandberg mtn. 54 21.08S 14.35E
Brande 19 55.57N 9.07E
Brandenburg 16 52.25N 12.34E
Brandfort 54 28.41S 26.27E
Brandon 39 49.50N 99.57W
Brandon Mtn. 10 52.14N 10.15W
Brasília 47 15.45S 47.57W
Braşov 17 45.40N 25.35E
Bratislava 17 48.10N 17.10E
Bratsk 23 56.20N101.15E
Braunschweig 16 52.15N 10.30E
Brava 53 1.02N 44.02E
Bray 10 53.12N 6.07W
Bray Head Kerry 10 51.53N 10.26W
Brazilian Highlands see Brasil, Planalto mts. 47
Brazos r. 41 28.55N 95.20W
Brazzaville 52 4.14S 15.10E
Breadalbane f. 11 56.30N 4.20W
Brechin 11 56.44N 2.40W
Brecon 9 51.57N 3.23W
Brecon Beacons mts. 9 51.53N 3.27W
Breda 16 51.35N 4.46E
Bredasdorp 54 34.31S 20.03E
Bregenz 16 47.31N 9.46E
Bremen 16 53.05N 8.48E
Bremerhaven 16 53.33N 8.35E
Brenner Pass 16 47.00N 11.30E
Brenta r. 16 45.25N 12.15E
Brescia 16 45.33N 10.12E
Bressay i. 11 60.08N 1.05W
Bressuire 12 46.50N 0.28W
Brest France 12 48.23N 4.30W
Brest U.S.S.R. 17 52.08N 23.40E
Brett, C. 29 35.15S174.20E
Brezhnev 22 55.42N 52.20E
Briançon 12 44.53N 6.39E
Bridgend 9 51.30N 3.35W
Bridgeport Conn. 44 41.12N 73.12W
Bridgetown 43 13.06N 59.37W
Bridgnorth 9 52.33N 2.25W
Bridgwater 9 51.08N 3.00W
Bridlington 8 54.06N 0.11W
Brig 16 46.19N 8.00E
Brigg 8 53.33N 0.30W
Bright 37 36.42S146.58E
Brighton 9 50.50N 0.09W
Brindisi 15 40.38N 17.57E
Brisbane 37 27.30S153.00E
Bristol 9 51.26N 2.35W
Bristol Channel 9 51.17N 3.20W
British Columbia d. 38 55.00N125.00W
British Virgin Is. 43 18.30N 64.30W
Britstown 54 30.34S 23.30E
Brive 12 45.09N 1.32E
Brixham 9 50.24N 3.31W
Brno 16 49.11N 16.39E
Broadway 9 52.02N 1.51W
Brockton 44 42.05N 71.01W
Brodick 11 55.34N 5.09W
Bromley 9 51.24N 0.02E
Bromsgrove 9 52.20N 2.03W
Brooks Range mts. 38 68.50N152.00W
Broom, Loch 11 57.52N 5.07W
Broome 32 17.58S122.15E
Brora 11 58.01N 3.52W
Brough England 8 54.32N 2.19W
Brough Scotland 11 60.29N 1.12W
Bruges see Brugge 16
Brugge 16 51.13N 3.14E
Brunei 27 4.56N114.58E
Brunswick Ga. 41 31.09N 81.21W
Bruny I. 35 43.15S147.16E
Brussels see Bruxelles 16
Bruxelles 16 50.50N 4.23E
Bryansk 20 53.15N 34.09E
Bua r. 53 12.42S 34.15E
Bucaramanga 46 7.08N 73.10W
Buchan Ness c. 11 57.28N 1.47W
Bucharest see Bucureşti 17
Buckhaven and Methil 8 56.11N 3.03W
Buckie 11 57.40N 2.58W
Buckingham 9 52.00N 0.59W
Buckinghamshire d. 9 51.50N 0.48W
Bucureşti 17 44.25N 26.06E
Budapest 17 47.30N 19.03E
Bude 9 50.49N 4.33W
Budjala 52 2.38N 19.48E
Buenaventura 46 3.54N 77.02W
Buenos Aires 49 34.40S 58.25W
Buffalo N.Y. 44 42.52N 78.55W
Buffalo Wyo. 40 44.21N106.40W
Builth Wells 9 52.09N 3.24W
Bujumbura 53 3.22S 29.21E
Bukama 52 9.16S 25.52E
Bukavu 53 2.30S 28.49E
Bukhara 22 39.47N 64.26E
Bukoba 53 1.20S 31.49E
Bula 27 3.07S130.27E
Bulawayo 54 20.10S 28.43E
Bulgaria 15 42.30N 25.00E
Buller r. 29 41.45S171.35E
Buller, Mt. 37 37.11S146.26E
Bulloo r. 36 28.43S142.27E
Buncrana 10 55.08N 7.27W
Bundaberg 34 24.50S152.21E
Bundoran 10 54.28N 8.17W
Bunguran i. 27 4.00N108.20E
Bunia 53 1.30N 30.10E
Burdur 21 37.44N 30.17E
Burg 16 52.17N 11.51E
Burgas 15 42.30N 27.29E
Burgos 13 42.21N 3.41W
Burgsvik 19 57.03N 18.16E
Burias i. 27 12.50N123.10E
Burkina 50 12.15N 1.30W
Burlington 44 43.19N 79.48W
Burma 25 21.45N 97.00E
Burnham-on-Sea 9 51.15N 3.00W
Burnie 35 41.03S145.55E
Burnley 8 53.47N 2.15W
Burra 36 33.40S138.57E
Burren Junction 37 30.08S148.59E
Burriana 13 39.54N 0.05W
Bursa 15 40.11N 29.04E
Būr Safājah 51 26.44N 33.56E
Būr Sa'īd 51 31.17N 32.18E
Būr Sūdān 51 19.39N 37.01E
Burton upon Trent 8 52.58N 1.39W
Buru i. 27 3.30S126.30E
Burundi 53 3.00S 30.00E
Bururi 53 3.58S 29.35E
Bury G.M. 8 53.36N 2.19W
Bury St. Edmunds 9 52.15N 0.42E
Būshehr 24 28.57N 50.52E
Bushmanland f. 54 29.25S 19.40E
Businga 52 3.16N 20.55E
Busira r. 52 0.05N 18.18E
Buta 52 2.50N 24.50E
Butari 53 2.38S 29.43E
Bute i. 11 55.51N 5.07W
Bute, Sd. of 11 55.44N 5.10W
Butiaba 53 1.48N 31.15E
Butte Mont. 40 46.00N112.31W
Buttevant 10 52.14N 8.41W
Butt of Lewis c. 11 58.31N 6.15W
Butuan 27 8.56N125.31E
Butung i. 27 5.00S122.50E
Buxton 8 53.16N 1.54W
Buzi r. 54 19.52S 34.00E
Bydgoszcz 17 53.16N 17.33E

C

Cabimas 46 10.26N 71.27W
Cabinda 52 5.34S 12.12E
Cabot Str. 39 47.00N 59.00W
Cabrera, Sierra mts. 13 42.10N 6.30W
Cabriel r. 13 39.13N 1.07W
Cáceres 13 39.29N 6.23W
Cachimo r. 52 7.02S 21.13E
Cachoeira do Sul 45 30.03S 52.52W
Cacin r. 13 37.10N 4.01W
Cacolo 52 10.09S 19.15E
Cader Idris mtn. 9 52.40N 3.55W
Cadí, Serra del mts. 13 42.12N 1.35E
Cadiz 27 10.57N123.18E
Cádiz 13 36.32N 6.18W
Caen 12 49.11N 0.22W
Caernarfon 8 53.08N 4.17W
Caerphilly 9 51.34N 3.13W
Cagliari 14 39.14N 9.07E
Caguas 43 18.08N 66.00W
Caha Mts. 10 51.44N 9.45W
Caherciveen 10 51.51N 10.14W
Cahir 10 52.23N 7.56W
Cahora Bassa Dam 53 15.36S 32.41E
Cahore Pt. 10 52.34N 6.12W
Cahors 12 44.28N 0.26E
Cahuapanas 46 5.15S 77.00W
Caibarién 43 22.31N 79.28W
Caicos Is. 43 21.30N 72.00W
Cairngorms mts. 11 57.04N 3.30W
Cairns 34 16.51S145.43E
Cairo see Al Qāhirah 51
Cairo Ill. 41 37.02N 89.02W
Cajamarca 46 7.09S 78.32W
Calabar 50 4.56N 8.22E
Calabozo 46 8.58N 67.28W
Calabria d. 15 39.00N 16.30E
Calahorra 13 42.18N 1.58W
Calais 7 50.57N 1.52E
Calamocha 13 40.54N 1.18W
Călăraşi 17 44.11N 27.21E
Calatayud 13 41.21N 1.39W
Calbayog 27 12.04N124.58E
Calcutta 25 22.32N 88.22E
Caledon r. 54 30.27S 26.12E
Calf of Man i. 8 54.03N 4.49W
Calgary 38 51.05N114.05W
Cali 46 3.24N 76.30W
Calicut 25 11.15N 75.45E
Caliente 40 37.36N114.31W
California d. 40 37.00N120.00W
California, Golfo de g. 42 28.30N112.30W
Callander 11 56.15N 4.13W
Callao 48 12.05S 77.08W
Caltagirone 14 37.14N 14.30E
Calulo 52 10.05S 14.56E
Calvi 12 42.34N 8.44E
Calvinia 54 31.29S 19.44E
Cam r. 9 52.34N 0.21E
Camacupa 52 12.01S 17.22E
Camagüey 43 21.25N 77.55W
Camarón, C. 43 15.59N 85.00W
Camberley 9 51.21N 0.45W
Cambodia 27 12.45N105.00E
Camborne 9 50.12N 5.19W
Cambrai 12 50.10N 3.14E
Cambrian Mts. 9 52.33N 3.33W
Cambridge 9 52.13N 0.08E
Cambridge G. 32 15.00S128.05E
Cambridgeshire d. 9 52.15N 0.05E
Camden U.K. 9 51.33N 0.10W
Camden N.J. 44 39.57N 75.07W
Camelford 9 50.37N 4.41W
Cameron Mts. 29 45.50S167.00E
Cameroon 50 5.30N 12.15E
Cameroun, Mont mtn. 50 4.20N 9.05E
Campana 49 34.10S 58.57W
Campbell, C. 29 41.45S174.15E
Campbelltown 37 34.04S150.49E
Campbeltown 11 55.25N 5.36W
Campeche 42 19.50N 90.30W
Campeche, Bahía de b. 42 19.30N 94.00W
Camperdown 36 38.15S143.14E
Campina Grande 47 7.15S 35.50W
Campinas 45 22.54S 47.06W
Campobasso 14 41.34N 14.39E
Campo Gallo 48 26.35S 62.50W
Campo Grande 48 20.24S 54.35W
Campos 45 21.45S 41.18W
Canada 38 60.00N105.00W
Canadian r. 41 35.20N 95.40W
Çanakkale 15 40.09N 26.26E
Çanakkale Boğazi str. 15 40.15N 26.30E
Canal du Midi 12 43.18N 2.00E
Canarias, Islas is. 50 29.00N 15.00W
Canaveral, C. 41 28.28N 80.28W
Canberra 37 35.18S149.08E
Candeleda 13 40.10N 5.14W
Cangamba 52 13.40S 19.50E
Cangzhou 26 38.15N116.58E
Çankiri 21 40.35N 33.37E
Canna i. 11 57.03N 6.30W
Cannes 12 43.33N 7.00E
Cannich 11 57.20N 4.45W
Cannock 9 52.42N 2.02W
Canōas 45 29.55S 51.10W
Canon City 40 38.27N105.14W
Cantabria, Sierra de mts. 13 42.40N 2.30W
Canterbury d. 29 43.30S172.00E
Canterbury 9 51.17N 1.05E
Canterbury Bight 29 44.15S172.00E
Can Tho 27 10.03N105.40E
Canton see Guangzhou 26
Canton Ohio 44 40.48N 81.23W
Caombo 52 8.45S 16.50E
Cape Barren I. 35 40.25S148.15E
Cape Breton I. 39 46.00N 61.00W
Cape Cod B. 44 41.50N 70.17W
Capelongo 52 14.28S 16.25E
Cape Town 54 33.55S 18.27E
Cape York Pen. 34 12.40S142.20E
Capri i. 14 40.33N 14.13E
Caprivi Strip f. 54 17.50S 23.10E
Caracas 46 10.35N 66.56W
Caravaca 13 38.06N 1.51W
Carcassonne 12 43.13N 2.21E
Carcross 38 60.11N134.41W
Cardabia 32 23.06S113.48E
Cárdenas 43 23.02N 81.12W
Cardenete 13 39.46N 1.42W
Cardiff 9 51.28N 3.11W
Cardigan 9 52.06N 4.41W
Carentan 12 49.18N 1.14W
Carhaix 12 48.16N 3.35W
Carhué 49 37.11S 62.45W
Caribbean Sea 43 15.00N 75.00W
Caribou Mts. 38 58.30N115.00W
Carlingford 10 54.03N 6.12W
Carlingford Lough 10 54.03N 6.09W
Carlisle 8 54.54N 2.55W
Carlow 10 52.50N 6.46W
Carlow d. 10 52.43N 6.50W
Carmarthen 9 51.52N 4.20W
Carmarthen B. 9 52.30N 4.30W
Carmel Head 8 53.24N 4.35W
Carmila 34 21.55S149.25E
Carmona 13 37.28N 5.38W
Carndonagh 10 55.15N 7.15W
Carnegie, L. 32 26.15S123.00E
Carnew 10 52.43N 6.31W
Carnot 50 4.59N 15.56E
Carnoustie 11 56.30N 2.44W
Carolina 43 18.23N 65.57W
Caroline Is. 30 5.00N147.00E
Carpathians mts. 17 48.45N 23.45E
Carpaţii Meridionali mts. 17 45.35N 24.40E
Carpentaria, G. of 34 14.00S139.00E
Carpentras 12 44.03N 5.03E
Carra, Lough 10 53.41N 9.15W
Carrara 14 44.04N 10.06E
Carrauntoohil mtn. 10 52.00N 9.45W
Carrickfergus 10 54.43N 5.49W
Carrickmacross 10 53.58N 6.43W
Carrick-on-Shannon 10 53.57N 8.06W
Carrick-on-Suir 10 52.21N 7.26W
Carrowmore Lough 10 54.11N 9.47W
Çarşamba 21 41.13N 36.43E
Carson City 40 39.10N119.46W
Carstairs 11 55.42N 3.41W
Cartagena Colombia 46 10.24N 75.33W
Cartagena Spain 13 37.36N 0.59W
Carterton 29 41.01S175.31E
Caruarú 47 8.15S 35.55W
Carvoeiro 46 1.24S 61.59W
Casablanca 50 33.39N 7.35W
Cascade Pt. 29 44.01S168.22E
Cascade Range mts. 40 44.00N121.30W
Caserta 14 41.06N 14.21E
Cashel Tipperary 10 52.31N 7.54W
Caspe 13 41.14N 0.03W
Casper 40 42.50N106.20W
Caspian Depression see Prikaspiyskaya Nizmennost ost 21
Caspian Sea 21 42.00N 51.00E
Castaños 42 26.48N101.26W
Castelo Branco 13 39.50N 7.30W
Casterton 36 37.35S141.25E
Castlebar 10 53.52N 9.19W
Castleblayney 10 54.08N 6.46W
Castle Douglas 11 54.56N 3.56W
Castleford 8 53.43N 1.21W
Castlemaine 36 37.05S144.19E
Castlerea 10 53.45N 8.30W
Castletown 8 54.04N 4.38W
Castres 12 43.36N 2.14E
Castries 43 14.01N 60.59W
Casula 53 15.26S 33.32E
Cataluña d. 13 42.00N 2.00E
Catamarca 48 28.30S 65.45W
Catanduanes i. 27 13.45N124.20E
Catanduva 45 21.03S 49.00W
Catania 14 37.31N 15.05E
Catete 52 9.09S 13.40E
Catterick 8 54.23N 1.38W
Caucasus Mts. see Kavkazskiy Khrebet mts. 21
Cavan 10 54.00N 7.22W
Cavan d. 10 53.58N 7.10W
Caxambu 45 21.59S 44.54W
Caxias do Sul 45 29.14S 51.10W
Caxito 52 8.32S 13.38E
Cayenne 47 4.55N 52.18W
Cayman Is. 43 19.00N 81.00W
Cazombo 52 11.54S 22.56E
Cebu i. 27 10.15N123.45E
Cecina 14 43.18N 10.30E
Cedar City 40 37.40N113.04W
Cedar Falls town 41 42.34N 92.26W
Cedar Rapids town 41 41.59N 91.31W
Ceduna 36 32.07S133.42E
Cefalù 14 38.01N 14.03E
Celaya 42 20.32N100.48W
Celebes i. see Sulawesi i. 27
Celebes Sea 27 3.00N122.00E
Celle 16 52.37N 10.05E
Celtic Sea 7 50.00N 8.00W
Cemaes Head 9 52.08N 4.42W
Central d. 11 56.10N 4.20W
Central African Republic 50 6.30N 20.00E
Central Auckland d. 29 36.45S174.45E
Centralia Ill. 41 38.32N 89.08W
Central Siberian Plateau see Sredne Sibirskoyf. f. 23
Cerignola 14 41.17N 15.53E
Cerro de Pasco 46 10.43S 76.15W
Cessnock 37 32.51S151.21E
Cetinje 15 42.24N 18.55E
Ceuta 13 35.53N 5.19W
Cévennes mts. 12 44.25N 4.05E
Chad 50 13.00N 19.00E
Chad, L. 50 13.30N 14.00E

Challans 12 46.51N 1.52W
Châlons-sur-Marne 12 48.58N 4.22E
Chalon-sur-Saône 12 46.47N 4.51E
Chambéry 12 45.34N 5.55E
Chambeshi r. 53 11.15S 30.37E
Chamonix 12 45.55N 6.52E
Champaign 41 40.07N 88.14W
Champlain, L. 44 44.45N 73.15W
Chandeleur Is. 41 29.50N 88.50W
Chandigarh 25 30.44N 76.47E
Changchun 26 43.51N125.15E
Changde 26 29.00N111.35E
Chang Jiang r. 26 31.40N121.15E
Changsha 26 28.09N112.59E
Channel Is. 9 49.28N 2.13W
Chanthaburi 27 12.35N102.05E
Chapala, Lago de l. 42 20.00N103.00W
Chapayevsk 20 52.58N 49.44E
Chard 9 50.52N 2.59W
Chardzhou 22 39.00N 63.34E
Charente r. 12 45.57N 1.00W
Charleroi 16 50.25N 4.27E
Charleston S.C. 41 32.48N 79.58W
Charleston W.Va. 44 38.23N 81.40W
Charlotte N.C. 41 35.05N 80.50W
Charlottesville 41 38.02N 78.29W
Charlottetown 39 46.14N 63.09W
Charlton 36 36.18S143.27E
Charolles 12 46.26N 4.17E
Chartres 12 48.27N 1.30E
Châteaubriant 12 47.43N 1.22W
Châteaudun 12 48.04N 1.20E
Châteauroux 12 46.49N 1.41E
Château-Thierry 12 49.03N 3.24E
Châtellerault 12 46.49N 0.33E
Chatham 9 51.23N 0.32E
Chatham Is. 30 44.00S176.35W
Châtillon-sur-Seine 16 47.52N 4.35E
Chattahoochee r. 41 30.52N 84.57W
Chattanooga 41 35.01N 85.18W
Chatteris 9 52.27N 0.03E
Chaumont 12 48.07N 5.08E
Cheboksary 20 56.08N 47.12E
Cheboygan 44 45.40N 84.28W
Chegutu 54 18.09S 30.07E
Chelmsford 9 51.44N 0.28E
Cheltenham 9 51.53N 2.07W
Chelyabinsk 22 55.10N 61.25E
Chemba 53 17.11S 34.53E
Chën, Gora mtn. 23 65.30N141.20E
Chengdu 26 30.41N104.05E
Chepstow 9 51.38N 2.40W
Cher r. 12 47.12N 2.04E
Cherbourg 12 49.38N 1.37W
Cheremkhovo 23 53.08N103.01E
Cherepovets 20 59.05N 37.55E
Cherkassy 21 49.27N 32.04E
Cherkessk 21 44.14N 42.05E
Chernigov 17 51.30N 31.18E
Chernovtsy 17 48.19N 25.52E
Chernyakhovsk 19 54.38N 21.49E
Chertsey 9 51.23N 0.27W
Cherwell r. 9 51.44N 1.15W
Chesapeake B. 41 38.40N 76.25W
Chesham 9 51.43N 0.38W
Cheshire d. 8 53.14N 2.30W
Chesil Beach f. 9 50.37N 2.33W
Chester 8 53.12N 2.53W
Chesterfield 8 53.14N 1.26W
Chetumal 43 18.30N 88.17W
Cheyenne Wyo. 40 41.08N104.50W
Chiai 26 23.29N120.27E
Chiang Mai 26 18.48N 98.59E
Chiavari 14 44.19N 9.19E
Chiba 28 35.36N140.07E
Chibemba 52 15.43S 14.07E
Chibia 52 15.10S 13.32E
Chibuto 54 24.41S 33.32E
Chicago 41 41.50N 87.45W
Chichester 9 50.50N 0.47W
Chicoutimi-Jonquière 44 48.26N 71.04W
Chieti 14 42.22N 14.12E
Chigubo 54 22.38S 33.18E
Chihuahua 42 28.40N106.06W
Chikwawa 53 16.00S 34.54E
Chilapa 42 17.38N 99.11W
Chile 48 32.30S 71.00W
Chillán 49 36.36S 72.07W
Chiloé, Isla de i. 49 43.00S 73.00W
Chilpancingo 42 17.33N 99.30W
Chiltern Hills 9 51.40N 0.53W
Chilumba 53 10.25S 34.18E
Chilwa, L. 53 15.15S 35.45E
Chimbote 46 9.04S 78.34W
Chimkent 22 42.16N 69.25E
Chimoio 54 19.04S 33.29E
China 26 33.00N103.00E
Chinandega 43 12.35N 87.10W
Chinati Peak 40 30.05N104.30W
Chinchoua 52 0.00 9.48E
Chindio 53 17.46S 35.23E
Chindwin r. 25 21.30N 95.12E
Chinga 53 15.14S 38.40E
Chingola 53 12.29S 27.53E
Chin Hills 26 22.30N 93.30E
Chinhoyi 54 17.22S 30.10E
Chipata 53 13.37S 32.40E
Chipera 53 15.20S 32.35E
Chipinge 54 20.12S 32.38E
Chippenham 9 51.27N 2.07W
Chipping Norton 9 51.56N 1.32W
Chir r. 21 48.34N 42.53E
Chiredzi r. 54 21.10S 31.50E
Chiromo 53 16.28S 35.10E
Chistopol 20 55.25N 50.38E
Chita 23 52.03N113.35E
Chitipa 53 9.41S 33.19E
Chitrāl 25 35.52N 71.58E
Chittagong 25 22.20N 91.50E
Chiumbe r. 52 6.37S 21.04E
Chiuta, L. 53 14.45S 35.50E
Chivhu 54 19.01S 30.53E
Chobe r. 54 17.48S 25.12E
Chojnice 17 53.42N 17.32E
Cholet 12 47.04N 0.53W
Choma 53 16.51S 27.04E
Chomutov 16 50.28N 13.25E
Ch'ŏngjin 26 41.55N129.50E
Chongqing 26 29.31N106.35E
Chorley 8 53.39N 2.39W
Chorzów 17 50.19N 18.56E
Christchurch New Zealand 29 43.33S172.40E
Christchurch U.K. 9 50.44N 1.47W
Christianshåb 39 68.50N 51.00W
Christmas I. 27 10.30S105.40E
Christmas I. see Kiritimati i. 31
Chu r. 22 45.00N 67.30E
Chudleigh 9 50.35N 3.36W
Chudovo 20 59.10N 31.41E
Chuiquimula 43 15.52N 89.50W
Chuna r. 23 58.00N 94.00E
Chunya 53 8.31S 33.28E
Chuquicamata 48 22.20S 68.56W
Chur 12 46.52N 9.32E
Churchill 39 58.45N 94.00W
Churchill r. Man. 39 58.20N 94.15W
Churchill r. Nfld. 39 53.20N 60.00W
Churchill, C. 39 58.50N 93.00W
Churchill L. 38 56.00N108.00W
Churchill Peak mtn. 38 58.10N125.00W
Church Stretton 9 52.32N 2.49W
Ciénaga 46 11.11N 74.15W
Cienfuegos 43 22.10N 80.27W
Cieza 13 38.14N 1.25W
Cimarron r. 41 36.15N 96.55W
Cinca r. 13 41.22N 0.20E
Cincinnati 44 39.10N 84.30W
Cirencester 9 51.43N 1.59W
Ciudad Bolívar 46 8.06N 63.36W
Ciudad Camargo 42 27.41N105.10W
Ciudad de México 42 19.25N 99.10W
Ciudadela 13 40.00N 3.50E
Ciudad Guayana 46 8.22N 62.40W
Ciudad Guerrero 42 28.33N107.28W
Ciudad Juárez 42 31.42N106.29W
Ciudad Madero 42 22.19N 97.50W
Ciudad Real 13 38.59N 3.55W
Ciudad Victoria 42 23.43N 99.10W
Civray 12 46.09N 0.18E
Çivril 21 38.18N 29.43E
Cizre 21 37.21N 42.11E
Clacton on Sea 9 51.47N 1.10E
Clampton 33 29.56S119.06E
Clara 10 53.21N 7.37W
Clare d. 10 52.52N 8.55W
Clare r. 10 53.17N 9.04W
Claremorris 10 53.44N 9.00W
Clarence r. 29 42.10S173.55E
Clarence Str. 32 12.00S131.00E
Clarke I. 35 40.30S148.10E
Clayton r. 36 29.06S137.59E
Clear I. 10 51.26N 9.30W
Cleethorpes 8 53.33N 0.02W
Clermont-Ferrand 12 45.47N 3.05E
Clevedon 9 51.26N 2.52W
Cleveland d. 8 54.37N 1.08W
Cleveland Ohio 44 41.30N 81.41W
Cleveland Hills 8 54.25N 1.10W
Cleveleys 8 53.52N 3.01W
Clew B. 10 53.50N 9.47W
Clifden 10 53.29N 10.02W
Clinton 29 46.13S169.23E
Cloghan Offaly 10 53.13N 7.54W
Clogher Head Kerry 10 52.09N 10.28W
Clonakilty 10 51.37N 8.54W
Clones 10 54.11N 7.16W
Clonmel 10 52.21N 7.44W
Cloud Peak mtn. 40 44.23N107.11W
Cloughton 8 54.20N 0.27W
Clovis N.Mex. 40 34.14N103.13W
Clowne 8 53.18N 1.16W
Clutha r. 29 46.18S169.05E
Clwyd d. 8 53.07N 3.20W
Clwyd r. 8 53.19N 3.30W
Clyde r. 11 55.58N 4.53W
Clydebank 11 55.53N 4.23W
Coast Mts. 38 55.30N128.00W
Coast Range mts. 40 40.00N123.00W
Coatbridge 11 55.52N 4.02W
Coatzacoalcos 42 18.10N 94.25W
Cobán 42 15.28N 90.20W
Cobar 37 31.32S145.51E
Cobh 10 51.50N 8.18W
Cobija 48 11.02S 68.44W
Cobourg 44 43.58N 78.11W
Coburg 16 50.15N 10.58E
Cochabamba 48 17.24S 66.09W
Cochin 25 9.56N 76.15E
Cochrane Ont. 44 49.04N 81.02W
Cockburn 36 32.05S141.00E
Coco r. 43 14.58N 83.15W
Cod, C. 44 41.42N 70.15W
Coen 34 13.56S143.12E
Coghinas r. 14 40.57N 8.50E
Cognac 12 45.42N 0.19W
Coimbatore 25 11.00N 76.57E
Coimbra 13 40.12N 8.25W
Coin 13 36.40N 4.45W
Colchester 9 51.54N 0.55E
Coldstream 11 55.39N 2.15W
Coleraine 10 55.08N 6.40W
Colesberg 54 30.43S 25.05E
Colima 42 19.14N103.41W
Coll i. 11 56.38N 6.34W
Collingwood 29 40.41S172.41E
Collin Top mtn. 10 54.58N 6.08W
Collon 10 53.47N 6.30W
Colmar 12 48.05N 7.21E
Colne r. Essex 9 51.50N 0.59E
Colo r. 37 33.26S150.53E
Cologne see Köln 16
Colombia 46 4.00N 72.30W
Colombo 25 6.55N 79.52E
Colón 46 9.21N 79.54W
Colonsay i. 11 56.04N 6.13W
Colorado r. Argentina 49 39.50S 62.02W
Colorado r. Ariz. 40 32.00N114.58W
Colorado d. 40 39.00N106.00W
Colorado r. Tex. 41 28.30N 96.00W
Colorado Plateau f. 40 35.45N112.00W
Colorado Springs town 40 38.50N104.40W
Columbia r. 40 46.10N123.30W
Columbia S.C. 41 34.00N 81.00W
Columbus Ga. 41 32.28N 84.59W
Columbus Ohio 44 39.59N 83.03W
Colville r. 38 70.06N151.30W
Colwyn Bay town 8 53.18N 3.43W
Comayagua 43 14.30N 87.39W
Comeragh Mts. 10 52.17N 7.34W
Commonwealth Territory d. 37 35.00S151.00E
Como 14 45.48N 9.04E
Como, Lago di l. 14 46.05N 9.17E
Comodoro Rivadavia 49 45.50S 67.30W
Comoros 53 12.15S 44.00E
Conakry 50 9.30N 13.43W
Concarneau 12 47.53N 3.55W
Concepción 49 36.50S 73.03W
Conception, Pt. 40 34.27N120.26W
Conchos r. 42 29.34N104.30W
Concord N.H. 44 43.12N 71.32W
Confolens 12 46.01N 0.40E
Congleton 8 53.10N 2.12W
Congo r. see Zaïre r. 52
Coningsby 8 53.07N 0.09W
Coniston 8 54.22N 3.06W
Conn, Lough 10 54.01N 9.15W
Connah's Quay town 8 53.13N 3.03W
Connecticut d. 44 41.45N 72.45W
Connecticut r. 44 41.17N 72.21W
Connemara f. 10 53.32N 9.56W
Conon r. 11 57.33N 4.33W
Consett 8 54.52N 1.50W
Constance, L. see Bodensee 16
Constanța 15 44.10N 28.31E
Constantina 13 37.54N 5.36W
Contas r. 47 14.15S 39.00W
Cook 35 30.37S130.25E
Cook Is. 30 15.00S160.00W
Cookstown 10 54.39N 6.46W
Cook Str. 29 41.15S174.30E
Cooktown 34 15.29S145.15E
Coolgardie 33 31.01S121.12E
Copán ruins 43 14.52N 89.10W
Copenhagen see København 19
Copiapó 48 27.22S 70.20W
Copper Belt f. 53 12.40S 28.00E
Coppermine r. 38 67.54N115.10W
Coppermine town 38 67.49N115.12W
Coquimbo 48 29.58S 71.21W
Coral Sea 34 14.30S149.30E
Corangamite, L. 36 38.10S143.25E
Corbeil 12 48.37N 2.29E
Corby 9 52.29N 0.41W
Córdoba Argentina 48 31.25S 64.10W
Córdoba Spain 13 37.53N 4.46W
Corfu i. see Kérkira i. 15
Corinthian 33 31.05S119.13E
Corinto 43 12.29N 87.14W
Cork 10 51.54N 8.28W
Cork d. 10 52.00N 8.40W
Corner Brook town 39 48.58N 57.58W
Cornwall d. 9 50.26N 4.40W
Cornwallis I. 39 75.00N 95.00W
Coromandel 29 36.46S175.30E
Coronation G. 38 68.00N112.00W
Corpus Christi 41 27.47N 97.26W
Corrib, Lough 10 53.26N 9.14W
Corrientes 48 27.30S 58.48W
Corse i. 12 42.00N 9.10E
Corse, Cap c. 12 43.00N 9.21E
Corsham 9 51.25N 2.11W
Corsica i. see Corse i. 12
Corte 12 42.18N 9.08E
Coruche 13 38.58N 8.31W
Corumbá 48 19.00S 57.27W
Corwen 8 52.59N 3.23W
Cosenza 14 39.17N 16.14E
Cosne 12 47.25N 2.55E
Costa Brava f. 13 41.30N 3.00E
Costa del Sol f. 13 36.30N 4.00W
Costa Rica 43 10.00N 84.00W
Côte d'Azur f. 12 43.20N 6.45E
Cotonou 50 6.24N 2.31E
Cotopaxi mtn. 46 0.40S 78.28W
Cotswold Hills 9 51.50N 2.00W
Cottbus 16 51.43N 14.21E
Coulonge r. 44 45.51N 76.45W
Coupar Angus 11 56.33N 3.17W
Coutances 12 49.03N 1.29W
Coventry 9 52.25N 1.31W
Covington Ky. 43 39.04N 84.30W
Cowdenbeath 11 56.07N 3.21W
Cowes 9 50.45N 1.18W
Cowra 37 33.50S148.45E
Coxim 48 18.28S 54.37W
Craboon 37 32.02S149.29E
Cradock 54 32.10S 25.35E
Craigavon 10 54.28N 6.25W
Craignure 11 56.28N 5.42W
Crail 11 56.16N 2.38W
Crailsheim 16 49.09N 10.06E
Cranbrook 38 49.29N115.48W
Cranston 44 41.47N 71.26W
Crawley 9 51.07N 0.10W
Cremona 14 45.08N 10.03E
Cres i. 14 44.50N 14.20E
Crest 12 44.44N 5.02E
Creston Iowa 41 41.04N 94.20W
Crete i. see Kriti i. 15
Creus, Cabo de c. 13 42.20N 3.19E
Creuse r. 12 47.00N 0.35E
Crewe 8 53.06N 2.28W
Crianlarich 11 56.23N 4.37W
Criccieth 8 52.55N 4.15W
Crieff 11 56.23N 3.52W
Crimea pen. see Krym pen. 21
Crinan 11 56.06N 5.34W
Cristóbal Colón mtn. 46 10.53N 73.48W
Crocodile r. Trans. 54 24.11S 26.48E
Cromarty 11 57.40N 4.02W
Cromarty Firth est. 11 57.41N 4.10W
Cromer 8 52.56N 1.18E
Cromwell 29 45.03S169.14E
Crookhaven 10 51.29N 9.45W
Croom 10 52.31N 8.43W
Crosby 8 54.11N 4.34W
Crotone 15 39.05N 17.06E
Crowl r. 37 31.58S144.53E
Crow's Nest 35 27.16S152.03E
Crowsnest Pass 38 49.40N114.41W
Croydon 9 51.23N 0.06W
Cuamba 53 14.48S 36.32E
Cuangar 52 17.34S 18.39E
Cuango r. see Kwango r. 52
Cuanza r. 52 9.20S 13.09E
Cua Rao 26 19.16N104.27E
Cuba 43 22.00N 79.00W
Cubango r. see Okavango r. 52
Cubia r. 52 16.00S 21.46E
Cuchi r. 52 15.23S 17.12E
Cúcuta 46 7.55N 72.31W
Cuddalore 25 11.43N 79.46E
Cuenca 46 2.54S 79.00W
Cuernavaca 42 18.57N 99.15W
Cuiabá r. 48 18.00S 57.25W
Cuillin Hills 11 57.12N 6.13W
Cuito r. 52 18.01S 20.50E
Culiacán 42 24.50N107.23W
Cullarin Range mts. 37 34.30S149.32E
Cullen 11 57.41N 2.50W
Cullera 13 39.10N 0.15W
Cullin Sd. 11 57.03N 6.13W
Culloden Moor 11 57.29N 3.55W
Culver, Pt. 33 32.52S124.41E
Cumberland r. 41 37.16N 88.25W
Cumberland, L. 41 37.00N 85.00W
Cumberland Sd. 39 65.00N 65.30W
Cumbernauld 11 55.57N 4.00W
Cumbria d. 8 54.30N 3.00W
Cumbrian Mts. 8 54.32N 3.05W
Cumnock 11 55.27N 4.15W
Cunene r. 52 17.15S 11.50E
Cuneo 14 44.22N 7.32E
Cupar 11 56.19N 3.01W
Curaçao i. 46 12.15N 69.00W
Curicó 49 34.59S 71.14W
Curitiba 45 25.24S 49.16W
Currane, Lough 10 51.50N 10.07W
Curvelo 45 18.45S 44.27W
Cushendall 10 55.06N 6.05W
Cuttack 25 20.30N 85.50E
Cuxhaven 16 53.52N 8.42E
Cuzco 46 13.32S 71.57W
Cwmbran 9 51.39N 3.01W
Cyclades is. see Kikládhes is. 15
Cyprus 24 35.00N 33.00E
Cyrenaica f. see Barqah f. 51
Czechoslovakia 16 49.30N 15.00E

D

Dacca see Dhaka 25
Dachau 16 48.15N 11.26E
Dagana 50 16.31N 15.30W
Da Hinggan Ling mts. 26 50.00N122.10E
Dajing 26 28.25N121.10E
Dakar 50 14.38N 17.27W
Dakhla 50 23.43N 15.57W
Dal r. 19 60.38N 17.27E
Dalbeattie 11 54.55N 3.49W
Dalby 35 27.11S151.12E
Dalkeith 11 55.54N 3.04W
Dallas Tex. 41 32.47N 96.48W
Dalmally 11 56.25N 4.58W
Dalmellington 11 55.19N 4.24W
Daloa 50 6.56N 6.28W
Dalrymple, Mt. 34 21.02S148.38E
Dalwhinnie 11 56.56N 4.15W
Damascus see Dimashk 24
Damāvand, Qolleh-ye mtn. 24 35.47N 52.04E
Damba 52 6.44S 15.17E
Dampier 32 20.45S116.50E
Danakil f. 51 13.00N 41.00E
Da Nang 27 16.04N108.13E
Danbury Conn. 44 41.24N 73.26W
Dande r. 52 8.30S 13.23E
Dandong 26 41.10N124.25E
Danlí 43 14.02N 86.30W
Dannevirke 29 40.12S176.08E
Danube r. 17 45.26N 29.38E
Danville Va. 41 36.34N 79.25W
Danzig, G. of 17 54.45N 19.15E
Dārān 24 33.00N 50.27E
Dardanelles see Çanakkale Boğazi str. 15
Dar es Salaam 53 6.51S 39.18E
Darfield 29 43.29S172.07E
Dargaville 29 35.57S173.53E
Dargo 37 37.30S147.16E
Darhan 26 49.34N106.23E
Darién, Golfo del g. 46 9.20N 77.30W
Darjeeling 25 27.02N 88.16E
Darling r. 36 34.05S141.57E
Darling Downs f. 35 28.00S149.45E
Darlington 8 54.33N 1.33W
Darmstadt 16 49.52N 8.30E
Dartmoor Forest hills 9 50.33N 3.55W
Dartmouth 9 50.21N 3.35W
Daru 34 9.04S143.12E
Darwen 8 53.42N 2.29W
Darwin 34 12.23S130.44E
Dasht-e Kavir des. 24 34.40N 55.00E
Dasht-e Lüt des. 24 31.30N 58.00E
Dasht-e Mārgow des. 24 30.45N 63.00E
Datong 26 40.10N113.15E
Dauphin 39 51.09N100.05W
Dauphiné, Alpes du mts. 12 44.35N 5.45E
Davao 27 7.05N125.38E
Davenport 41 41.40N 90.36W
Daventry 9 52.16N 1.10W
Davis Str. 39 66.00N 58.00W
Davos 16 46.47N 9.50E
Dawlish 9 50.34N 3.28W
Dawna Range mts. 27 17.00N 98.00E
Dawson 38 64.04N139.24W
Dawson Creek town 38 55.44N120.15W
Dawson Range f. 38 62.40N139.00W
Dax 12 43.43N 1.03W
Dayton Ohio 44 39.45N 84.10W
Daytona Beach town 41 29.11N 81.01W
Dead Sea 24 31.25N 35.30E
Deal 9 51.13N 1.25E
Dearborn 44 42.18N 83.14W
Death Valley f. 40 36.00N116.45W
Deauville 12 49.21N 0.04E
Decatur Ill. 41 39.44N 88.57W
Deccan f. 25 18.30N 77.30E
Děčín 16 50.48N 14.15E
Dedza 53 14.20S 34.24E
Dee r. D. and G. 11 54.50N 4.05W
Dee r. Grampian 11 57.07N 2.04W
Dee r. Wales 8 53.13N 3.05W
Deepdale 32 21.42S116.11E
Dehra Dūn 25 30.19N 78.02E
Dej 17 47.08N 23.55E
Dekese 52 3.25S 21.24E
Delano 40 35.45N119.16W
Delaware d. 44 39.10N 75.30W
Delaware r. 44 39.20N 75.25W
Delft 16 52.01N 4.23E
Delhi 25 28.40N 77.13E
Delicias 42 28.10N105.30W
Del Rio 40 29.23N100.56W
Delta Utah 40 39.22N112.35W
Demba 52 5.28S 22.14E
Denbigh 8 53.11N 3.25W
Den Helder 16 52.58N 4.46E
Denia 13 38.51N 0.07E
Deniliquin 37 35.33S144.58E
Denizli 21 37.46N 29.05E
Denmark 19 55.50N 10.00E
Denver 40 39.45N104.58W
Derbent 21 42.03N 48.18E
Derby 8 52.55N 1.28W
Derbyshire d. 8 52.55N 1.28W
Derg, Lough Donegal 10 54.37N 7.55W
Derg, Lough Tipperary 10 52.57N 8.18W
Derrynasaggart Mts. 10 51.58N 9.15W
Derryveagh Mts. 10 55.00N 8.07W
Derwent r. Cumbria 8 54.38N 3.34W
Derwent r. N. Yorks. 8 53.44N 0.57W
Deseado r. 49 47.45S 65.50W
Des Moines Iowa 41 41.35N 93.35W
Dessau 16 51.51N 12.15E
Dete 54 18.39S 26.49E
Detroit 44 42.23N 83.05W
Deutsche Bucht b. 16 54.00N 8.15E
Deva 17 45.54N 22.55E
Deventer 16 52.15N 6.10E
Deveron r. 11 57.40N 2.30W
Devizes 9 51.21N 2.00W
Devon d. 9 50.50N 3.40W
Devon I. 39 75.00N 86.00W
Dewsbury 8 53.42N 1.38W
Dhaka 25 23.43N 90.25E
Dhodhekánisos is. 15 37.00N 27.00E
Dholpur 25 26.42N 77.54E
Diamantino 45 14.25S 56.29W
Dibaya 52 6.31S 22.57E
Dickinson 40 46.54N102.48W
Didcot 9 51.36N 1.14W
Dieppe 12 49.55N 1.05E
Digne 12 44.05N 6.14E
Dijlah r. 24 31.00N 47.27E
Dijon 12 47.20N 5.02E
Dikili 15 39.05N 26.52E
Dikwa 50 12.01N 13.55E
Dili 27 8.35S125.35E
Dillon 40 45.14N112.38W
Dilolo 52 10.39S 22.20E
Dimashk 24 33.30N 36.19E
Dimbelenge 52 5.32S 23.04E
Dimitrovgrad 15 42.01N 25.34E
Dinan 12 48.27N 2.02W
Dinant 16 50.16N 4.55E
Dingle 10 52.09N 10.17W
Dingwall 11 57.35N 4.26W
Diourbel 50 14.30N 16.10W
Dipolog 27 8.34N123.28E
Dirē Dawa 51 9.35N 41.50E
Disappointment, L. 32 23.30S122.55E
Disaster B. 37 37.20S149.58E
Disko i. 39 69.45N 53.00W
Diss 9 52.23N 1.06E
Diyarbakir 21 37.55N 40.14E
Dja r. 52 1.38N 16.03E
Djado 50 21.00N 12.20E
Djambala 52 2.33S 14.38E
Djelfa 50 34.43N 3.14E
Djibouti 51 12.00N 42.50E
Djibouti town 51 11.35N 43.11E
Djolu 52 0.35N 22.28E
Djugu 53 1.55N 30.31E
Dnepr r. 17 50.00N 31.00E
Dnepropetrovsk 21 48.29N 35.00E
Dnestr r. 17 46.21N 30.20E
Dno 20 57.50N 30.00E
Doboj 17 44.44N 18.02E
Doce r. 45 19.32S 39.57W
Dodecanese is. see Dhodhekánisos is. 15
Dodge City 40 37.45N100.02W
Dodoma 53 6.10S 35.40E
Doha see Ad Dawhah 24
Dokkum 16 53.20N 6.00E
Dole 12 47.05N 5.30E
Dolgellau 9 52.44N 3.53W
Dolisie 52 4.09S 12.40E
Dolomiti mts. 14 46.25N 11.50E
Dombås 19 62.05N 9.08E
Dombe Grande 52 13.00S 13.06E
Dominica 43 15.30N 61.30W
Dominican Republic 43 18.00N 70.00W
Don r. England 8 53.41N 0.50W
Don r. Scotland 11 57.10N 2.05W
Don r. U.S.S.R. 21 47.06N 39.16E
Donaghadee 10 54.39N 5.33W
Donald 36 36.25S143.04E
Donau r. W. Germany see Danube r. 16
Doncaster 8 53.31N 1.09W
Donegal 10 54.39N 8.06W
Donegal d. 10 54.52N 8.00W
Donegal Pt. 10 52.43N 9.38W
Donetsk 21 48.00N 37.50E
Dongchuan 26 26.10N103.02E
Donggala 27 0.48S119.45E
Donington 8 52.55N 0.12W
Doon, Loch 11 55.15N 4.23W
Dorchester 9 50.52N 2.28W
Dordogne r. 12 45.03N 0.34W
Dordrecht 16 51.48N 4.40E
Dori 50 14.03N 0.02W
Dorking 9 51.14N 0.20W
Dornie 11 57.16N 5.31W
Dornoch 11 57.52N 4.02W
Dornoch Firth est. 11 57.50N 4.04W
Dorset d. 9 50.48N 2.25W
Dortmund 16 51.32N 7.27E
Douai 12 50.22N 3.05E
Douala 50 4.05N 9.43E
Douarnenez 12 48.05N 4.20W
Doubs r. 12 46.57N 5.03E
Douentza 50 14.58N 2.48W
Douglas 8 54.09N 4.29W
Doumé 50 4.16N 13.30E
Dounreay 11 58.35N 3.42W
Dourados 48 22.09S 54.52W
Douro r. 13 41.10N 8.40W
Dove r. Derbys. 8 52.50N 1.35W
Dover 9 51.07N 1.19E
Dovey r. 9 52.33N 3.56W
Dowa 53 13.40S 33.55E
Down d. 10 54.20N 6.00W
Downham Market 9 52.36N 0.22E
Downpatrick 10 54.21N 5.43W
Downpatrick Head 10 54.20N 9.22W
Dowra 10 54.11N 8.02W
Drachten 16 53.06N 6.05E
Draguignan 12 43.32N 6.28E
Drakensberg mts. 54 30.00S 29.05E
Dráma 15 41.09N 24.11E
Drammen 19 59.44N 10.15E
Drava r. 17 45.34N 18.56E
Drayton 35 27.40S151.50E
Dresden 16 51.03N 13.45E
Dreux 12 48.44N 1.23E
Drina r. 17 44.53N 19.20E
Drogheda 10 53.42N 6.23W
Droitwich 9 52.16N 2.10W
Dronne r. 12 45.02N 0.09W
Drumheller 38 51.28N112.40W
Drum Hills 10 52.03N 7.42W
Drummondville 44 45.52N 72.30W
Drummore 11 54.41N 4.54W
Drymen 11 56.04N 4.27W
Dua r. 52 3.12N 20.55E
Dubai see Dubayy 24
Dubawnt r. 39 62.50N102.00W
Dubayy 24 25.13N 55.17E
Dubbo 37 32.16S148.41E
Dubica 16 45.11N 16.48E
Dublin 10 53.21N 6.18W
Dublin d. 10 53.20N 6.18W
Dubrovnik 15 42.40N 18.07E
Dubuque 41 42.31N 90.41W
Dudinka 23 69.27N 86.13E
Dudley 9 52.30N 2.05W
Duero r. Spain see Douro r. 13
Dufftown 11 57.27N 3.09W
Duisburg 16 51.26N 6.45E
Dukou 26 26.33N101.44E
Duleek 10 53.39N 6.24W
Dülmen 16 51.51N 7.16E
Duluth 41 46.50N 92.10W
Dumbarton 11 55.57N 4.35W
Dumfries 11 55.04N 3.37W
Dumfries and Galloway d. 11 55.05N 3.40W
Duna r. Hungary see Danube r. 17
Dunărea r. Romania see Danube r. 17
Dunav r. Bulgaria see Danube r. 17
Dunav r. Yugo. see Danube r. 17
Dunbar 11 56.00N 2.31W
Dunblane 11 56.12N 3.59W
Dunboyne 10 53.26N 6.30W
Duncansby Head 11 58.39N 3.01W
Dundalk 10 54.01N 6.25W
Dundee 11 56.28N 3.00W
Dunedin 29 45.52S170.30E
Dunfermline 11 56.04N 3.29W
Dungannon 10 54.31N 6.47W
Dungarvan 10 52.06N 7.39W
Dungeness c. 9 50.55N 0.58E
Dungiven 10 54.56N 6.56W
Dungu 53 3.40N 28.40E
Dunkeld 11 56.34N 3.36W
Dunkerque 16 51.02N 2.23E
Dunkirk see Dunkerque 16
Dunkwa 50 5.59N 1.45W
Dun Laoghaire 10 53.17N 6.09W
Dunleer 10 53.49N 6.24W
Dunmahon 10 52.09N 7.23W
Dunnet Head 11 58.40N 3.23W
Dunoon 11 55.57N 4.57W
Duns 11 55.47N 2.20W
Dunshaughlin 10 53.30N 6.34W
Dunstable 9 51.53N 0.32W
Dunstan Mts. 29 44.45S169.45E
Durance r. 12 43.55N 4.48E
Durango 42 24.01N104.00W
Durban 54 29.50S 30.59E
Düren 16 50.48N 6.30E
Durham 8 54.47N 1.34W
Durham d. 8 54.42N 1.45W
Durmitor mtn. 15 43.08N 19.03E
Durness 11 58.33N 4.45W
Durrow 10 52.51N 7.25W
Dursey Head 10 51.35N 10.15W
D'Urville I. 29 40.45S173.50E
Dushanbe 22 38.38N 68.51E
Düsseldorf 16 51.13N 6.47E
Dvina r. 22 57.03N 24.02E
Dyfed d. 9 52.00N 4.17W
Dzerzhinsk R.S.F.S.R. 20 56.15N 43.30E
Dzhambul 22 42.50N 71.25E
Dzhankoy 21 45.42N 34.23E

E

Eabamet L. 41 51.30N 87.55W
Eagle Pass town 40 28.44N100.31W
Ealing 9 51.31N 0.20W
Earn r. 11 56.21N 3.18W
Earn, Loch 11 56.23N 4.12W
Easingwold 8 54.08N 1.11W
Easky 10 54.17N 8.58W
Eastbourne 9 50.46N 0.18E
East C. 29 37.45S178.30E
East China Sea 26 29.00N125.00E
East Coast d. 29 38.20S177.45E
Easter I. see Pascua, Isla de i. 31
East Germany 16 52.15N 12.30E
East Grinstead 9 51.08N 0.01W
East Kilbride 11 55.46N 4.09W
East Lansing 44 42.45N 84.30W
Eastleigh 9 50.58N 1.21W
East London 54 33.00S 27.54E
Eastmain 39 52.15N 78.30W
Eastmain r. 39 52.15N 78.30W
Easton Penn. 44 40.41N 75.13W
East Retford 8 53.19N 0.55W
East Sussex d. 9 50.56N 0.12E
Eau-Claire, Lac à l' l. 39 56.10N 74.30W
Ebbw Vale 9 51.47N 3.12W
Ebola r. 52 3.12N 21.00E
Ebolowa 52 2.56N 11.11E
Ebro r. 13 40.43N 0.54E
Ecclefechan 8 55.03N 3.18W
Echuca 37 36.10S144.20E
Écija 13 37.33N 5.04W
Ecuador 46 1.40S 79.00W
Eddystone Pt. 35 40.58S148.12E
Edea 52 3.47N 10.15E
Eden 37 37.04S149.54E
Eden r. Cumbria 8 54.57N 3.02W
Edenderry 10 53.21N 7.05W
Ederny 10 54.32N 7.40W
Édhessa 15 40.47N 22.03E
Edinburgh 11 55.57N 3.13W
Edirne 15 41.40N 26.35E
Edmonton 38 53.34N113.25W
Edmundston 44 47.22N 68.20W
Edremit 15 39.35N 27.02E
Edward, L. 53 0.30S 29.30E
Edwards Plateau f. 40 30.30N100.30W
Egersund 19 58.27N 6.00E
Egmont, Mt. 29 39.20S174.05E
Egridir 21 37.52N 30.51E
Egypt 51 26.30N 29.30E
Eidsvold 34 25.23S151.08E
Eigg i. 11 56.53N 6.09W
Eighty Mile Beach f. 32 19.00S121.00E
Eil, Loch 11 56.51N 5.12W
Eildon Resr. 37 37.10S146.00E
Eindhoven 16 51.26N 5.30E
Eisenach 16 50.59N 10.19E
Eisenhut mtn. 16 47.00N 13.45E
Eisleben 16 51.32N 11.33E
Ejin Qi 26 41.50N100.50E
Eksjö 19 57.40N 14.47E
El Aaiún 50 27.10N 13.11W
Elands r. Trans. 54 24.52S 29.20E
El Arenal 13 39.30N 2.45E
El Asnam 50 36.20N 1.30E
Elâzig 21 38.41N 39.14E
Elba i. 14 42.47N 10.17E
Elbe r. 16 53.33N 10.00E
Elbert, Mt. 40 39.05N106.27W
Elbeuf 12 49.17N 1.01E
Elbistan 21 38.14N 37.11E
Elbrus mtn. 21 43.21N 42.29E
Elburz Mts. see Alborz, Reshteh-ye Kūhhā-ye ye 51
Elche 13 38.16N 0.41W
Elcho I. 34 11.55S135.45E
Elde r. 16 53.17N 12.40E
El Dorado Ark. 41 33.12N 92.40W
Elektrostal 20 55.46N 38.30E
El Ferrol 13 43.29N 8.14W
Elgin 11 57.39N 3.20W
El Golea 50 30.35N 2.51E
Elkhart Ind. 44 41.52N 85.56W
Elkins W.Va. 44 38.55N 79.51W
Elko 40 40.50N115.46W
Ellen, Mt. 40 38.06N110.50W
Ellesmere I. 39 78.00N 82.00W
Ellesmere Port 8 53.17N 2.55W
Ellon 11 57.22N 2.05W
Elmali 21 36.43N 29.56E
Elmshorn 16 53.46N 9.40E
Eloy 40 32.45N111.33W
El Paso 40 31.45N106.30W
El Real 43 8.06N 77.42W
El Salvador 43 13.30N 89.00W
Elvas 13 38.53N 7.10W
Elverum 19 60.53N 11.34E
Ely Nev. 40 39.15N114.53W
Elyria 44 41.22N 82.06W
Emba r. 21 46.38N 53.00E
Embleton 8 55.30N 1.37W
Embu 53 0.32S 37.28E
Emden 16 53.23N 7.13E
Emory Peak mtn. 40 29.15N103.19W
Empangeni 54 28.45S 31.54E
Empedrado 48 27.59S 58.47W
Emporia Kans. 41 38.24N 96.10W
Ems r. 16 53.14N 7.25E
Emyvale 10 54.20N 6.59W
Encarnación 45 27.20S 55.50W
Endicott Mts. 38 68.00N152.00W
Enfield 9 51.40N 0.05W
Engels 21 51.30N 46.07E
Enggano i. 27 5.20S102.15E
England 8 53.00N 2.00W
English Channel 9 50.15N 1.00W
Enkhuizen 16 52.42N 5.17E
Enköping 19 59.38N 17.04E
Enna 14 37.34N 14.15E
Ennis 10 52.51N 9.00W
Enniscorthy 10 52.30N 6.35W
Enniskillen 10 54.21N 7.40W
Ennistymon 10 52.56N 9.18W
Enschede 16 52.13N 6.54E
Ensenada 49 34.51S 57.55W
Ensenada Baja Calif. Norte 42 31.53N116.35W
Entebbe 53 0.08N 32.29E
Enugu 50 6.20N 7.29E
Epernay 16 49.02N 3.58E
Épinal 12 48.10N 6.28E
Epping 9 51.42N 0.07E
Epsom 9 51.20N 0.16W
Equatorial Guinea 52 2.00N 10.00E
Erdre r. 12 47.27N 1.34W
Erechim 45 27.35S 52.15W
Eregli Konya 21 37.30N 34.02E
Eregli Zonguldak 21 41.17N 31.26E
Erenhot 26 43.48N112.00E
Erfurt 16 50.58N 11.02E
Ergani 21 38.17N 39.44E
Erie 44 42.07N 80.05W
Erie, L. 44 42.15N 81.00W
Erigavo 51 10.40N 47.20E
Eriskay i. 11 57.04N 7.17W
Eritrea f. 51 15.30N 38.00E
Ermelo 54 26.30S 29.59E
Errigal Mtn. 10 55.02N 8.08W
Erzincan 21 39.44N 39.30E
Erzurum 21 39.57N 41.17E
Esbjerg 19 55.28N 8.27E
Escondido r. 43 11.58N 83.45W
Escuintla 42 14.18N 90.47W
Eşfahān 24 32.42N 51.40E
Esher 9 51.23N 0.22W
Eshowe 54 28.53S 31.29E
Esk r. N. Yorks. 8 54.29N 0.37W
Eskilstuna 19 59.22N 16.30E
Eskimo Point town 39 61.10N 94.15W
Eskişehir 21 39.46N 30.30E
Esperance 33 33.49S121.52E
Espiritu Santo i. 30 15.50S166.50E
Espungabera 54 20.28S 32.48E
Esquel 49 42.55S 71.20W
Essen 16 51.27N 6.57E
Essex d. 9 51.46N 0.30E
Estepona 13 36.26N 5.09W
Estevan 38 49.09N103.00W
Eston 8 54.34N 1.07W
Estoril 13 38.42N 9.23W
Estremoz 13 38.50N 7.35W
Étaples 12 50.31N 1.39E
Ethiopia 51 10.00N 39.00E
Etive, Loch 11 56.27N 5.15W
Etna, Monte mtn. 14 37.43N 14.59E
Etosha Pan f. 54 18.50S 16.20E
Euboea see Évvoia i. 15
Eucla 33 31.40S128.51E
Euclid 44 41.34N 81.33W
Eugene 40 44.03N123.07W
Euphrates r. see Al Furāt r. 24
Eureka Calif. 40 40.49N124.10W
Euroa 37 36.46S145.35E
Europa, Picos de mts. 13 43.10N 4.40W
Euskirchen 16 50.40N 6.47E
Evale 52 16.24S 15.50E
Evansville 44 38.00N 87.33W
Everard, C. 37 37.50S149.16E
Everest, Mt. 25 27.59N 86.56E
Evesham 9 52.06N 1.57W
Evje 19 58.36N 7.51E
Évora 13 38.34N 7.54W
Évreux 12 49.03N 1.11E
Évvoia i. 15 38.30N 23.50E
Ewe, Loch 11 57.48N 5.38W
Exe r. 9 50.40N 3.28W
Exeter 9 50.43N 3.31W
Exmoor Forest hills 9 51.08N 3.45W
Exmouth 9 50.37N 3.24W
Eye 9 52.19N 1.09E
Eyemouth 11 55.52N 2.05W
Eyre, L. 36 28.30S137.25E

F

Fåborg 19 55.06N 10.15E
Faenza 16 44.17N 11.52E
Fagernes 19 60.59N 9.17E
Fairbanks 38 64.50N147.50W
Fairborn 44 39.48N 84.03W
Fair Isle 11 59.32N 1.38W
Faisalābād 25 31.25N 73.05E
Faizābād 25 37.05N 70.40E
Fakenham 8 52.50N 0.51E
Falaise 12 48.54N 0.11W
Falcarragh 10 55.08N 8.06W
Falkenberg 19 56.54N 12.28E
Falkirk 11 56.00N 3.48W
Falkland Is. 49 51.45W 59.00W
Fall River town 44 41.43N 71.08W
Falmouth 9 50.09N 5.05W
Falster i. 19 54.48N 11.58E
Falun 19 60.36N 15.38E

Fannich, Loch 11 57.38N 5.00W
Faradje 53 3.45N 29.43E
Fareham 9 50.52N 1.11W
Farewell, C. 29 40.30S172.35E
Fargo 41 46.52N 96.59W
Farnborough 9 51.17N 0.46W
Farne Is. 8 55.38N 1.36W
Farnham 9 51.13N 0.49W
Faro 13 37.01N 7.56W
Faroe Is. 18 62.00N 7.00W
Fårösund 19 57.52N 19.03E
Farrell 44 41.13N 80.31W
Farsund 19 58.05N 6.48E
Farvel, Kap c. 39 60.00N 44.20W
Fáurei 17 45.04N 27.15E
Fauske 18 67.17N 15.25E
Favignana i. 14 37.57N 12.19E
Faxe r. 18 63.15N 17.15E
Fayetteville N.C. 41 35.03N 78.53W
Fdérik 50 22.30N 12.30W
Feale r. 10 52.28N 9.37W
Fécamp 12 49.45N 0.23E
Feeagh, Lough 10 53.56N 9.35W
Fehmarn i. 16 54.30N 11.05E
Feira 53 15.30S 30.27E
Feldkirch 16 47.15N 9.38E
Felixstowe 9 51.58N 1.20E
Feodosiya 21 45.03N 35.23E
Fergana 22 40.23N 71.19E
Fergus Falls town 41 46.18N 96.00W
Fermanagh d. 10 54.21N 7.40W
Fermoy 10 52.08N 8.17W
Ferrara 14 44.49N 11.38E
Ferret, Cap c. 12 44.42N 1.16W
Fès 50 34.05N 5.00W
Feshi 52 6.08S 18.12E
Fetlar i. 11 60.37N 0.52W
Fife d. 11 56.10N 3.10W
Fife Ness c. 11 56.17N 2.36W
Figeac 12 44.32N 2.01E
Figueira da Foz 13 40.09N 8.51W
Figueres 13 42.16N 2.57E
Fiji 30 18.00S178.00E
Filey 8 54.13N 0.18W
Findhorn r. 11 57.38N 3.37W
Findlay 44 41.02N 83.40W
Finisterre, Cabo de c. 13 42.54N 9.16W
Finland 20 64.30N 27.00E
Finland, G. of 19 59.30N 24.00E
Finlay r. 38 56.30N124.40W
Finn r. 10 54.50N 7.30W
Firenze 14 43.46N 11.15E
Firth of Clyde est. 11 55.35N 4.53W
Firth of Forth est. 11 56.05N 3.00W
Firth of Lorn est. 11 56.20N 5.40W
Firth of Tay est. 11 56.24N 3.08W
Fishguard 9 51.59N 4.59W
Fitzroy Crossing 32 18.13S125.33E
Fizi 53 4.18S 28.56E
Flagstaff 40 35.12N111.38W
Flåm 19 60.50N 7.07E
Flamborough Head 8 54.06N 0.05W
Flannan Is. 11 58.16N 7.40W
Flathead L. 40 47.50N114.05W
Fleetwood 8 53.55N 3.01W
Flen 19 59.04N 16.35E
Flensburg 16 54.47N 9.27E
Flinders r. 34 17.30S140.45E
Flinders I. Tas. 35 40.00S148.00E
Flinders Range mts. 36 31.25S138.45E
Flin Flon 39 54.47N101.51W
Flint U.K. 8 53.15N 3.07W
Flint U.S.A. 44 43.03N 83.40W
Flint r. Ga. 41 30.52N 84.35W
Flinton 35 27.54S149.34E
Florence see Firenze 14
Florence, L. 36 28.52S138.08E
Flores i. 27 8.40S121.20E
Flores, Laut sea 27 7.00S121.00E
Flores Sea see Flores, Laut sea 27
Florianópolis 45 27.35S 48.34W
Florida d. 41 29.00N 82.00W
Flórina 15 40.48N 21.25E
Florö 19 61.36N 5.00E
Flushing see Vlissingen 16
Focşani 17 45.40N 27.12E
Foggia 14 41.28N 15.33E
Foix 12 42.57N 1.35E
Folgares 52 14.55S 15.03E
Folkestone 9 51.05N 1.11E
Fond du Lac 38 59.20N107.09W
Fontainebleau 12 48.24N 2.42E
Fontenay 12 46.28N 0.48W
Forbes 37 33.24S148.03E
Foreland Pt. 9 51.15N 3.47W
Forest of Bowland hills 8 53.57N 2.30W
Forest of Dean f. 9 51.48N 2.32W
Forfar 11 56.38N 2.54W
Formby Pt. 8 53.34N 3.07W
Formentera i. 13 38.41N 1.30E
Formosa see Taiwan 26
Forres 11 57.37N 3.38W
Forrest 33 30.49S128.03E
Fort Albany 39 52.15N 81.35W
Fortaleza 47 3.45S 38.35W
Fort Augustus 11 57.09N 4.41W
Fort Beaufort 54 32.46S 26.36E
Fort Chimo 39 58.10N 68.15W
Fort Chipewyan 38 58.46N111.09W
Fort Collins 40 40.35N105.05W
Fort-de-France 43 14.36N 61.05W
Fort Frances 39 48.37N 93.23W
Fort George 39 53.50N 79.01W
Fort Good Hope 38 66.16N128.37W
Forth r. 11 56.06N 3.48W
Fort Lauderdale 41 26.08N 80.08W
Fort Maguire 53 13.38S 34.59E
Fort McMurray 38 56.45N111.27W
Fort McPherson 38 67.29N134.50W
Fort Myers 41 26.39N 81.51W
Fort Nelson 38 58.48N122.44W
Fort Norman 38 64.55N125.29W
Fort Portal 53 0.40N 30.17E
Fort Randall 38 55.10N162.47W
Fort Reliance 38 62.45N109.08W
Fort Resolution 38 61.10N113.39W
Fortrose 11 57.34N 4.09W
Fort St. John 38 56.14N120.55W
Fort Scott 41 37.52N 94.43W
Fort Severn 39 56.00N 87.40W
Fort Simpson 38 61.46N121.15W
Fort Smith d. 38 63.30N118.00W
Fort Smith U.S.A. 41 35.22N 94.27W
Fort Vermilion 38 58.22N115.59W
Fort Wayne 44 41.05N 85.08W
Fort William 11 56.49N 5.07W
Fort Worth 41 32.45N 97.20W
Fort Yukon 38 66.35N145.20W
Fougères 12 48.21N 1.12W
Foula i. 11 60.08N 2.05W
Foulness I. 9 51.35N 0.55E
Foulwind, C. 29 41.45S171.30E
Foveaux Str. 29 46.40S168.00E
Fowey 9 50.20N 4.39W
Foxe Channel 39 65.00N 80.00W
Foxton 29 40.27S175.18E
Foyle r. 10 55.00N 7.20W
Foyle, Lough 10 55.05N 7.10W
Foz do Iguaçu 45 25.33S 54.31W
Franca 45 20.33S 47.27W
France 12 47.00N 2.00E
Franceville 52 1.38S 13.31E
Francistown 54 21.12S 27.29E
Frankfort 54 27.15S 28.30E
Frankfurt E. Germany 16 52.20N 14.32E
Frankfurt W. Germany 16 50.06N 8.41E
Franz Josef Land is. see Frantsa Iosifa, Zemlya ya 22
Fraser r. B.C. 38 49.05N123.00W
Fraserburg 54 31.55S 21.29E
Fraserburgh 11 57.42N 2.00W
Fredericia 19 55.35N 9.46E
Fredericksburg Va. 41 38.18N 77.30W
Fredericton 44 45.57N 66.40W
Frederikshåb 39 62.05N 49.30W
Frederikshavn 19 57.26N 10.32E
Fredrikstad 19 59.13N 10.57E
Freeport 43 26.40N 78.30W
Freetown 50 8.30N 13.17W
Freiburg 16 48.00N 7.52E
Fréjus 12 43.26N 6.44E
Fremantle 33 32.07S115.44E
Freshford 10 52.44N 7.23W
Fresno 40 36.41N119.57W
Fribourg 16 46.50N 7.10E
Friedrichshafen 16 47.39N 9.29E
Frobisher Bay town 39 63.45N 68.30W
Frohavet est. 18 63.55N 9.05E
Frome 9 51.16N 2.17W
Frome, L. 36 30.48S139.48E
Fröya i. 18 63.45N 8.45E
Frunze 22 42.53N 74.46E
Fuerte r. 42 25.42N109.20W
Fuji san mtn. 28 35.22N138.44E
Fukui 26 36.04N136.12E
Fukuoka 26 33.39N130.21E
Fulda 16 50.35N 9.45E
Funabashi 28 35.42N139.59E
Funchal 50 32.38N 16.54W
Fundy, B. of 44 45.00N 66.00W
Furancungo 53 14.51S 33.38E
Furneaux Group is. 35 40.15S148.15E
Fürstenwalde 16 52.22N 14.04E
Fürth 16 49.28N 11.00E
Fushun 26 41.50N123.55E
Fuyu 26 45.12N124.49E
Fuzhou 26 26.09N119.21E
Fyne, Loch 11 55.55N 5.23W

G

Gabela 52 10.52S 14.24E
Gabès 50 33.52N 10.06E
Gabon 52 0.00 12.00E
Gabon r. 52 0.15N 10.00E
Gaborone 54 24.45S 25.55E
Gadsden 41 34.00N 86.00W
Gaeta 14 41.13N 13.35E
Gagnoa 50 6.04N 5.55W
Gagnon 39 51.55N 68.10W
Gaillac 12 43.54N 1.53E
Gainesville Fla. 41 29.37N 82.31W
Gainsborough 8 53.23N 0.46W
Gairdner, L. 36 31.30S136.00E
Gairloch 11 57.43N 5.40W
Galana r. 53 3.12S 40.09E
Galapagos, Islas is. 31 0.30S 90.30W
Galashiels 11 55.37N 2.49W
Galaţi 17 45.27N 27.59E
Galena Alas. 38 64.43N157.00W
Galesburg 41 40.58N 90.22W
Galle 25 6.01N 80.13E
Gállego r. 13 41.40N 0.55W
Gallipoli 15 40.02N 18.01E
Galloway f. 11 55.00N 4.28W
Gallup 40 35.32N108.46W
Galston 11 55.36N 4.23W
Galty Mts. 10 52.20N 8.10W
Galveston 41 29.17N 94.48W
Galvez 48 32.03S 61.14W
Galway 10 53.17N 9.04W
Galway d. 10 53.25N 9.00W
Gambia 50 13.30N 15.00W
Gambia r. 50 13.28N 15.55W
Gamboma 52 1.50S 15.58E
Ganda 52 12.58S 14.39E
Gandajika 52 6.46S 23.58E
Gander 39 48.58N 54.34W
Gandía 13 38.59N 0.11W
Ganga r. 25 23.22N 90.32E
Ganges r. see Ganga r. 25
Ganzhou 26 25.49N114.50E
Gao 50 16.19N 0.09W
Gap 12 44.33N 6.05E
Gara, Lough 10 53.57N 8.27W
Gard r. 12 43.52N 4.40E
Garda, Lago di l. 14 45.40N 10.40E
Garies 54 30.34S 18.00E
Garissa 53 0.27S 39.49E
Garmisch Partenkirchen 16 47.30N 11.05E
Garonne r. 12 45.00N 0.37W
Garoua 50 9.17N 13.22E
Garron Pt. 10 55.03N 5.57W
Garry L. 39 66.00N100.00W
Garut 27 7.15S107.55E
Garvão 13 37.42N 8.21W
Garve 11 57.37N 4.41W
Garvie Mts. 29 45.15S169.00E
Gary 44 41.34N 87.20W
Gascogne, Golfe de g. 12 44.00N 2.40W
Gascony, G. of see Gascogne, Golfe de 12
Gascoyne r. 32 25.00S113.40E
Gaspé 39 48.50N 64.30W
Gaspé, Péninsule de pen. 44 48.30N 65.00W
Gata, Sierra de mts. 13 40.20N 6.30W
Gatehouse of Fleet 11 54.53N 4.12W
Gateshead 8 54.57N 1.35W
Gatineau r. 44 45.27N 75.40W
Gavá 13 41.18N 2.00E
Gävle 19 60.40N 17.10E
Gávrion 15 37.52N 24.46E
Gawler 36 34.38S138.44E
Gcuwa 54 32.20S 28.09E
Gdańsk 17 54.22N 18.38E
Gdov 20 58.48N 27.52E
Gdynia 17 54.31N 18.30E
Geel 16 51.10N 5.00E
Geelong 36 38.10S144.26E
Geidam 50 12.55N 11.55E
Gelsenkirchen 16 51.30N 7.05E
Gemena 52 3.14N 19.48E
Gemlik 21 40.26N 29.10E
General Pico 49 35.38S 63.46W
Geneva see Genève 16
Geneva, L. see Léman, Lac l. 16
Genève 16 46.13N 6.09E
Genoa see Genova 14
Genoa, G. of see Genova, Golfo di g. 14
Genova 14 44.24N 8.54E
Gent 16 51.02N 3.42E
George 54 33.57S 22.27E
George, L. N.S.W. 37 35.07S149.22E
George Town Tas. 35 41.04S146.48E
Georgetown Cayman Is. 43 19.20N 81.23W
Georgetown Guyana 46 6.46N 58.10W
George Town Malaysia 27 5.30N100.16E
Georgia d. 41 33.00N 83.00W
Gera 16 50.51N 12.11E
Geraldine 29 44.05S171.15E
Geraldton 33 28.49S114.36E
Germiston 54 26.14S 28.10E
Geyve 21 40.32N 30.18E
Ghana 50 8.00N 1.00W
Ghanzi 54 21.42S 21.39E
Ghardaïa 50 32.20N 3.40E
Ghāt 50 24.59N 10.11E
Gibraltar 13 36.07N 5.22W
Gibraltar, Str. of 13 36.00N 5.25W
Gibson Desert 32 24.30S123.00E
Giessen 16 50.35N 8.42E
Gifu 28 35.25N136.45E
Gigha i. 11 55.41N 5.44W
Gijón 13 43.32N 5.40W
Gila r. 40 32.45N114.30W
Gilé 53 16.10S 38.17E
Gilgandra 37 31.42S148.40E
Gilgit 25 35.54N 74.20E
Gill, Lough 10 54.15N 8.14W
Gillingham Kent 9 51.24N 0.33E
Girdle Ness 11 57.06N 2.02W
Giresun 21 40.55N 38.25E
Girona 13 41.59N 2.49E
Gironde r. 12 45.35N 1.00W
Girvan 11 55.15N 4.51W
Gisborne 29 38.41S178.02E
Gizhiga 23 62.00N160.34E
Gladstone Qld. 34 23.52S151.16E
Glåma r. 19 59.15N 10.55E
Glasgow 11 55.52N 4.15W
Glastonbury 9 51.09N 2.42W
Glazov 20 58.09N 52.42E
Glen Affric f. 11 57.15N 5.03W
Glen Coe f. 11 56.40N 5.03W
Glendale Calif. 40 34.09N118.20W
Glendive 40 47.08N104.42W
Glengarriff 10 51.45N 9.33W
Glen Garry f. Highland 11 57.03N 5.04W
Glen Head 10 54.44N 8.46W
Glen Innes 37 29.42S151.45E
Glen Mór f. 11 57.15N 4.30W
Glenrothes 11 56.12N 3.10W
Glenshee f. 11 56.45N 3.25W
Głogów 16 51.40N 16.06E
Gloucester 9 51.52N 2.15W
Gloucestershire d. 9 51.45N 2.00W
Goa d. 25 15.30N 74.00E
Goat Fell mtn. 11 55.37N 5.12W
Gobi des. 26 45.00N108.00E
Godalming 9 51.11N 0.37W
Godāvari r. 25 16.40N 82.15E
Godhavn 39 69.20N 53.30W
Godthåb 39 64.10N 51.40W
Göksun 21 38.03N 36.30E
Golden B. 29 40.45S172.50E
Golden Vale f. 10 52.30N 8.07W
Golspie 11 57.58N 3.58W
Goma 53 1.37S 29.10E
Gombe r. 53 4.43S 31.30E
Gongga Shan mtn. 26 29.30N101.30E
Good Hope, C. of 54 34.21S 18.28E
Goole 8 53.42N 0.52W
Goose L. 40 41.55N120.25W
Göppingen 16 48.43N 9.39E
Gorakhpur 25 26.45N 83.22E
Gore 29 46.06S168.58E
Gori 21 41.59N 44.05E
Gorki see Gor'kiy 20
Gor'kiy 20 56.20N 44.00E
Gorzów Wielkopolski 16 52.42N 15.12E
Gosford 37 33.25S151.18E
Goslar 16 51.54N 10.25E
Gospić 16 44.34N 15.23E
Gosport 9 50.48N 1.08W
Göteborg 19 57.43N 11.58E
Gotha 16 50.57N 10.43E
Gothenburg see Göteborg 19
Gotland i. 19 57.30N 18.33E
Göttingen 16 51.32N 9.57E
Goulburn r. 37 36.08S144.30E
Gourdon 12 44.45N 1.22E
Gouré 50 13.59N 10.15E
Gournay 12 49.29N 1.44E
Gourock Range mts. 37 35.45S149.25E
Gower pen. 9 51.37N 4.10W
Goya 48 29.10S 59.20W
Goyder r. 34 12.38S135.11E
Gozo i. 14 36.03N 14.16E
Grahamstown 54 33.18S 26.30E
Grampian d. 11 57.22N 2.35W
Grampian Mts. 11 56.55N 4.00W
Granada 13 37.10N 3.35W
Granby 44 45.23N 72.44W
Gran Canaria i. 50 28.00N 15.30W
Gran Chaco f. 48 22.00S 60.00W
Grand r. S.Dak. 40 45.40N100.32W
Grand Bahama I. 43 26.35N 78.00W
Grand Canyon f. 40 36.15N113.00W
Grand Cayman i. 43 19.20N 81.30W
Grande r. 48 15.10S 64.55W
Grande r. Minas Gerais 48 20.00S 51.00W
Grande Comore i. 53 11.35S 43.20E
Grande Prairie town 38 55.10N118.52W
Grand Forks 41 47.57N 97.05W
Grand Island town 40 40.56N 98.21W
Grand Junction 40 39.04N108.33W
Grand Manan I. 44 44.38N 66.50W
Grand Rapids town Mich. 44 42.57N 85.40W
Grand St. Bernard, Col du pass 16 45.52N 7.11E
Grand Teton mtn. 40 43.45N110.50W
Grangemouth 11 56.01N 3.44W
Grantham 8 52.55N 0.39W
Grantown-on-Spey 11 57.20N 3.38W
Grants Pass town 40 42.26N123.20W
Granville 12 48.50N 1.35W
Graskop 54 24.55S 30.50E
Grasse 12 43.40N 6.56E
Gravesend 9 51.27N 0.24E
Gray 12 47.27N 5.35E
Grays 9 51.29N 0.20E
Graz 16 47.05N 15.22E
Great Artesian Basin f. 34 26.30S143.02E
Great Australian Bight 33 33.10S129.30E
Great Barrier I. 29 36.15S175.30E
Great Barrier Reef f. 34 16.30S146.30E
Great Basin f. 40 39.00N115.30W
Great Bear L. 38 66.00N120.00W
Great Blasket I. 10 52.05N 10.32W
Great Dividing Range mts. 37 29.00S152.00E
Great Driffield 8 54.01N 0.26W
Greater London d. 9 51.31N 0.06W
Greater Manchester d. 8 53.30N 2.18W
Great Falls town 40 47.30N111.16W
Great Karoo f. 54 32.40S 22.20E
Great Kei r. 54 32.39S 28.23E
Great L. 35 41.50S146.43E
Great Malvern 9 52.07N 2.19W
Great Namaland f. 54 25.30S 17.20E
Great Ouse r. 8 52.47N 0.23E
Great Salt L. 40 41.10N112.40W
Great Sandy Desert 32 20.30S123.35E
Great Slave L. 38 61.30N114.20W
Great Victoria Desert 33 29.00S127.30E
Great Whernside mtn. 8 54.09N 1.59W
Great Yarmouth 9 52.40N 1.45E
Greece 15 39.00N 22.00E
Greeley 40 40.26N104.43W
Green r. 40 38.20N109.53W
Greenhills 33 31.58S117.01E
Greenland 39 68.00N 45.00W
Greenlaw 11 55.43N 2.28W
Greenock 11 55.57N 4.45W
Greensboro N.C. 41 36.03N 79.50W
Greenville S.C. 41 34.52N 82.25W
Grenå 19 56.25N 10.53E
Grenada 46 12.07N 61.40W
Grenada i. 43 12.15N 61.45W
Grenoble 12 45.11N 5.43E
Gretna 11 55.00N 3.04W
Grey r. 29 42.28S171.13E
Greymouth 29 42.28S171.12E
Grey Range mts. 35 27.00S143.35E
Greystones 10 53.09N 6.04W
Grim, C. 35 40.45S144.45E
Grimsby 8 53.35N 0.05W
Grodno 17 53.40N 23.50E
Groningen 16 53.13N 6.35E
Groot r. C.P. r. 54 33.58S 25.03E
Groote Eylandt i. 34 14.00S136.40E
Grootfontein 54 19.32S 18.07E
Grossenbrode 16 54.23N 11.07E
Gross Glockner mtn. 16 47.05N 12.50E
Groundhog r. 44 49.43N 81.58W
Groznyy 21 43.21N 45.42E
Guadalajara 42 20.30N103.20W
Guadalcanal i. 30 9.32S160.12E
Guadalete r. 13 36.37N 6.15W
Guadalmena r. 13 38.00N 3.50W
Guadalquivir r. 13 36.50N 6.20W
Guadalupe 42 25.41N100.15W
Guadalupe, Isla de i. 40 29.00N118.25W
Guadarrama r. 13 39.55N 4.10W
Guadarrama, Sierra de mts. 13 41.00N 3.50W
Guadeloupe i. 43 16.20N 61.40W
Guadiana r. 13 37.10N 7.36W
Guadix 13 37.19N 3.08W
Guaíra 48 24.04S 54.15W
Gualeguay 49 33.10S 59.20W
Gualeguaychu 49 33.00S 58.30W
Guam i. 30 13.30N144.40E
Guangxi Zhuangzu d. 26 23.30N109.00E
Guangzhou 26 23.08N113.20E
Guaporé r. 48 12.00S 65.15W
Guarapuava 45 25.22S 51.28W
Guarda 13 40.32N 7.17W
Guardo 13 42.47N 4.50W
Guatemala 43 15.40N 90.00W
Guatemala town 42 14.38N 90.22W
Guaviare r. 46 4.00N 67.35W
Guayaquil 46 2.13S 79.54W
Guaymas 42 27.59N110.54W
Gubin 16 51.59N 14.42E
Guecho 13 43.21N 3.01W
Guéret 12 46.10N 1.52E
Guernsey i. 9 49.27N 2.35W
Guiana 47 3.40N 53.00W
Guiana Highlands 46 4.00N 59.00W
Guildford 9 51.14N 0.35W
Guilin 26 25.20N110.10E
Guinea 50 10.30N 10.30W
Guinea, G. of 50 2.00N 1.00W
Guinea Bissau 50 12.00N 15.30W
Güines 43 22.50N 82.02W
Guingamp 12 48.34N 3.09W
Güiria 46 10.37N 62.21W
Guiyang 26 26.31N106.39E
Gujarat d. 25 22.20N 70.30E
Gulu 53 2.46N 32.21E
Gundagai 37 35.07S148.05E
Gungu 52 5.43S 19.20E
Gunnedah 37 30.59S150.15E
Gürün 21 38.44N 37.15E
Guruve 53 16.42S 30.40E
Guyana 46 4.40N 59.00W
Gwādar 24 25.07N 62.19E
Gwai r. 54 17.59S 26.55E
Gwalior 25 26.13N 78.10E
Gwanda 54 20.59S 29.00E
Gweebarra B. 10 54.52N 8.28W
Gwent d. 9 51.44N 3.00W
Gweru 54 19.25S 29.50E
Gwynedd d. 8 53.00N 4.00W
Györ 17 47.41N 17.40E

H

Haarlem 16 52.22N 4.38E
Haddington 11 55.57N 2.47W
Hadramawt f. 24 16.30N 49.30E
Hagerstown 44 39.39N 77.43W
Ha Giang 26 22.50N105.00E
Hague, Cap de la c. 12 49.44N 1.56W
Haikou 26 20.03N110.27E
Hā'il 24 27.31N 41.45E
Hailsham 9 50.52N 0.17E
Hainan i. 27 19.00N109.30E
Haines Alas. 38 59.11N135.23W
Hai Phòng 26 20.48N106.40E
Haiti 43 19.00N 73.00W
Hakkâri 21 37.36N 43.45E
Hakodate 26 41.46N140.44E
Ḥalab 24 36.14N 37.10E
Halberstadt 16 51.54N 11.04E
Halden 19 59.09N 11.23E
Haliburton Highlands 44 45.03N 78.03W
Halifax Canada 39 44.38N 63.35W
Halifax U.K. 8 53.43N 1.51W
Halifax B. 34 18.50S146.30E
Halle 16 51.28N 11.58E
Hall's Creek town 32 18.17S127.44E
Hallstavik 19 60.03N 18.36E
Halmahera i. 27 0.45N128.00E
Halmstad 19 56.39N 12.50E
Hälsingborg 19 56.03N 12.42E
Haltwhistle 8 54.58N 2.27W
Hamamatsu 28 34.42N137.44E
Hamar 19 60.48N 11.06E
Hamburg 16 53.33N 10.00E
Hameln 16 52.06N 9.21E
Hamersley Range mts. 32 22.00S118.00E
Hami 26 42.40N 93.30E
Hamilton r. 35 27.12S135.28E
Hamilton Canada 44 43.15N 79.51W
Hamilton New Zealand 29 37.46S175.18E
Hamilton U.K. 11 55.46N 4.10W
Hamilton Ohio 44 39.23N 84.33W
Hammerfest 18 70.40N 23.42E
Hampshire d. 9 51.03N 1.20W
Handa 28 34.53N136.56E
Handeni 53 5.25S 38.04E
Hangzhou 26 30.14N120.08E
Hannibal Mo. 41 39.41N 91.25W
Hannover 16 52.23N 9.44E
Hà Nôi 26 21.01N105.53E
Hanoi see Hà Nôi 26
Hanover 54 31.04S 24.25E
Haparanda 18 65.50N 24.10E
Ḥaraḍ 24 24.12N 49.08E
Harare 54 17.49S 31.04E
Harbin 26 45.45N126.41E
Hardangerfjorden est. 19 60.10N 6.00E
Harding 54 30.34S 29.52E
Hargeysa 51 9.31N 44.02E
Har Hu l. 26 38.20N 97.40E
Hari r. 27 1.00S104.15E
Harlech 8 52.52N 4.08W
Harlow 9 51.47N 0.08E
Harris i. 11 57.50N 6.55W
Harris, Sd. of 11 57.43N 7.05W
Harrisburg Penn. 44 40.16N 76.52W
Harrogate 8 53.59N 1.32W
Harrow 9 51.35N 0.21W
Harstad 18 68.48N 16.30E
Hartford 44 41.45N 72.42W
Hartland Pt. 9 51.01N 4.32W
Hartlepool 8 54.42N 1.11W
Harwich 9 51.56N 1.18E
Haryana d. 25 29.15N 76.30E
Haslemere 9 51.05N 0.41W
Hässleholm 19 56.09N 13.46E
Hastings New Zealand 29 39.39S176.52E
Hastings U.K. 9 50.51N 0.36E
Hatfield 9 51.46N 0.13W
Hattiesburg 41 31.25N 89.19W
Hauge 19 58.18N 6.15E
Haugesund 19 59.25N 5.18E
Hauraki G. 29 36.30S175.00E
Havana see La Habana 43
Havant 9 50.51N 0.59W
Haverfordwest 9 51.48N 4.59W
Haverhill 9 52.06N 0.27E
Havre 40 48.34N109.45W
Hawaii d. 40 21.00N156.00W
Hawaii i. Hawaii 40 19.30N155.30W
Hawaiian Is. 40 21.00N157.00W
Hawea, L. 29 44.30S169.15E
Hawera 29 39.35S174.19E
Hawick 11 55.25N 2.47W
Hawke, C. 37 32.12S152.33E
Hawke B. 29 39.18S177.15E
Hawthorne 40 38.13N118.37W
Hay 37 34.31S144.31E
Hayes r. 39 57.00N 92.30W
Hay-on-Wye 9 52.04N 3.09W
Hazelton 38 55.16N127.18W
Hazleton 44 40.58N 75.59W
Heanor 8 53.01N 1.20W
Hebel 37 28.55S147.49E
Hebron 39 58.05N 62.30W
Heerenveen 16 52.57N 5.55E
Hefei 26 31.50N117.16E
Heidelberg 16 49.25N 8.42E
Heilbron 54 27.16S 27.57E
Heilbronn 16 49.08N 9.14E
Hekou 26 22.39N103.57E
Helena 40 46.35N112.00W
Helensburgh 11 56.01N 4.44W
Helmsdale r. 11 58.05N 3.39W
Helsingfors see Helsinki 19
Helsingör 19 56.02N 12.37E
Helsinki 19 60.08N 25.00E
Helston 9 50.07N 5.17W
Hemel Hempstead 9 51.46N 0.28W
Hemsedal 19 60.52N 8.34E
Henares r. 13 40.26N 3.35W
Hendaye 12 43.22N 1.46W
Hengelo 7 52.16N 6.46E
Hengyang 26 26.52N112.35E
Herāt 24 34.20N 62.12E
Hereford 9 52.04N 2.43W
Hereford and Worcester d. 9 52.08N 2.30W
Herford 16 52.07N 8.40E
Hermidale 37 31.33S146.44E
Herne Bay town 9 51.23N 1.10E
Herning 19 56.08N 8.59E
Hertford 9 51.48N 0.05W
Hertfordshire d. 9 51.51N 0.05W
Hexham 8 54.58N 2.06W
Heysham 8 54.03N 2.53W
Heywood 8 53.36N 2.13W
Highland d. 11 57.42N 5.00W
High Peak mtn. 8 53.22N 1.48W
High Wycombe 9 51.38N 0.46W
Hikurangi mtn. 29 37.50S178.10E
Hildesheim 16 52.09N 9.58E
Hillston 37 33.30S145.33E
Hilo Hawaii 40 19.42N155.04W
Hilversum 16 52.14N 5.12E
Himachal Pradesh d. 25 32.05N 77.15E
Himalaya mts. 25 29.00N 84.30E
Ḥimş 24 34.44N 36.43E
Hinckley 9 52.33N 1.21W
Hindmarsh, L. 36 36.03S141.53E
Hindu Kush mts. 25 36.40N 70.00E
Hiroshima 26 34.23N132.27E
Hirson 12 49.56N 4.05E
Hispaniola i. 43 19.00N 71.00W
Hitchin 9 51.57N 0.16W
Hjälmaren l. 19 59.15N 15.45E
Hjörring 19 57.28N 9.59E
Hobart 35 42.54S147.18E
Ho Chi Minh City see Thành Pho Ho Chí Min 27
Hof 16 50.19N 11.56E
Höfn 18 64.16N 15.10W
Hofors 19 60.33N 16.17E
Hohhot 26 40.42N111.38E
Hokitika 29 42.42S170.59E
Hokkaidō i. 26 43.60N143.00E
Holland Mich. 44 42.46N 86.06W
Holstebro 19 56.21N 8.38E
Holt 8 52.55N 1.04E
Holyhead 8 53.18N 4.38W
Holy I. England 8 55.41N 1.47W
Holy I. Wales 8 53.15N 4.38W
Holywood 10 54.38N 5.50W
Homer Alas. 38 59.40N151.37W
Homer Tunnel 29 44.40S168.15E
Homoine 54 23.45S 35.09E
Honduras 43 14.30N 87.00W
Honfleur 12 49.25N 0.14E
Hong Kong 26 22.15N114.15E
Hongshui He r. 26 23.20N110.04E
Honiton 9 50.48N 3.13W
Honolulu Hawaii 40 21.19N157.50W
Honshū i. 26 36.00N138.00E
Hoopstad 54 27.48S 25.52E
Hoorn 16 52.38N 5.03E
Hoover Dam 40 36.01N114.45W
Hopetoun Vic. 36 35.43S142.20E
Hopetown 54 29.37S 24.04E
Horn, C. see Hornos, Cabo de c. 49
Horncastle 8 53.13N 0.08W
Hornos, Cabo de c. 49 55.47S 67.00W
Hornsea 8 53.55N 0.10W
Horsens 19 55.52N 9.52E
Horsham 9 51.04N 0.20W
Hospitalet de Llobregat 13 41.20N 2.06E
Hotan 25 37.07N 79.57E
Hotazel 54 27.16S 22.57E
Hoting 18 64.07N 16.10E
Houndé 50 11.34N 3.31W
Houston Tex. 41 29.45N 95.25W
Hovd 26 46.40N 90.45E
Hove 9 50.50N 0.10W
Howe, C. 37 37.30S149.59E
Howitt, Mt. 37 37.15S146.40E
Howrah 25 22.35N 88.20E
Hoy i. 11 58.51N 3.17W
Huabei Pingyuan f. 26 36.32N108.14E
Huambo 52 12.47S 15.44E
Huancayo 46 12.05S 75.12W
Huang He r. 26 38.00N118.40E
Huánuco 46 9.55S 76.11W
Hubli 25 15.20N 75.14E
Hucknall 8 53.03N 1.12W
Huddersfield 8 53.38N 1.49W
Hudiksvall 19 61.44N 17.07E
Hudson r. 44 40.42N 74.02W
Hudson B. 39 58.00N 86.00W
Hudson Str. 39 62.00N 70.00W
Hue 27 16.28N107.40E
Huelva 13 37.15N 6.56W
Huelva r. 13 37.25N 6.00W
Huesca 13 42.02N 0.25W
Hughenden 34 20.51S144.12E
Huiarau Range mts. 29 38.20S177.15E
Huixtla 42 15.09N 92.30W
Hull 44 45.26N 75.45W
Hultsfred 19 57.29N 15.50E
Humansdorp 54 34.02S 24.45E
Humber r. 8 53.40N 0.12W
Humberside d. 8 53.48N 0.35W
Humboldt r. 40 40.02N118.31W
Hün 50 29.06N 15.57E
Hungary 17 47.30N 19.00E
Hüngnam 26 39.49N127.40E
Hunsrück mts. 16 49.44N 7.05E
Hunstanton 8 52.57N 0.30E
Huntingdon 9 52.20N 0.11W
Huntsville Ala. 41 34.44N 86.35W
Huron, L. 44 44.30N 82.15W
Huskvarna 19 57.48N 14.16E
Husum 16 54.29N 9.04E
Hwange 54 18.22S 26.29E
Hyde 8 53.26N 2.06W
Hyderābād India 25 17.22N 78.26E
Hyderābād Pakistan 25 25.22N 68.22E
Hyères 12 43.07N 6.08E
Hyndman Peak 40 43.46N113.55W
Hythe Kent 9 51.04N 1.05E

I

Ibadan 50 7.23N 3.56E
Ibagué 46 4.25N 75.20W
Ibarra 46 0.23N 78.05W
Ibi 50 8.11N 9.44E
Ibicaraí 47 14.52S 39.37W
Ibina r. 53 1.00N 28.40E
Ibiza i. 13 39.00N 1.23E
Ibotirama 47 12.13S 43.12W
Iceland 18 64.45N 18.00W
Ichinomiya 28 35.18N136.48E
Idah 50 7.05N 6.45E
Idaho d. 40 45.00N115.00W
Ídhra i. 15 37.20N 23.32E
Ierápetra 15 35.00N 25.45E
Iesi 14 43.32N 13.15E
Iesolo 14 45.32N 12.38E
Igoumenítsa 15 39.32N 20.14E
Iguaçu r. 45 25.33S 54.35W
Iguala 42 18.21N 99.31W
Iisalmi 18 63.34N 27.11E
IJsselmeer l. 16 52.45N 5.20E
Ijuí 45 28.23S 53.55W
Ikaría i. 15 37.35N 26.10E
Ikelemba r. 52 0.08N 18.19E
Ilebo 52 4.20S 20.35E
Ilesha Oyo 50 7.38N 4.45E
Ilfracombe 9 51.13N 4.08W
Iligan 27 8.12N124.13E
Ilkley 8 53.56N 1.49W
Illinois d. 41 40.00N 89.00W
Ilminster 9 50.55N 2.56W
Ilorin 50 8.32N 4.34E
Imala 53 14.39S 39.34E
Immingham 8 53.37N 0.12W
Imphāl 25 24.47N 93.55E
Inca 13 39.43N 2.54E
Inch'on 26 37.30N126.38E
India 25 23.00N 78.00E
Indiana d. 44 40.00N 86.15W
Indianapolis 44 39.45N 86.10W
Indian Ocean 27
Indonesia 27 6.00S118.00E
Indore 25 22.43N 75.50E
Indre r. 12 47.16N 0.19W
Indus r. 25 24.20N 67.47E
Inebolu 21 41.57N 33.45E
Ingende 52 0.17S 18.58E
Ingham 34 18.35S146.12E
Ingleborough mtn. 8 54.10N 2.23W
Inhambane 54 23.51S 35.29E
Inisheer i. 10 53.04N 9.32W
Inishmaan i. 10 53.06N 9.36W
Inishmore i. 10 53.08N 9.43W
Inishowen Pen. 10 55.08N 7.20W
Inishturk i. 10 53.43N 10.08W
Inner Hebrides is. 11 56.50N 6.45W
Inner Mongolia d. see Nei Monggol d. 26
Innsbruck 16 47.17N 11.25E
Interlaken 16 46.42N 7.52E
Inuvik 38 68.16N133.40W
Inuvik d. 38 68.00N130.00W
Inveraray 11 56.24N 5.05W
Inverbervie 11 56.51N 2.17W
Invercargill 29 46.26S168.21E
Inverell 37 29.46S151.10E
Invergordon 11 57.42N 4.10W
Inverness 11 57.27N 4.15W
Inverurie 11 57.17N 2.23W
Inzia r. 52 3.47S 17.57E
Ioánnina 15 39.39N 20.49E
Iona i. 11 56.20N 6.25W
Ionian Is. see Iónioi Nísoi is. 15
Ionian Sea 15 38.30N 18.45E
Iónioi Nísoi is. 15 38.45N 20.00E
Ios i. 15 36.42N 25.20E
Iowa d. 41 42.00N 93.00W
Iowa City 41 41.39N 91.30W
Ipiaú 47 14.07S 39.43W
Ipoh 27 4.36N101.02E
Ipswich Australia 37 27.38S152.40E
Ipswich U.K. 9 52.04N 1.09E
Iquitos 46 3.51S 73.13W
Iráklion 15 35.20N 25.08E
Iran 24 32.00N 54.30E
Iraq 24 33.00N 44.00E
Iringa 53 7.49S 35.39E
Irish Sea 10 53.30N 5.40W
Irkutsk 23 52.18N104.15E
Iron Gate f. 17 44.40N 22.30E
Iron Mts. 10 54.10N 7.56W
Irosin 27 12.45N124.02E
Irrapatana 36 29.03S136.28E
Irrawaddy r. 27 15.50N 95.00E
Irtysh r. 22 61.00N 68.40E
Irún 13 43.20N 1.48W
Irvine 11 55.37N 4.40W
Isangi 52 0.48N 24.03E
Isar r. 16 48.48N 12.57E
Ischia i. 14 40.43N 13.54E
Isère r. 12 45.02N 4.54E
Isfahan see Eşfahān 24
Ishim r. 22 57.50N 71.00E
Isiro 53 2.50N 27.40E
Iskenderun 21 36.37N 36.08E
Iskür r. 15 43.42N 24.27E
Isla r. 11 56.32N 3.22W
Islāmābād 25 33.40N 73.10E
Islands, B. of 29 35.15S174.15E
Islay i. 11 55.45N 6.20W
Isle of Portland f. 9 50.32N 2.25W
Isle of Wight d. 9 50.40N 1.17W
Israel 24 32.00N 35.00E
Issoire 12 45.33N 3.15E
Istanbul 24 41.02N 28.58E
Itabira 45 19.39S 43.14W
Itabuna 47 14.48S 39.18W
Itaituba 47 4.17S 55.59W
Italy 14 43.00N 12.00E
Itapetinga 47 15.17S 40.16W
Itaqui 45 29.07S 56.33W
Ithaca 44 42.26N 76.30W
Itháki 15 38.23N 20.42E
Ituiutaba 45 19.00S 49.25W
Ituri r. 53 1.45N 27.06E
Ivaí r. 45 23.20S 53.23W
Ivalo r. 18 68.43N 27.36E
Ivanhoe 36 32.56S144.22E
Ivanovo R.S.F.S.R. 20 57.00N 41.00E
Ivigtût 39 61.10N 48.00W
Ivindo 52 0.02S 12.13E
Iviza i. see Ibiza i. 13
Ivory Coast 50 7.00N 5.30W
Izmail 24 45.20N 28.50E
Izmir 24 38.24N 27.09E
Izmit 21 40.48N 29.55E

J

Jabalón r. 13 38.55N 4.07W
Jabalpur 25 23.10N 79.57E
Jaca 13 42.34N 0.33W
Jackson Mich. 44 42.15N 84.24W
Jackson Miss. 41 32.20N 90.11W
Jacksonville Fla. 41 30.20N 81.40W
Jacques Cartier, Mt. 44 49.00N 65.55W
Jacuí r. 45 29.56S 51.13W
Jaffa, C. 36 36.58S139.39E
Jaffna 25 9.38N 80.02E
Jagdalpur 25 19.04N 82.02E
Jaipur 25 26.53N 75.50E
Jakarta 27 6.08S106.45E
Jalapa 42 19.45N 96.48W
Jalón r. 13 41.47N 1.02W
Jamaica 43 18.00N 77.00W
Jamālpur 25 24.55N 89.56E
James r. S.Dak. 41 42.50N 97.15W
James B. 39 53.00N 80.00W
Jammu 25 32.42N 74.52E
Jammu & Kashmir 25 34.45N 76.00E
Jāmnagar 25 22.28N 70.04E
Jämsänkoski 19 61.55N 25.11E
Jamshedpur 25 22.48N 86.11E
Jāndula r. 13 38.08N 4.08W
Janesville 41 42.42N 89.02W

Logroño 13 42.28N 2.26W
Loir r. 12 47.29N 0.32W
Loire r. 12 47.18N 2.00W
Loja 13 3.59S 79.16W
Loka 52 0.20N 17.57E
Lokitaung 53 4.15N 35.45E
Lokja 50 7.49N 6.44E
Lokolo r. 52 0.45S 19.36E
Lokoro r. 52 1.40S 18.29E
Lolland i. 19 54.46N 11.30E
Lomami r. 52 0.45N 24.10E
Lomas de Zamora 49 34.46S 58.24W
Lombok i. 27 8.30S116.20E
Lomé 50 6.10N 1.21E
Lomela r. 52 0.14S 20.45E
Lomié 52 3.09N 13.35E
Lomond, Loch 11 56.07N 4.36W
London 21 42.59N 81.14W
London U.K. 9 51.32N 0.06W
Londonderry 10 55.00N 7.21W
Londonderry d. 10 55.00N 7.00W
Londonderry, C. 32 13.58S126.55E
Londrina 48 23.30S 51.13W
Long Beach town Calif. 40 33.57N118.15W
Long Eaton 8 52.54N 1.16W
Longford 10 53.44N 7.48W
Longford d. 10 53.42N 7.45W
Long I. 44 40.46N 73.00W
Long L. 44 49.29N 86.44W
Longniddry 11 55.58N 2.53W
Longreach 34 23.26S144.15E
Longtown 8 55.01N 2.59W
Lonsdale, L. 36 37.05S142.15E
Looe 9 50.51N 4.26W
Lookout, C. 41 34.34N 76.34W
Loongana 33 30.57S127.02E
Loop Head r. 52 1.20N 20.22E
Lopari r. 52 1.20N 20.22E
Lopez, C. 52 0.36S 8.40E
Lop Nur l. 26 40.30N 90.30E
Lorain 41 41.28N 82.11W
Loralai 25 30.22N 68.36E
Lorca 13 37.40N 1.41W
Lordsburg 40 32.22N108.43W
Lorient 12 47.45N 3.21W
Lorne 36 38.34S144.01E
Los Angeles 40 34.00N118.17W
Los Blancos 13 37.37N 0.48W
Lossiemouth 11 57.43N 3.18W
Lot r. 12 44.17N 0.22E
Lothian d. 11 55.50N 3.00W
Lotoi r. 52 1.30S 18.30E
Lotsani r. 54 22.42S 28.11E
Louangphrabang 26 19.53N102.10E
Loudéac 12 48.11N 2.45W
Loudima 52 4.06S 13.05E
Loughborough 8 52.47N 1.11W
Loughrea 10 53.12N 8.35W
Loughros More B. 10 54.48N 8.32W
Louisburgh 10 53.46N 9.49W
Louisiana d. 41 31.00N 92.30W
Louis Trichardt 54 23.03S 29.54E
Louisville Ky. 44 38.13N 85.48W
Lourdes 12 43.06N 0.02W
Louth d. 10 53.55N 6.30W
Louth 8 53.23N 0.00
Lovat r. 20 58.06N 31.37E
Lovech 15 43.08N 24.44E
Lovoi r. 53 8.14S 26.40E
Lovua r. 52 6.08S 20.35E
Lowa r. Kivu 52 1.25S 25.55E
Lowell 44 42.39N 71.18W
Lower Hutt 29 41.13S174.55E
Lower Lough Erne 10 54.28N 7.48W
Lowestoft 9 52.29N 1.44E
Łowicz 17 52.06N 19.55E
Loxton 36 34.38S140.38E
Loyauté, Îles is. 30 21.00S167.00E
Luachimo r. 52 6.32S 20.57E
Luama r. 53 4.45S 26.55E
Luanda 52 8.50S 13.20E
Luanginga r. 52 15.11S 23.05E
Luangwa r. Central 53 15.32S 30.28E
Luanshya 53 13.09S 28.24E
Luao 52 10.41S 22.09E
Luapula r. 52 9.25S 28.36E
Luarca 13 43.33N 6.31W
Lubango 52 14.52S 13.30E
Lubao 52 5.19S 25.43E
Lubbock 40 33.35N101.53W
Lübeck 16 53.52N 10.40E
Lubefu r. 52 4.05S 23.00E
Lubilash r. 52 4.59S 23.25E
Lublin 17 51.18N 22.31E
Lubudi r. K.Occidental 52 4.00S 21.23E
Lubudi r. Shaba 52 9.57S 25.59E
Lubumbashi 53 11.44S 27.29E
Lubutu 52 0.48S 26.19E
Luce B. 11 54.45N 4.47W
Lucena 13 37.25N 4.29W
Lučenec 17 48.20N 19.40E
Lucero 42 30.50N106.30W
Luckenwalde 16 52.05N 13.11E
Lucknow 25 26.51N 80.55E
Lüda 26 38.49N121.48E
Lüderitz 54 26.37S 15.09E
Ludhiana 25 30.55N 75.51E
Ludington 44 43.58N 86.27W
Ludlow 9 52.23N 2.42W
Ludvika 19 60.09N 15.11E
Ludwigshafen 16 49.29N 8.27E
Luebo 52 5.16S 21.27E
Luenge r. 52 16.58S 21.15E
Lufeng 26 23.01N115.35E
Lufira r. 52 8.15S 26.30E
Lufkin 41 31.21N 94.47W
Luga 20 58.42N 29.49E
Lugano 14 46.01N 8.57E
Lugenda r. 53 11.23S 38.30E
Lugo 13 43.00N 7.33W
Lugoj 17 45.42N 21.56E
Luiana r. 52 22.43S 28.11E
Luilu r. 52 0.15S 19.00E
Luiro r. 18 67.18N 27.28E
Luga r. 52 7.15S 22.27E
Lukala 52 5.23S 13.02E
Lukanga Swamp f. 53 14.15S 27.30E
Lukenie r. 52 2.43S 18.12E
Lukuga r. 53 5.37S 26.58E
Lukula r. 52 5.23S 13.00E
Lule r. 18 65.34N 22.10E
Luleå 18 65.35N 22.10E
Lulonga r. 52 0.42N 18.26E
Lulua r. 52 5.03S 21.07E
Lumsden 29 45.44S168.26E
Lund 19 55.42N 13.11E
Lundazi 53 12.19S 33.11E

Lundi r. 54 21.20S 32.23E
Lundy i. 9 51.10N 4.41W
Lüneburg 16 53.15N 10.24E
Lunga r. 52 14.28S 26.27E
Lungwebungu r. 52 14.20S 23.15E
Luofo 53 0.12S 29.15E
Luoyang 26 34.48N112.25E
Lurgan 10 54.28N 6.21W
Lurio 53 13.30S 40.30E
Lurio r. 53 13.32S 40.31E
Lusaka 53 15.20S 28.14E
Lusambo 52 4.59S 23.26E
Lushoto 53 4.48S 38.20E
Lusk 40 42.47N104.26W
Lutong, Selat str. 27 3.00S118.00E
Lutsk 17 50.42N 25.15E
Lutterworth 8 52.28N 1.12W
Luvua r. 53 6.45S 27.00E
Luwegu r. 53 8.30S 37.28E
Luwingu 53 10.13S 30.05E
Luxembourg 16 49.50N 6.15E
Luxembourg town r. 16 49.37N 6.08E
Luxor see Al Uqsur 51
Luzern 16 47.03N 8.17E
Luzhou 26 28.48N105.23E
Luziânia 47 16.18S 47.57W
Luzon i. 27 17.50N121.00E
Lvov 17 49.50N 24.00E
Lybster 11 58.18N 3.18W
Lycksele 18 64.36N 18.40E
Lydenburg 54 25.06S 30.27E
Lyme B. 9 50.40N 2.55W
Lyme Regis 9 50.44N 2.57W
Lymington 9 50.46N 1.32W
Lyndhurst 36 30.19S 138.24E
Lynn 44 42.28N 70.57W
Lynn Lake town 39 56.51N101.01W
Lynton 9 51.14N 3.50W
Lyon 12 45.46N 4.50E
Lyons r. 32 25.02S115.09E
Lysekil 19 58.16N 11.26E
Lytham St. Anne's 8 53.45N 3.01W
Lyubertsy 20 55.38N 37.58E

M

Maamakeogh mtn. 10 54.17N 9.29W
Maamturk Mts. 10 53.32N 9.42W
Ma'an 24 30.11N 35.43E
Maas r. 16 51.44N 4.42E
Mabel Creek town 35 29.01S134.17E
Mablethorpe 8 53.21N 0.14E
Macalister r. 37 37.55S146.50E
Macapá 47 0.04N 51.04W
Macaroni r. 36 16.36S141.30E
Macau 26 22.11N113.33E
Macclesfield 8 53.16N 2.09W
Macdonald, L. 32 23.30S129.00E
Macdonnell Ranges mts. 34 23.45S133.20E
Macduff 11 57.40N 2.29W
Macedon mtn. 37 37.27S144.34E
Maceió 47 9.40S 35.44W
Macerata 14 43.18N 13.30E
Macfarlane, L. 36 31.55S136.42E
Macgillycuddy's Reeks mts. 10 52.00N 9.43W
Machattie, L. 34 24.50S139.48E
Macheke 54 18.08S 31.49E
Machrihanish 11 55.25N 5.44W
Machynlleth 9 52.35N 3.51W
Macintyre r. 37 28.50S150.50E
Mackay, L. 32 22.30S149.10E
Mackenzie Australia 34 22.48S149.15E
Mackenzie Canada 38 69.20N134.00W
Mackenzie Mts. 38 64.00N130.00W
Mackinnon Road town 53 3.50S 39.03E
Maclear 54 31.04S 28.21E
Macleay r. 37 30.52S153.01E
Macomer 14 40.16N 8.45E
Mâcon 12 46.18N 4.50E
Macon Ga. 41 32.47N 83.37W
Macpherson Range mts. 37 28.15S153.00E
Macquarie r. 37 30.07S147.24E
Macquarie Marshes 37 30.50S147.32E
Macroom 10 51.54N 8.58W
Macumba r. 35 27.55S137.15E
Madagascar 3 17.00S 46.00E
Madawaska 44 47.21N 68.20W
Madeira r. 50 32.45N 17.00W
Madeira r. 46 3.50S 59.00W
Madeira, Arquipélago da is. 50 32.40N 16.45W
Madeleine, Îles de la is. 39 47.30N 61.45W
Madhya Pradesh d. 25 23.30N 78.30E
Madison Wisc. 41 43.04N 89.22W
Mado Gashi 53 0.40N 39.11E
Madras 25 13.05N 80.18E
Madre del Sur, Sierra mts. 42 17.00N100.00W
Madrid 13 40.25N 3.43W
Madukani 53 3.57S 35.49E
Madura i. 27 7.02S113.20E
Madurai 25 9.55N 78.07E
Maestra, Sierra mts. 43 20.10N 76.30W
Mafeteng 54 29.51S 27.13E
Mafia I. 53 7.50S 39.50E
Mafikeng 54 25.52S 25.36E
Magadi 53 1.53S 36.18E
Magallanes, Estrecho de str. 49 53.00S 71.00W
Magalluf 13 39.30N 2.31E
Magangué 46 9.14N 74.46W
Magdalena r. 46 10.56N 74.58W
Magdeburg 16 52.08N 11.36E
Magee, I. 10 54.48N 5.44W
Magelang 27 7.28S110.11E
Magellan's Str. see Magallanes, Estrecho de str. 49
Magerøya i. 18 71.03N 25.45E
Maggiore, Lago i. 14 46.00N 8.40E
Magherafelt 10 54.45N 6.38W
Magnitogorsk 20 53.28N 59.06E
Magué 53 15.46S 31.42E
Mahaddaq Weyne 53 2.58N 45.32E
Mahagi 52 2.15S 32.00E
Mahalapye 54 23.06S 26.50E
Mahārāshtra d. 25 19.40N 76.00E
Mahdia 46 5.10N 59.12W
Mahia Pen. 29 39.10S177.50E
Mahón 13 39.55N 4.18E
Maidenhead 9 51.32N 0.44W
Maidstone 9 51.17N 0.32E
Maiduguri 50 11.53N 13.16E
Maiko r. 52 0.15N 25.35E
Main r. 16 50.00N 8.19E

Main Barrier Range mts. 36 31.25S141.25E
Mai Ndombe l. 52 2.00S 18.20E
Maine d. 44 45.15N 69.15W
Mainland i. Orkney Is. 11 59.00N 3.10W
Mainz 16 50.00N 8.16E
Maipo mtn. 49 34.10N 69.50W
Maitland N.S.W. 37 32.33S151.33E
Majene 27 3.33S118.59E
Majorca i. see Mallorca i. 13
Majuba Hill 54 27.26S 29.48E
Makarikari Salt Pan f. 54 20.50S 25.45E
Makasar, Selat str. 27 3.00S118.00E
Makeyevka 21 48.01N 38.00E
Makhachkala 21 42.59N 47.30E
Makó 17 46.13N 20.30E
Makran f. 24 26.30N 61.20E
Makurdi 50 7.44N 8.35E
Malabo 52 3.45N 8.48E
Malacca, Str. of 27 3.00N100.30E
Málaga 13 36.43N 4.25W
Malakal 51 9.31N 31.40E
Malakand 25 34.34N 71.56E
Malanje 52 9.36S 16.21E
Mälaren I. 19 59.30N 17.12E
Malawi 53 12.00S 34.30E
Malawi, L. 53 12.00S 34.30E
Malaysia 27 5.00N110.00E
Malbork 17 54.02N 19.01E
Maldives 24 6.20N 73.00E
Maldon 9 51.43N 0.41E
Maldonado 45 34.57S 54.59W
Maléa, Ákra c. 15 36.27N 23.11E
Malebo Pool f. 52 4.15S 15.25E
Malema 53 14.55S 37.09E
Mali 50 16.00N 3.00W
Malindi 53 3.14S 40.08E
Malin Head 10 55.23N 7.24W
Malin More 10 54.43N 8.48W
Mallacoota Inlet b. 37 37.34S149.43E
Mallaig 11 57.00N 5.50W
Mallorca i. 13 39.35N 3.00E
Mallow 10 52.08N 8.39W
Malmesbury 54 33.28S 18.43E
Malmö 19 55.36N 13.00E
Malone 44 44.51N 74.17W
Malonga 52 10.26S 23.10E
Malpas 36 34.44S140.43E
Malta 14 35.55N 14.25E
Maltby 8 53.25N 1.12W
Malton 8 54.09N 0.48W
Mambasa 53 1.20N 29.05E
Mambilima Falls town 53 10.32S 28.45E
Mamore r. 48 12.00S 65.15W
Mamuju 27 2.41S118.55E
Man 50 7.31N 7.37W
Man, Isle of 8 54.15N 4.30W
Manacor 13 39.34N 3.12E
Manado 27 1.30N124.58E
Managua 43 12.06N 86.18W
Managua, Lago de l. 43 12.10N 86.30W
Manakara 53 22.08S 48.01E
Manaus 46 3.06S 60.00W
Manchester 8 53.30N 2.15W
Manchurian Plain f. see Dongbei Pingyuan f. 26
Mandal 16 58.02N 7.27E
Mandalay 26 21.58N 96.04E
Mandalgovi 26 45.40N106.10E
Mandeb, Bâb el Str. 24 13.00N 43.10E
Mandurah 33 32.31S115.41E
Manfred 36 33.21S143.50E
Manfredonia, Golfo di g. 14 41.35N 16.05E
Mangalia 17 43.50N 28.35E
Mangalore 25 12.54N 74.51E
Mangaweka 29 38.49S175.48E
Mangnai 26 37.52N 91.26E
Mango 50 10.23N 0.30E
Mangochi 53 14.29S 35.15E
Manhiça 54 25.24S 32.49E
Maniamba 53 12.44S 35.05E
Manica 54 19.00S 33.00E
Manila 27 14.36N120.59E
Manildra 37 33.12S148.41E
Maningrida 34 12.03S134.13E
Manipur d. 25 25.00N 93.40E
Manisa 15 38.37N 27.28E
Manistee r. 44 44.14N 86.20W
Manitoba d. 39 54.00N 96.00W
Manitoba, L. 39 51.33N 99.00W
Manitoulin I. 44 45.45N 82.30W
Manizales 46 5.03N 75.32W
Manjimup 33 34.15S116.06E
Manly 37 33.47S151.17E
Mann r. 34 12.20S134.07E
Mannahill 36 32.26S139.59E
Mannar, G. of 25 8.20N 79.00E
Mannheim 16 49.30N 8.28E
Mannin B. 10 53.28N 10.06W
Mannum 36 34.50S139.20E
Manokwari 27 0.53S134.05E
Manono 53 7.18S 27.24E
Manorhamilton 10 54.18N 8.10W
Manresa 13 41.43N 1.50E
Mansa 53 11.10S 28.52E
Mansel I. 39 62.00N 80.00W
Mansfield 8 53.08N 1.12W
Mantova 14 45.10N 10.47E
Mänttä 19 62.02N 24.38E
Manukau Harbour est. 29 37.10S174.00E
Manus i. 30 2.05S147.00E
Manyara, L. 53 3.40S 35.50E
Manych r. 21 47.14N 40.20E
Manyinga r. 52 13.28S 24.25E
Manzanares 13 39.00N 3.23W
Manzanillo 43 20.21N 77.21W
Manzhouli 26 49.36N117.28E
Manzini 54 26.29S 31.24E
Maoke, Pegunungan mts. 27 4.00S138.30E
Maoming 26 21.50N110.58E
Mapai 54 22.51S 32.00E
Mappi 27 7.06S139.23E
Maputo 54 25.58S 32.35E
Maputo r. 54 26.11S 32.34E
Maquela do Zombo 52 6.06S 15.12E
Mar, Serra do mts. 45 23.00S 44.40W
Maracaibo 46 10.44N 71.37W
Maracaju, Serra de mts. 45 21.38S 55.10W
Maracay 46 10.20N 67.28W
Maradi 50 13.29N 7.10E

Marahuaca, Cerro mtn. 46 3.37N 65.25W
Marajó, Ilha de i. 47 1.00S 49.40W
Maralal 53 1.15N 36.48E
Maramba 52 17.40S 25.50E
Maranoa r. 35 27.55S148.30E
Marão 54 24.21S 34.07E
Marathon 15 38.10N 23.59E
Marbella 13 36.31N 4.53W
Marble Bar 32 21.16S119.45E
Marburg 16 50.49N 8.36E
March 9 52.33N 0.05E
Marchant Hill 36 32.16S138.49E
Mar Chiquita l. 48 30.42S 62.36W
Mardan 25 34.12N 72.02E
Mar del Plata 49 38.00S 57.32W
Marden 9 51.11N 0.30E
Mardie 32 21.14S115.57E
Mardin 21 37.19N 40.43E
Maree, Loch 11 57.41N 5.28W
Mareeba 34 17.00S145.26E
Marettimo i. 14 37.58N 12.05E
Margaret r. 36 29.26S137.00E
Margarita, Isla de i. 46 11.00N 64.00W
Margate 9 51.23N 1.24E
Maria i. 34 14.52S135.40E
Mariana Is. 30 16.00N145.30E
Marianao 43 23.03N 82.29W
Marie-Galante i. 43 15.54N 61.11W
Mariental 54 24.38S 17.58E
Marília 45 22.13S 50.20W
Maringá 45 23.36S 52.02W
Maringa r. 52 1.13N 19.50E
Maringue 54 17.55S 34.24E
Marinha Grande 13 39.45N 8.55W
Mariscal Estigarribia 45 22.03S 60.35W
Maritsa r. 15 41.00N 26.15E
Market Drayton 8 52.55N 2.30W
Market Harborough 9 52.29N 0.55W
Market Rasen 8 53.24N 0.20W
Market Weighton 8 53.52N 0.04W
Markha r. 23 63.37N110.00E
Marlborough d. 29 41.40S173.40E
Marlborough 9 51.26N 1.44W
Marmande 12 44.30N 0.10E
Marmara i. 15 40.38N 27.37E
Marmara, Sea of see Marmara Denizi sea 15
Marmara Denizi sea 15 40.45N 28.15E
Marmaris 15 36.50N 28.17E
Marne r. 12 48.40N 2.25E
Marnoo 36 36.40S142.55E
Maroua 50 10.35N 14.20E
Marquard 54 28.39S 27.25E
Marquesas Is. see Marquises, Îles is. 31
Marquises, Îles is. 31 9.00S139.30W
Marra r. 37 30.05S147.05W
Marrakech 50 31.49N 8.00W
Marree 36 29.40S138.04E
Marrupa 53 13.10S 37.30E
Marsabit 53 2.20N 37.59E
Marsala 14 37.48N 12.27E
Marsden 37 33.46S147.35E
Marseille 12 43.18N 5.22E
Marshall Tex. 41 32.33N 94.22W
Marshall Is. 30 10.00N172.00E
Martaban, G. of 25 15.10N 96.30E
Martés, Sierra mts. 13 39.10N 1.00W
Martha's Vineyard i. 44 41.25N 70.40W
Martigny 16 46.07N 7.05E
Martinique i. 43 14.40N 61.00W
Martin Pt. 38 70.10N143.50W
Marton 29 40.04S175.25E
Mary Kathleen 34 20.48S140.00E
Maryland d. 44 39.00N 76.45W
Maryport 8 54.43N 3.30W
Masai Steppe f. 53 4.30S 37.00E
Masaka 53 0.20S 31.46E
Masasi 53 10.43S 38.48E
Masbate i. 27 12.00N123.30E
Maseru 54 29.19S 27.29E
Mashhad 24 36.16N 59.34E
Mashonaland f. 54 18.20S 32.00E
Masi-Manimba 52 4.47S 17.54E
Masindi 53 1.41N 31.45E
Masirah i. 24 20.30N 58.50E
Mask, Lough 10 53.38N 9.22W
Masqat 24 23.36N 58.38E
Mason City 41 43.10N 93.10W
Massachusetts d. 44 42.15N 71.50W
Massangena 54 21.33S 33.03E
Massif Central mts. 12 45.00N 3.30E
Massinga 54 23.20S 35.25E
Masterton 29 40.57S175.39E
Masuku 52 0.20S 13.20E
Masvingo 54 20.10N 30.49E
Matabeleland f. 54 19.50S 28.15E
Matadi 52 5.50S 13.36E
Matagorda B. 41 28.30N 96.20W
Matakana I. 29 37.35S176.15E
Matam 50 15.40N 13.15W
Matamata 29 37.49S175.46E
Matamoros Tamaulipas 42 25.50N 97.31W
Matandu r. 53 8.44S 39.22E
Matanzas 43 23.04N 81.35W
Mataura r. 29 46.34S168.45E
Matawai 29 38.21S177.32E
Matehuala 42 23.40N100.40W
Matlock 8 53.08N 1.32W
Mato Grosso 48 15.00S 59.57W
Mato Grosso, Planalto do 48 16.00S 54.00W
Matope 53 15.20S 34.57E
Matopo Hills 54 20.28S 28.30E
Matrah 24 23.37N 58.30E
Matsue 26 35.29N133.00E
Matsusaka 28 34.34N136.32E
Matsuyama 26 33.50N132.47E
Mattagami r. 44 50.43N 81.29W
Matterhorn mtn. 12 45.58N 7.38E
Maude 36 34.27S144.21E
Maui i. Hawaii 40 20.45N156.15W
Maumere 27 8.35S122.13E
Mauna Kea mtn. 31 19.50N155.28W
Mauna Loa mtn. 31 19.29N155.36W
Mauritania 50 20.00N 10.00W
Mavinga 52 15.47S 20.21E
Mayaguana I. 43 22.30N 73.00W
Mayagüez 43 18.13N 67.09W
Maya Mts. 43 16.30N 89.00W
Mayenne d. 12 48.15N 0.37W
Mayenne r. 12 47.30N 0.37W
Maykop 21 44.37N 40.48E
Mayo d. 10 53.47N 9.07W
Mayo, Plains of f. 10 53.46N 9.05W

Mayo Landing 38 63.45N135.45W
Mayor I. 29 37.15S176.15E
Mayotte, Île i. 53 12.50S 45.10E
Mayumba 52 3.23S 10.38E
Mazabuka 53 15.50S 27.47E
Mazatenango 42 14.31N 91.30W
Mazatlán 42 23.11N106.25W
Mazowe r. 54 16.38N 33.25E
Mazowe 54 17.30S 30.58E
Mbabane 54 26.19S 31.08E
M'Baiki 52 3.53N 18.01E
Mbala 53 8.50S 31.24E
Mbale 53 1.04N 34.12E
Mbanza Congo 52 6.18S 14.16E
Mbarara 52 0.36S 30.40E
Mbeya 53 8.54S 33.29E
Mbinda 52 2.11S 12.55E
M'bridge r. 52 7.12S 12.55E
Mbuji Mayi 52 6.08S 23.39E
Mbulamuti 53 0.50N 33.05E
McArthur r. 34 15.54S136.40E
McClintock Channel 39 71.20N102.00W
McClure Str. 38 74.30N116.00W
McConaughy, L. 40 41.20N102.00W
McCook 40 40.15N100.45W
McGrath 38 62.58N155.40W
Mchinja 53 9.44S 39.45E
Mchinji 53 13.48S 32.55E
McIlwraith Range mts. 34 14.00S143.10E
McKeesport 44 40.21N 79.52W
McKinley, Mt. 38 63.00N151.00W
Meath d. 10 53.32N 6.40W
Meaux 12 48.58N 2.54E
Mecca see Makkah 24
Meconta 53 15.00S 39.50E
Medan 27 3.35N 98.39E
Mededsiz mtn. 21 37.33N 34.38E
Medellín 46 6.15N 75.36W
Médenine 50 33.24N 10.25E
Mederdra 50 16.55N 15.40W
Medford Oreg. 40 42.20N122.52W
Medicine Hat 38 50.03N110.41W
Medina see Al Madinah 24
Medina del Campo 13 41.20N 4.55W
Medina de Ríoseco 13 41.53N 5.03W
Mediterranean Sea 50 37.00N 15.00E
Medveditsa r. 21 49.35N 42.45E
Medway r. 9 51.24N 0.31E
Meekatharra 32 26.35S118.30E
Meerut 25 28.59N 77.42E
Mégara 15 38.00N 23.20E
Meghalaya d. 25 25.30N 91.00E
Meiktila 26 20.53N 95.50E
Meiningen 16 50.34N 10.25E
Meissen 16 51.10N 13.28E
Meknès 50 33.53N 5.37W
Mekong r. 26 10.00N106.40E
Melanesia is. 30 5.00N165.00E
Melbourne 37 37.45S144.58E
Melfi 14 40.59N 15.39E
Melilla 13 35.17N 2.57W
Melitopol 21 46.51N 35.22E
Mellerud 19 58.42N 12.28E
Melmore Pt. 10 55.15N 7.49W
Melo 45 32.22S 54.10W
Melrose 11 55.36N 2.43W
Melton Mowbray 8 52.46N 0.53W
Melun 12 48.32N 2.40E
Melvich 11 58.33N 3.55W
Melville B. 34 12.10S136.32E
Melville I. 34 11.30S131.00E
Melville Pen. 39 68.00N 84.00W
Melvin, Lough 54 54.26N 8.12W
Memba 53 14.16S 40.30E
Memmingen 16 47.59N 10.11E
Memphis Tenn. 41 35.05N 90.00W
Menai Str. 8 53.17N 4.20W
Mendawai r. 27 3.17S113.20E
Mende 12 44.32N 3.30E
Mendip Hills 9 51.15N 2.40W
Mendocino, C. 40 40.26N124.24W
Mendoza 49 32.54S 68.50W
Menindee 36 32.23S142.30E
Menongue 52 14.40S 17.41E
Menorca i. 13 40.00N 4.00E
Mentawai, Kepulauan is. 27 2.50S 99.00E
Menton 12 43.47N 7.30E
Menzies 33 29.41S121.02E
Meppel 16 52.42N 6.12E
Meppen 16 52.41N 7.17E
Merano 14 46.41N 11.10E
Merauke 27 8.30S140.22E
Merbein 36 34.11S142.04E
Merced 40 37.17N120.29W
Mere 9 51.05N 2.16W
Meredith 36 37.50S144.05E
Mergui 27 12.26N 98.38E
Mergui Archipelago is. 27 11.15N 98.00E
Meribah 36 34.42S140.53E
Mérida 43 20.59N 89.39W
Meridian 41 32.21N 88.42W
Merino 36 37.45S141.35E
Merrick mtn. 11 55.08N 4.29W
Mersea I. 9 51.47N 0.58E
Merseburg 16 51.22N 12.00E
Mersey r. 8 53.22N 2.37W
Merseyside d. 8 53.28N 3.00W
Mersin 21 36.47N 34.37E
Mersing 27 2.25N103.50E
Merthyr Tydfil 9 51.45N 3.23W
Merton 9 51.25N 0.12W
Meru 53 0.03N 37.38E
Meru mtn. 53 3.15S 36.44E
Merzifon 21 40.52N 35.28E
Mesa 40 33.25N111.50W
Meshchera r. see Néstos r. 15
Meta r. 46 6.10N 67.30W
Metković 15 43.03N 17.38E
Metz 12 49.07N 6.11E
Meuse r. Belgium see Maas r. 16
Mexborough 8 53.29N 1.18W
Mexicali 42 32.26N115.30W
Mexico 42 20.00N100.00W
Mexico, G. of 42 25.00N 90.00W
Mexico City see Ciudad de México 42
Mezen 21 65.50N 44.20E
Miami Fla. 41 25.45N 80.10W
Mianyang Sichuan 26 31.26N104.45E
Miass 20 55.00N 60.00E
Michigan d. 44 44.00N 85.00W
Michigan, L. 44 44.00N 87.00W
Michurinsk 20 52.54N 40.30E
Micronesia is. 30 8.00N160.00E

Mongolia 26 46.30N104.00E
Mongu 52 15.10S 23.09E
Monifieth 11 56.29N 2.50W
Mid Glamorgan d. 9 51.38N 3.25W
Monkoto 52 1.39S 20.41E
Monmouth 9 51.48N 2.43W
Monroe La. 41 32.31N 92.06W
Monrovia 50 6.20N 10.46W
Mons 16 50.27N 3.57E
Montana d. 40 47.00N110.00W
Montargis 12 48.00N 2.44E
Montauban 12 44.01N 1.20E
Montbrison 12 45.37N 4.04E
Mont Cenis, Col du pass 12 45.15N 6.55E
Mont de Marsan town 12 43.54N 0.30W
Monte Azul town 45 15.53S 42.53W
Monte Carlo 12 43.44N 7.25E
Montecristo i. 14 42.20N 10.19E
Montego Bay town 43 18.27N 77.56W
Montélimar 12 44.33N 4.45E
Monterey B. 40 36.45N122.00W
Montería 46 8.45N 75.54W
Montero 48 17.20S 63.15W
Monterrey 42 25.40N100.20W
Monte Santu, Capo di c. 14 40.05N 9.44E
Montes Claros 45 16.45S 43.52W
Montevideo 49 34.53S 56.11W
Montgomery Ala. 41 32.22N 86.20W
Montijo 13 38.42N 8.59W
Montluçon 12 46.20N 2.36E
Montmagny 44 46.56N 70.28W
Montmédy 12 49.31N 5.21E
Montmorillon 12 46.26N 0.52E
Montoro 13 38.02N 4.23W
Montpellier 12 43.36N 3.53E
Montpelier Vt. 44 44.16N 72.35W
Montreal 44 45.30N 73.36W
Montreal r. 44 47.14N 84.39W
Montrejeau 12 43.05N 0.33E
Montreuil 12 50.28N 1.46E
Montreux 16 46.27N 6.55E
Montrose 11 56.43N 2.29W
Montsant, Sierra de mts. 13 41.20N 1.00E
Montserrat i. 43 16.45N 62.14W
Monywa 26 22.05N 95.15E
Monza 14 45.35N 9.16E
Monze 53 16.16S 27.28E
Monzón 13 41.52N 0.10E
Moora 33 30.39S116.01E
Moore, L. 33 29.30S117.30E
Moorfoot Hills 11 55.43N 3.03W
Moorhead 41 46.51N 96.44W
Moosehead L. 44 45.40N 69.40W
Moose Jaw 38 50.23N105.35W
Mootwingee 36 31.52S141.14E
Mopti 50 14.29N 4.10W
Morādābād 25 28.50N 78.47E
Moralana 36 31.42S138.12E
Morar, Loch 11 56.56N 4.00W
Moray Firth est. 11 57.35N 5.15W
Morecambe 8 54.03N 2.52W
Morecambe B. 8 54.05N 3.00W
Morelia 42 19.40N101.11W
Morella 13 40.37N 0.06W
Morena, Sierra mts. 13 38.10N 5.00W
Moreton I. 35 27.10S153.25E
Morez 12 46.31N 6.02E
Morgan 36 34.02S139.40E
Morgan City 41 29.41N 91.13W
Morkalla 36 34.22S141.10E
Morlaix 12 48.35N 3.50W
Mornington I. 34 16.33S139.24E
Morocco 50 31.00N 5.00W
Morogoro 53 6.47S 37.40E
Moroni 53 11.40S 43.19E
Morotai i. 27 2.10N128.30E
Moroto 53 2.32N 34.41E
Morpeth 8 55.10N 1.40W
Morrinsville 29 37.39S175.32E
Mortagne 12 48.32N 0.33E
Mortlake town 36 38.05S142.48E
Morundah 37 34.56S146.18E
Morven 34 26.26S147.05E
Morvern f. 11 56.37N 5.45W
Moscow see Moskva 20
Mosel r. 16 50.23N 7.37E
Mosgiel 29 45.53S170.22E
Moshi 53 3.20S 37.21E
Mosjøen 18 65.50N 13.10E
Moskva 20 55.45N 37.42E
Moskva r. 20 55.08N 38.50E
Mosquitos, Costa de f. 43 13.00N 84.00W
Moss 19 59.26N 10.42E
Mossaka 52 1.20S 16.44E
Mossburn 29 45.41S168.18E
Mossgiel 37 33.18S144.05E
Mossman 34 16.28S145.22E
Mossoró 47 5.10S 37.18W
Most 16 50.31N 13.39E
Mostar 15 43.20N 17.50E
Motagua r. 43 15.56N 87.45W
Motala 19 58.33N 15.03E
Motherwell 11 55.48N 4.00W
Mouila 52 1.50S 11.02E
Moulamein 36 35.03S144.05E
Moulins 12 46.34N 3.20E
Moulmein 27 16.55N 97.49E
Moundou 50 8.34N 16.05E
Mountain Ash 9 51.42N 3.22W
Mount Barker town W.A. 33 34.36S117.37E
Mount Bellew town 10 53.28N 8.30W
Mount Darwin town 53 16.46S 31.35W
Mount Douglas town 34 21.31S146.50E
Mount Eba town 36 30.12S135.33E
Mount Fletcher town 54 30.41S 28.30E
Mount Gambier town 36 37.51S140.50E
Mount Goldsworthy town 32 20.20S119.31E
Mount Isa town 34 20.50S139.29E
Mount Magnet town 33 28.06S117.50E
Mountmellick 10 53.08N 7.21W
Mount Newman town 32 23.20S119.40E
Mount's B. 9 50.05N 5.25W
Mount Sturgeon town 34 20.08S144.00E
Mount Swan town 34 22.31S135.00E
Mount Vernon town 32 24.09S118.10E
Mount Willoughby 36 27.58S134.08E
Mourne Mts. 10 54.10N 6.02W
Moussoro 50 13.39N 16.29E
Moxico 52 11.50S 20.05E
Moy r. 10 54.10N 9.09W
Moyale 53 3.31N 39.04E
Moyowosi r. 53 4.59S 30.58E

zambique 54 17.30S 35.45E
zdok 21 43.45N 44.43E
zyr 17 52.02N 29.10E
ama r. 52 0.59S 15.40E
anda 53 6.21S 31.01E
ika 53 11.52S 31.30E
orokoso 53 9.22S 30.06E
ouya 52 2.38S 16.08E
wapwa 53 6.23S 36.38E
a r. 20 58.28N 31.20E
akuja 53 7.21S 30.37E
sensk 20 53.18N 36.35E
wara 53 10.17S 40.11E
ang Chiang Rai 25 19.56N 99.51E
ang Nakhon Sawan 27 7.22N104.45E
bende 53 0.30N 31.24E
chinga Mts. 53 12.15S 31.00E
ck i. 11 56.50N 6.14W
cojo 53 12.05S 40.26E
danjiang 26 44.36N129.42E
fulira 53 12.30S 28.12E
gía 13 43.06N 9.14W
ğla 15 37.12N 28.22E
hlhausen 16 51.12N 10.27E
ine Bheag town 10 52.42N 6.58W
ir, L. 33 34.30S116.30E
kachevo 17 48.26N 22.45E
kah 27 2.56N112.02E
kawa 34 9.48S150.00E
kinbudin 33 30.52S118.08E
lanje Mts. 53 15.57S 35.33E
lchén 49 37.43S 72.14W
lgrave I. 34 10.07S142.08E
lhacén mtn. 13 37.04N 3.22W
lhouse 12 47.45N 7.21E
ll i. 11 56.28N 5.56W
ll, Sd. of str. 11 56.32N 5.55W
llaghareirk Mts. 10 52.19N 9.06W
llaghmore mtn. 10 54.51N 6.51W
llaley 37 31.06S149.55E
llet Pen. 10 54.12N 10.04W
llingar 10 53.31N 7.21W
ll of Galloway c. 11 54.39N 4.52W
ll of Kintyre c. 11 55.17N 5.45W
lobezi 54 16.49S 25.09E
ltān 25 30.11N 71.29E
ltyfarnham 10 53.37N 7.25W
mbwa 53 14.57S 27.01E
na i. 27 5.00S122.30E
ünchen 16 48.08N 11.35E
uncie 44 40.11N 85.23W
ungari 54 17.12S 33.31E
ungbere 53 2.40N 28.25E
unich see München 16
ünster N.-Westfalen 16 51.58N 7.37E
uonio 18 67.57N 23.42E
uonio r. 18 67.10N 23.40E
ur r. Austria see Mura r. 16
ura r. 16 46.18N 16.53E
uranga 53 0.43S 37.10E
urchison r. 32 27.30S114.10E
urcia 13 37.59N 1.08W
ureş r. 17 46.16N 20.10E
uret 12 43.28N 1.19E
urewa 54 17.40S 31.47E
urmansk 20 68.59N 33.08E
urom 20 55.04N 42.04E
uroran 26 42.21N140.59E
urray r.S.A. 36 35.23S139.20E
urray r.W.A. 33 32.35S115.46E
urray Bridge town 36 35.10S139.17E
urrumbidgee r. 36 34.38S143.10E
urrurundi 37 31.47S150.51E
urtoa 36 36.40S142.31E
urwāra 25 23.51N 80.24E
uş 21 38.45N 41.30E
uscat see Masqaţ 24
usgrave Ranges mts. 32 26.10S131.50E
ushie 52 2.59S 16.55E
usi r. 27 2.20S104.57E
uskegon 44 43.13N 86.15W
uskogee 41 35.45N 95.21W
usoma 53 1.31S 33.48E
Musselburgh 11 55.57N 3.04W
Mussende 52 10.33S 16.02E
Mustjala 19 58.28N 22.14E
Mut 21 36.38N 33.27E
Mutare 54 18.59S 32.40E
Muyinga 53 2.48S 30.21E
Muzaffarpur 25 26.07N 85.24E
Mvuma 54 19.16S 30.30E
Mwanza 52 7.51S 26.43E
Mwaya Mbeya 53 9.33S 33.56E
Mweka 52 4.51S 21.34E
Mwene Ditu 52 7.04S 23.27E
Mwenezi r. 54 22.42S 31.45E
Mweru, L. 53 9.00S 28.40E
Mwinilunga 52 11.44S 24.24E
Myrdal 19 60.44N 7.08E
Mysore 25 12.18N 76.37E
Mytishchi 20 55.54N 37.47E
Mzimba 53 12.00S 33.39E

N

Naas 10 53.13N 6.41W
Nacala 53 14.34S 40.41E
Nachingwea 53 10.21S 38.46E
Naestved 19 55.14N 11.46E
Nāgāland d. 25 26.10N 94.30E
Nagano d. 28 35.33N137.50E
Nagasaki 26 32.45N129.52E
Nāgercoil 25 8.11N 77.30E
Nagles Mts. 10 52.06N 8.26W
Nagoya 28 35.10N136.55E
Nāgpur 25 21.09N 79.06E
Nagykanizsa 17 46.27N 17.01E
Naha 26 26.10N127.40E
Nain 39 56.30N 61.45W
Nairn 11 57.35N 3.52W
Nairobi 53 1.17S 36.50E
Naivasha 53 0.44S 36.26E
Nakatsugawa 28 35.29N137.30E
Nakhodka 23 42.53N132.54E
Nakhon Ratchasima 27 14.58N102.06E
Nakskov 19 54.50N 11.09E
Nakuru 53 0.16S 36.04E
Nalchik 21 43.31N 43.38E
Nalón r. 13 43.35N 6.06W
Namacurra 53 17.35S 37.00E
Namanga 53 2.33S 36.48E
Namangan 22 40.59N 71.41E
Namapa 53 13.48S 39.44E
Namaponda 53 15.51S 39.52E
Namarroi 53 15.58S 36.55E
Nam Co l. 25 30.45N 90.30E
Nam Dinh 26 20.21N106.09E
Namecala 53 12.50S 39.38E
Nametil 53 15.41S 39.30E
Namib Desert 54 23.00S 15.20E
Namibe 52 15.10S 12.10E
Namibia 54 21.30S 16.45E
Namlea 27 3.15S127.07E
Nampula 53 15.09S 39.14E
Namsos 18 64.28N 11.30E
Namur 16 50.28N 4.52E
Namutoni 54 18.48S 16.58E
Namwaia 52 15.44S 26.25E
Nanaimo 38 49.08N123.58W
Nanchang 26 28.37N115.57E
Nancy 12 48.42N 6.12E
Nānder 25 19.09N 77.20E
Nandewar Range mts. 37 30.20S150.45E
Nānga Parbat mtn. 25 35.10N 74.35E
Nanjing 26 32.02N118.52E
Nan Ling mts. 26 25.10N110.00E
Nanning 26 22.48N108.10E
Nantes 12 47.14N 1.35W
Nantucket I. 44 41.16N 70.03W
Nantwich 8 53.05N 2.31W
Nanyang 26 33.07N112.30E
Nanyuki 53 0.01N 37.03E
Napier 29 39.29S176.58E
Naples see Napoli 14
Napoli 14 40.50N 14.14E
Napoli, Golfo di g. 14 40.42N 14.15E
Nara 28 34.41N135.50E
Naracoorte 36 36.58S140.46E
Nārāyanganj 25 23.37N 90.30E
Narbonne 12 43.11N 3.00E
Narembeen 33 32.04S118.23E
Nares Str. 39 78.30N 75.00W
Narmada r. 25 21.40N 73.00E
Narodnaya mtn. 20 65.00N 61.00E
Narok 53 1.04S 35.54E
Narrabri 37 30.20S149.49E
Narrandera 37 34.36S146.34E
Narran L. 37 29.40S147.25E
Narrogin 33 32.58S117.10E
Narva 20 59.22N 28.17E
Narvik 18 68.26N 17.25E
Nasarawa 50 8.35N 7.44E
Nashua N.H. 44 42.46N 71.27W
Nashville 41 36.10N 86.50W
Näsijärvi l. 19 61.37N 23.42E
Nāsik 25 19.59N 73.48E
Nāşir, Buḩayrat l. 24 22.40N 32.00E
Nassau 43 25.03N 77.20W
Nasser, L. see Nāşir, Buḩayrat l. 51
Nässjö 19 57.39N 14.41E
Natal 47 5.46S 35.15W
Natchez 41 31.22N 91.24W
Nauru 30 0.32S166.55E
Nava r. 53 1.45N 27.06E
Navalmoral de la Mata 13 39.54N 5.33W
Navan 10 53.39N 6.42W
Naver r. 11 58.32N 4.14W
Navlya 20 52.51N 34.30E
Navojoa 42 27.06N109.26W
Návpaktos 15 38.24N 21.49E
Návplion 15 37.33N 22.47E
Navrongo 50 10.51N 1.03W
Náxos i. 15 37.03N 25.30E
Nazas r. 42 25.34N103.25W
Nazilli 21 37.55N 28.20E
Ndalatando 52 9.12S 14.54E
N'Dendé 52 2.20S 11.23E
N'Djamena 50 12.10N 14.59E
Ndjolé 52 0.07S 10.45E
Ndola 53 12.58S 28.39E
Neagh, Lough 10 54.36N 6.25W
Neath 9 51.39N 3.49W
Nebit-Dag 21 39.31N 54.24E
Nebraska d. 40 41.30N100.00W
Neches r. 41 29.55N 93.50W
Neckar r. 16 49.32N 8.26E
Necochea 49 38.31S 58.46W
Necuto 52 4.55S 12.38E
Needles 40 34.51N114.36W
Nefyn 8 52.55N 4.31W
Negotin 17 44.14N 22.33E
Negrais, C. 25 16.00N 94.12E
Negro r. 49 40.50S 63.00W
Negro r. 46 3.00S 59.55W
Negro r. 49 33.27S 58.20W
Negros i. 27 10.00N123.00E
Neijiang 26 29.29N105.03E
Nei Monggol d. 26 41.00N112.00E
Neisse r. 16 52.05N 14.42E
Neiva 46 2.58N 75.15W
Neksö 19 55.04N 15.09E
Nellore 25 14.29N 80.00E
Nelson r. 39 57.00N 93.20W
Nelson d. 29 41.40S172.20E
Nelson 8 53.50N 2.14W
Nelson, C. 36 38.27S141.35E
Nelspruit 54 25.27S 30.58E
Néma 50 16.32N 7.12W
Neman r. 19 55.18N 21.23E
Nemours 12 48.16N 2.41E
Nenagh 10 52.52N 8.13W
Nenana 38 64.35N149.20W
Nene r. 8 52.49N 0.12E
Nepal 25 28.00N 84.00E
Nephin Beg Range mts. 10 54.00N 9.37W
Nera r. 14 42.33N 12.43E
Neretva r. 15 43.02N 17.28E
Neriquinha 52 15.50S 21.40E
Ness, Loch 11 57.16N 4.30W
Netherlands 16 52.00N 5.30E
Netherlands Antilles 43 12.30N 69.00W
Neto r. 15 39.12N 17.08E
Neubrandenburg 16 53.33N 13.16E
Neuchâtel 16 47.00N 6.56E
Neuchâtel, Lac de l. 16 46.55N 6.55E
Neufchâtel 12 49.44N 1.26E
Neuquén r. 49 39.02S 68.07W
Neuse r. 41 35.04N 77.04W
Neustrelitz 16 53.22N 13.05E
Neuwied 16 50.26N 7.28E
Nevada d. 40 39.00N117.00W
Nevada, Sierra mts. Spain 13 37.04N 3.20W
Nevada, Sierra mts. U.S.A. 40 37.30N119.00W
Nevel 20 56.00N 29.59E
Nevers 12 47.00N 3.09E
Nevertire 37 31.52S147.47E
Nevşehir 21 38.38N 34.43E
New Amsterdam 47 6.18N 57.30W
Newark N.J. 44 40.44N 74.11W
Newark-on-Trent 8 53.06N 0.48E
New Bedford 44 41.38N 70.56W
New Bern 41 35.05N 77.04W
Newbiggin-by-the-Sea 8 55.11N 1.30W
New Brunswick d. 44 46.30N 66.15W
New Brunswick 44 40.29N 74.27W
Newburgh 44 41.30N 74.00W
Newbury 9 51.24N 1.19W
New Caledonia is. see Nouvelle Calédonie is. 30
Newcastle Australia 37 32.55S151.46E
Newcastle U.K. 10 54.13N 5.53W
Newcastle Emlyn 9 52.02N 4.29W
Newcastle-under-Lyme 8 53.02N 2.15W
Newcastle upon Tyne 8 54.58N 1.36W
Newcastle West 10 52.26N 9.04W
New Delhi 25 28.36N 77.12E
New England Range mts. 37 30.30S151.50E
Newent 9 51.56N 2.24W
New Forest f. 9 50.50N 1.35W
Newfoundland d. 39 55.00N 60.00W
Newfoundland i. 39 48.30N 56.00W
New Galloway 11 55.05N 4.09W
New Guinea i. 27 5.00S140.00E
New Hampshire d. 44 43.35N 71.40W
Newhaven 9 50.47N 0.04E
New Haven 44 41.18N 72.55W
New Jersey d. 44 40.15N 74.30W
New London Conn. 44 41.21N 72.06W
Newmarket 9 52.15N 0.23E
Newmarket on Fergus 10 52.46N 8.55W
New Mexico d. 40 34.00N106.00W
New Norfolk 35 42.46S147.02E
New Orleans 41 30.00N 90.03W
New Plymouth 29 39.03S174.04E
Newport Mayo 10 53.53N 9.34W
Newport Tipperary 10 52.42N 8.25W
Newport Dyfed 9 52.01N 4.51W
Newport Essex 9 51.58N 0.13E
Newport Gwent 9 51.34N 2.59W
Newport Hants. 9 50.43N 1.18W
Newport R.I. 44 41.13N 71.18W
Newquay 9 50.24N 5.06W
New Quay 9 52.13N 4.22W
New Radnor 9 52.15N 3.10W
New Romney 9 50.59N 0.58E
New Ross 10 52.24N 6.57W
Newry 10 54.11N 6.21W
New Scone 11 56.25N 3.25W
New South Wales d. 37 32.40S147.40E
Newton Abbot 9 50.32N 3.37W
Newton Aycliffe 8 54.36N 1.34W
Newtonmore 11 57.04N 4.08W
Newton Stewart 11 54.57N 4.29W
Newtown 9 52.31N 3.19W
Newtownabbey 10 54.39N 5.57W
Newtownards 10 54.35N 5.41W
Newtown Butler 10 54.12N 7.22W
Newtown St. Boswells 11 55.35N 2.40W
Newtownstewart 10 54.43N 7.25W
New York 44 40.40N 73.50W
New York d. 44 43.00N 75.00W
New Zealand 29 41.00S175.00E
Nezhin 17 51.03N 31.54E
Ngami, L. 54 20.32S 22.38E
Ngamiland f. 54 20.00S 22.30E
N'Gao 52 2.28S 15.40E
Ngaoundéré 50 7.20N 13.35E
Ngaruawahia 29 37.40S175.09E
Ngaruroro r. 29 39.34S176.54E
N'Giva 52 17.03S 15.47E
Ngong 53 1.22S 36.40E
Ngonye Falls f. 52 16.35S 23.39E
Ngozi 53 2.52S 29.50E
Nguigmi 50 14.00N 13.06E
Nha Trang 27 12.15N109.10E
Nhill 36 36.20S141.40E
Niagara Falls town 44 43.06N 79.02W
Niamey 50 13.32N 2.05E
Niangara 53 3.47N 27.54E
Niassa d. 53 13.00S 36.30E
Nicaragua 43 13.00N 85.00W
Nicaragua, Lago de l. 43 11.30N 85.30W
Nicastro 14 38.58N 16.16E
Nice 12 43.42N 7.16E
Nicobar Islands 25 8.00N 93.30E
Nicosia see Levkosía 24
Nicoya, Golfo de g. 43 9.30N 85.00W
Nid r. 19 58.24N 8.48E
Nigde 21 37.58N 34.42E
Niger 50 17.00N 9.30E
Niger r. 50 4.15N 6.05E
Nigeria 50 9.00N 7.30E
Niigata 26 37.58N139.02E
Niiza 28 35.48N139.34E
Nijmegen 16 51.50N 5.52E
Nikel 18 69.20N 30.00E
Nikiniki 27 9.49S124.29E
Nikki 50 9.55N 3.18E
Nikolayev 21 46.57N 32.00E
Nikolayevsk-na-Amure 23 53.20N140.44E
Nikopol 21 47.34N 34.25E
Niksar 21 40.35N 36.59E
Nīl, An r. 51 31.30N 30.25E
Nile r. see Nīl, An r. 51
Niles Mich. 44 41.51N 86.15W
Nilgiri Hills 25 11.30N 77.30E
Nîmes 12 43.50N 4.21E
Ningbo 26 29.56N121.32E
Niobrara r. 40 42.45N 98.10W
Nioro 50 15.12N 9.35W
Niort 12 46.19N 0.27W
Nipigon, L. 44 49.50N 88.30W
Nipissing, L. 44 46.17N 80.00W
Niš 15 43.20N 21.54E
Niterói 45 22.54S 43.06W
Nith r. 11 55.00N 3.35W
Niue i. 30 19.02S169.52W
Nizāmābād 25 18.40N 78.05E
Nizhneudinsk 23 54.55N 99.00E
Nizhnevartovsk 22 60.57N 76.40E
Nizhniy Tagil 20 58.00N 60.00E
Njombe r. 53 7.02S 35.55E
Njoro 53 5.16S 36.30E
Nkhata Bay town 53 11.37S 34.20E
Nkhotakota 53 12.55S 34.19E
Nkungwe Mt. 53 6.15S 29.54E
Noatak 38 67.34N162.59W
Nogales 42 31.20N111.00W
Nogent-le-Rotrou 12 48.19N 0.50E
Noguera Ribagorçana r. 13 41.27N 0.25E
Noirmoutier, Île de i. 12 47.00N 2.15W
Nokia 19 61.28N 23.30E
Nola 52 3.28N 16.08E
Noma Omuramba r. 54 19.14S 22.15E
Nome 38 64.30N165.30W
Noorvik 38 66.50N161.14W
Nordenham 16 53.30N 8.29E
Nordfriesische Inseln is. 16 54.30N 8.00E
Nordvik 23 73.40N110.50E
Nore r. 10 52.25N 6.58W
Norfolk d. 9 52.39N 1.00E
Norfolk Va. 41 36.54N 76.18W
Norfolk Broads f. 8 52.43N 1.35E
Norilsk 23 69.21N 88.02E
Normanton 34 17.40S141.05E
Norman Wells 38 65.19N126.46W
Nörresundby 19 57.04N 9.56E
Norris L. 41 36.20N 83.55W
Norristown 44 40.07N 75.20W
Norrköping 19 58.36N 16.11E
Norrtälje 19 59.46N 18.42E
Norseman 33 32.15S121.47E
Norte, C. 47 1.40N 49.55W
Northallerton 8 54.20N 1.26W
Northam 33 31.41S116.40E
Northampton 9 52.14N 0.54W
Northamptonshire d. 9 52.18N 0.55W
North Battleford 38 52.47N108.19W
North Bay town 44 46.19N 79.28W
North Bend Oreg. 40 43.26N124.14W
North Berwick 11 56.04N 2.43W
North C. 29 34.28S173.00E
North Canadian r. 41 35.30N 95.45W
North Carolina d. 41 35.30N 79.00W
North Channel 10 55.15N 5.52W
North China Plain f. see Huabei Pingyuan f. 26
North Dakota d. 40 47.00N100.00W
North Downs hills 9 51.18N 0.40E
Northern Ireland d. 10 54.40N 6.45W
Northern Territory d. 34 20.00S133.00E
North Esk r. 11 56.45N 2.25W
North Foreland c. 9 51.23N 1.26E
North Frisian Is. see Nordfriesische Inseln is. 16
North I. 29 39.00S175.00E
Northiam 9 50.59N 0.39E
North Korea 26 40.00N128.00E
Northland d. 29 35.25S174.00E
North Platte r. 40 41.09N100.55W
North Ronaldsay i. 11 59.23N 2.26W
North Sea 7 56.00N 5.00E
North Sporades see Voríai Sporádhes is. 15
North Taranaki Bight b. 29 38.45S174.15E
North Tawton 9 50.48N 3.55W
North Uist i. 11 57.35N 7.20W
Northumberland d. 8 55.12N 2.00W
North Walsham 8 52.49N 1.22E
Northway 38 62.58N142.00W
North West Highlands 11 57.30N 5.15W
North West River town 39 53.30N 60.10W
Northwest Territories d. 39 66.00N 95.00W
Northwich 8 53.16N 2.30W
North York Moors hills 8 54.21N 0.50W
North Yorkshire d. 8 54.14N 1.14W
Norton Sound b. 38 63.50N164.00W
Norwalk Conn. 44 41.07N 73.25W
Norway 18 65.00N 13.00E
Norway House town 39 53.59N 97.50W
Norwich 9 52.38N 1.17E
Noss Head 11 58.28N 3.03W
Noteć r. 16 52.44N 15.26E
Nottingham 8 52.57N 1.10W
Nottinghamshire d. 8 53.10N 1.00W
Nouadhibou 50 20.54N 17.01W
Nouakchott 50 18.09N 15.58W
Nouméa 30 22.16S166.27E
Nouvelle Anvers 52 1.38N 19.10E
Nouvelle Calédonie is. 30 21.30S165.30E
Nova Gaia 52 10.09S 17.35E
Nova Iguaçu 45 22.45S 43.27W
Novara 14 45.27N 8.37E
Nova Scotia d. 39 45.00N 64.00W
Nova Sofala 54 20.09S 34.24E
Novaya Ladoga 20 60.09N 32.15E
Novelda 13 38.24N 0.45W
Novgorod 20 58.30N 31.20E
Novi Pazar 15 43.08N 20.28E
Novi Sad 17 45.16N 19.52E
Novocherkassk 21 47.25N 40.05E
Novograd Volynskiy 17 50.34N 27.32E
Novogrudok 17 53.35N 25.50E
Novo Hamburgo 45 29.37S 51.07W
Novokazalinsk 22 45.48N 62.06E
Novokuznetsk 22 53.45N 87.12E
Novomoskovsk R.S.F.S.R. 20 54.06N 38.15E
Novorossiysk 21 44.44N 37.46E
Novoshakhtinsk 21 47.46N 39.55E
Novosibirsk 22 55.04N 82.55E
Novouzensk 21 50.29N 48.08E
Novyy Port 22 67.38N 72.33E
Nowa Ruda 16 50.34N 16.30E
Nowa Sól 16 51.49N 15.41E
Nowra 37 35.54S150.36E
Nowy Sącz 17 49.39N 20.40E
Noyon 12 49.35N 3.00E
Nsanje 53 16.55S 35.12E
Nubian Desert 51 21.00N 34.00E
Nueces r. 41 27.55N 97.30W
Nueva Gerona 43 21.53N 82.49W
Nuevitas 43 21.34N 77.18W
Nuevo Laredo 42 27.30N 99.30W
Nu Jiang r. China see Salween r. 26
Nuku'alofa 31 21.07S175.12W
Nullarbor Plain f. 33 31.30S128.00E
Numazu 28 35.06N138.52E
Nuneaton 9 52.32N 1.29W
Nungo 53 13.25S 37.45E
Nunivak I. 38 60.00N166.30W
Nürnberg 16 49.27N 11.05E
Nusaybin 21 37.05N 41.11E
Nuweveldberge mts. 54 32.15S 21.50E
Nyahururu Falls town 53 0.04N 36.22E
Nyakanazi 53 3.05S 31.16E
Nyala 51 12.01N 24.50E
Nyamandhlovu 54 19.50S 28.15E
Nyanga r. 52 3.00S 10.17E
Nyanza 53 2.20S 29.42E
Nyborg 19 55.19N 10.48E
Nybro 19 56.45N 15.54E
Nyeri 53 0.22S 36.56E
Nyika Plateau f. 53 10.25S 33.50E
Nyköping 19 58.45N 17.00E
Nylstroom 54 24.42S 28.24E
Nynäshamn 19 58.54N 17.57E
Nyong r. 52 3.15N 9.55E
Nyons 12 44.22N 5.08E
Nyunzu 53 5.55S 28.00E
Nzega 53 4.13S 33.09E
Nzeto 52 7.13S 12.56E

O

Oahe Resr. 40 45.45N100.20W
Oakland Calif. 40 37.50N122.15W
Oakville 44 43.27N 79.41W
Oamaru 29 45.07S170.58E
Oaxaca 42 17.05N 96.41W
Ob r. 20 66.50N 69.00E
Oba 44 49.04N 84.07W
Oban 11 56.26N 5.28W
Obbia 51 5.20N 48.30E
Oberá 48 27.30S 55.07W
Obi i. 27 1.45S127.30E
Ocaña 46 8.16N 73.21W
Ocean I. see Banaba i. 30 0.52S169.35E
Ochil Hills 11 56.16N 3.25W
Ocotal 43 13.37N 86.31W
Ocotlán 42 20.21N102.42W
Ocua 53 13.40S 39.46E
Oda 50 5.55N 0.56W
Odawara 28 35.15N139.10E
Odda 19 60.04N 6.33E
Ödemiş 15 38.12N 28.00E
Odense 19 55.24N 10.23E
Odenwald mts. 16 49.40N 9.20E
Oder r. E. Germany see Odra r. 16
Odessa 24 46.30N 30.46E
Odorhei 17 46.18N 25.18E
Ofanto r. 14 41.22N 16.12E
Offaly d. 10 53.15N 7.30W
Offenbach 16 50.06N 8.46E
Offenburg 16 48.29N 7.57E
Ōgaki 28 35.21N136.37E
Ogbomosho 50 8.05N 4.11E
Ogden Utah 40 41.14N111.59W
Ogeechee r. 41 32.54N 81.05W
Ognon r. 12 47.20N 5.37E
Ogoja 50 6.40N 8.45E
Ogooué r. 52 1.00S 9.05E
Ogosta r. 15 43.44N 23.51E
Ogulin 16 45.17N 15.14E
Ohio d. 44 40.15N 82.45W
Ohio r. 44 36.59N 89.08W
Ohře r. 16 50.32N 14.08E
Ohrid 15 41.06N 20.48E
Oise r. 12 49.00N 2.10E
Ojocaliente 42 22.35N102.18W
Ojo de Agua 48 29.30S 63.44W
Oka r. 20 56.09N 43.00E
Okahandja 54 21.58S 16.44E
Okanogan r. 40 47.45N120.05W
Okavango r. 54 18.30S 22.04E
Okavango Basin f. 54 19.30S 22.30E
Okazaki 28 34.57N137.10E
Okeechobee, L. 41 27.00N 80.45W
Okefenokee Swamp f. 41 30.40N 82.40W
Okehampton 9 50.44N 4.01W
Okere r. 53 1.37N 33.53E
Okha 23 53.35N142.50E
Okhotsk 23 59.20N143.15E
Okhotsk, Sea of 23 55.00N150.00E
Okinawa jima i. 26 26.30N128.00E
Okipoko r. 54 18.40S 16.03E
Oklahoma d. 41 35.00N 97.00W
Oklahoma City 41 35.28N 97.33W
Öland i. 19 56.45N 16.38E
Olary 36 32.18S140.19E
Olavarría 49 36.57S 60.20W
Oldenburg Nschn. 16 53.08N 8.13E
Oldham 8 53.33N 2.08W
Old Head of Kinsale c. 10 51.37N 8.33W
Olenëk r. 23 73.00N120.00E
Oléron, Île d' i. 12 45.55N 1.16W
Olga 23 43.46N135.14E
Olhão 13 37.01N 7.50W
Olifants r. C.P. 54 31.42S 18.10E
Olifants r. Trans. 54 24.08S 32.39E
Ólimbos 15 35.44N 27.11E
Ólimbos mtn. 15 40.04N 22.20E
Oliva 48 32.05S 63.35W
Olivares 13 39.45N 2.21W
Olney 9 52.09N 0.42W
Olomouc 17 49.36N 17.16E
Oloron 12 43.12N 0.35W
Olot 13 42.11N 2.30E
Olsztynek 17 53.36N 20.17E
Olteţ r. 17 44.13N 24.28E
Olympus mtn. see Ólimbos mtn. 15
Omagh 10 54.36N 7.20W
Omaha 41 41.15N 96.00W
Oman 24 22.30N 57.30E
Oman, G. of 24 25.00N 58.00E
Omaruru 54 21.25S 15.57E
Omdurman see Umm Durmān 51
Omolon r. 23 68.50N158.30E
Omsk 22 55.00N 73.22E
Omulew r. 17 53.05N 21.32E
Oña 13 42.44N 3.25W
Onega r. 20 63.59N 38.11E
Onitsha 50 6.10N 6.47E
Onslow 32 21.41S115.12E
Ontario d. 39 52.00N 86.00W
Ontario Oreg. 40 44.02N116.58W
Ontario, L. 44 43.45N 78.00W
Oostende 16 51.13N 2.55E
Opole 17 50.40N 17.56E
Oporto see Porto 13
Opotiki 29 38.00S177.18E
Oradea 17 47.03N 21.55E
Oran 50 35.45N 0.38W
Orange 12 44.08N 4.48E
Orange r. 54 28.38S 16.38E
Orangeburg 41 33.28N 80.53W
Oranjemund 54 28.35S 16.26E
Orbost 37 37.42S148.30E
Orchila i. 43 11.52N 66.10W
Ord r. 32 15.30S128.30E
Ordu 21 41.00N 37.52E
Orduña 13 43.00N 3.00W
Ordzhonikidze 21 43.02N 44.43E
Örebro 19 59.17N 15.13E
Oregon d. 40 44.00N120.00W
Öregrund 19 60.20N 18.26E
Orekhovo-Zuyevo 20 55.47N 39.00E
Orel 20 52.58N 36.04E
Orenburg 20 51.50N 55.00E
Orense 13 42.20N 7.52W
Orihuela 13 38.05N 0.56W
Orinoco r. 46 9.00N 61.30W
Orissa d. 25 20.20N 84.00E
Oristano 14 39.53N 8.36E
Orizaba 42 18.51N 97.08W
Orkney Is. d. 11 59.00N 3.00W
Orlando 41 28.33N 81.21W
Orléans 12 47.54N 1.54E
Ormond 29 38.35S177.58E
Ormskirk 8 53.35N 2.53W
Orne r. 12 49.17N 0.10W
Örnsköldsvik 18 63.17N 18.50E
Oromocto 44 45.50N 66.28W
Orosei 14 40.23N 9.40E
Oroville Wash. 40 48.57N119.27W
Orsha 20 54.30N 30.23E
Orsk 20 51.13N 58.35E
Orşova 17 44.42N 22.22E
Orthez 12 43.29N 0.46W
Oryakhovo 15 43.42N 23.58E
Ōsaka 28 34.40N135.30E
Osh 22 40.37N 72.49E
Oshawa 44 43.54N 78.51W
Ō shima i. Tosan 28 34.43N139.24E
Oshogbo 50 7.50N 4.35E
Oshwe 52 3.27S 19.32E
Osijek 15 45.35N 18.43E
Oskarshamn 19 57.16N 16.26E
Oskol r. 21 49.08N 37.10E
Oslo 19 59.56N 10.45E
Osmancik 21 40.58N 34.50E
Osmaniye 21 37.04N 36.15E
Osnabrück 16 52.17N 8.03E
Osorno 49 40.35S 73.14W
Ossa, Mt. 35 41.52S146.04E
Ostashkov 20 57.09N 33.10E
Ostend see Oostende 16
Österdal r. 19 61.03N 14.30E
Österö i. 18 62.10N 7.00W
Östersund 18 63.10N 14.40E
Ostrava 17 49.50N 18.15E
Ostrov 20 57.22N 28.22E
Ostrów Mazowiecka 17 52.50N 21.51E
Osuna 13 37.14N 5.06W
Oswestry 8 52.52N 3.03W
Otago d. 29 45.10S169.20E
Otago Pen. 29 45.48S170.45E
Otavi 54 19.37S 17.21E
Otju 54 18.15S 13.18E
Otra r. 19 58.09N 8.00E
Otranto 15 40.09N 18.30E
Otranto, Str. of 15 40.10N 19.00E
Otta 19 61.46N 9.32E
Ottawa 44 45.25N 75.43W
Ottawa r. 44 45.20N 73.58W
Ottawa Is. 39 59.50N 80.00W
Otter r. 9 50.38N 3.19W
Otterburn 8 55.14N 2.10W
Ottumwa 41 41.02N 92.26W
Otway, C. 36 38.51S143.34E
Ouachita r. 41 33.10N 92.10W
Ouachita Mts. 41 34.40N 94.30W
Ouagadougou 50 12.20N 1.40W
Ouahigouya 50 13.31N 2.21W
Ouargla 50 32.00N 5.16E
Oudtshoorn 54 33.35S 22.11E
Ouessant, Île d' i. 12 48.28N 5.05W
Ouesso 52 1.38N 16.03E
Oughter, Lough 10 54.01N 7.28W
Oujda 50 34.41N 1.45W
Oulu 18 65.01N 25.28E
Oulu r. 18 65.01N 25.25E
Oulujärvi l. 18 64.20N 27.15E
Oundle 9 52.28N 0.28W
Ourinhos 45 23.00S 49.54W
Ouse r. Humber. 8 53.41N 0.42W
Outer Hebrides is. 11 57.40N 7.35W
Outjo 54 20.07S 16.10E
Ouyen 36 35.06S142.22E
Ovamboland f. 54 17.45S 16.00E
Oviedo 13 43.21N 5.50W
Owando 52 0.30S 15.48E
Owen Falls Dam 53 0.30N 33.07E
Owen Stanley Range mts. 34 9.30S148.00E
Oxelösund 19 58.40N 17.06E
Oxford 9 51.45N 1.15W
Oxfordshire d. 9 51.46N 1.10W
Oxley 36 34.11S144.10E
Oykel r. 11 57.53N 4.21W
Oymyakon 23 63.30N142.44E
Ozark Plateau 41 36.00N 93.35W

P

Paarl 54 33.44S 18.58E
Pachuca 42 20.10N 98.44W
Pacific Ocean 31
Padang 27 0.55S100.21E
Paderborn 16 51.43N 8.44E
Padova 14 45.27N 11.52E
Padre I. 41 27.00N 97.20W
Padstow 9 50.33N 4.57W
Padua see Padova 16
Paeroa 29 37.23S175.41E
Paible 11 57.35N 7.27W
Paihia 29 35.16S174.05E
Päijänne l. 19 61.35N 25.30E
Paisley 11 55.50N 4.26W
Pakanbaru 27 0.33N101.20E
Pakistan 25 31.00N 70.00E
Pakwach 53 2.27N 31.18E
Palana 23 59.05N159.59E
Palapye 54 22.33S 27.07E
Palawan i. 27 9.30N118.30E
Paldiski 19 59.20N 24.06E
Palembang 27 2.59S104.50E
Palencia 13 42.01N 4.34W
Palermo 14 38.09N 13.22E
Palliser, C. 29 41.35S175.15E
Palma 13 39.36N 2.39E
Palma, Bahía de b. 13 39.30N 2.40E
Palma del Río 13 37.43N 5.17W
Palmas, Golfo di g. 14 39.00N 8.30E
Palmerston North 29 40.20S175.39E
Palmi 14 38.22N 15.50E
Palmira 46 3.33N 76.17W
Palm Springs town 40 33.49N116.34W
Palmyras Pt. 25 20.46N 87.02E
Pamiers 12 43.07N 1.36E
Pamir mts. 22 38.00N 73.30E
Pampa 40 35.32N100.58W
Pampas f. 49 34.00S 64.00W
Pamplona 13 42.49N 1.39W
Panama 43 9.00N 80.00W
Panamá town 43 8.57N 79.30W
Panamá, Golfo de g. 43 8.30N 79.00W
Panama City 41 30.10N 85.41W
Panay i. 27 11.10N122.30E
Panevežys 19 55.44N 24.21E
Pangi 52 3.10S 26.38E
Pangnirtung 39 66.05N 65.45W
Pantano del Esla l. 13 41.40N 5.50W
Pantelleria i. 14 36.48N 12.00E
Paola 14 39.21N 16.03E
Papeete 31 17.32S149.34W
Papenburg 16 53.03N 7.23E
Paracatu r. 45 16.30S 45.10W
Paraguaçu r. 47 12.35S 38.59W
Paraguarí 45 25.36S 57.06W
Paraguay r. 45 27.30S 58.50W
Paraguay 45 23.00S 57.00W
Paraíba r. 45 21.45S 41.10W
Parakou 50 9.23N 2.40E
Paramaribo 47 5.52N 55.14W
Paraná 49 31.45S 60.30W
Paraná r. 49 34.00S 58.30W
Paranã r. 47 12.30S 48.10W
Paranaguá 45 25.32S 48.36W
Paranaíba r. 45 20.00S 51.00W
Paranapanema r. 45 22.30S 53.03W
Paranapiacaba, Serra mts. 45 24.30S 49.15W
Paranavaí 45 23.02S 52.36W
Paraparaumu 29 40.55S175.00E
Pardo r. Bahia 45 15.40S 39.38W
Pardo r. Mato Grosso 45 21.56S 52.07W
Pardo r. São Paulo 45 20.10S 48.36W
Pardubice 16 50.03N 15.45E
Paris 12 48.52N 2.20E
Parkano 19 62.01N 23.01E
Parker Dam 40 34.25N114.05W
Parkersburg 44 39.17N 81.33W
Parkes 37 33.10S148.13E
Parma 14 44.48N 10.18E
Parnaíba r. 47 2.58S 41.47W
Parnassós mtn. 15 38.33N 22.35E
Pärnu r. 19 58.23N 24.29E
Paroo r. 36 31.30S143.34E
Páros i. 15 37.04N 25.11E
Parral 49 36.09S 71.50W
Parramatta 37 33.50S150.57E
Parry Is. 39 76.00N102.00W
Parseta r. 16 54.12N 15.33E
Parthenay 12 46.39N 0.14W
Partry Mts. 10 53.40N 9.30W
Parys 54 26.54S 27.26E
Pasadena Calif. 40 34.10N118.09W
Pascua, Isla de i. 31 27.08S109.23W
Passau 16 48.35N 13.28E
Passo Fundo 45 28.16S 52.20W
Passos 45 20.45S 46.38W
Patagonia f. 49 42.20S 67.00W
Pate I. 53 2.08S 41.02E
Paterson 44 40.55N 74.10W
Pathfinder Resr. 40 42.25N106.55W
Patía r. 46 1.54N 78.30W
Patkai Hills 25 26.30N 95.30E
Pátmos i. 15 37.20N 26.33E
Patna 25 25.36N 85.07E
Patos de Minas 45 18.35S 46.32W
Pátrai 15 38.15N 21.45E
Patraïkós Kólpos g. 15 38.15N 21.35E
Patrickswell 10 52.36N 8.43W
Patuca r. 43 15.50N 84.18W
Pau 12 43.18N 0.22W
Pauillac 12 45.12N 0.44W
Pavia 14 45.10N 9.10E
Pavlodar 22 52.21N 76.59E
Paysandú 49 32.19S 58.05W
Peace r. 38 59.00N111.26W
Peace River town 38 56.15N117.18W
Peak Hill town N.S.W. 37 32.47S148.13E
Pearl r. 41 30.15N 89.25W
Pebane 53 17.14S 38.10E
Peć 15 42.40N 20.17E
Pechenga 18 69.28N 31.04E
Pechora r. 20 68.10N 54.00E
Pechorskoye More sea 20 69.00N 55.00E
Pecos r. 40 29.45N101.25W
Pécs 17 46.05N 18.14E
Pedro Juan Caballero 45 22.30S 55.44W
Peebinga 36 34.55S140.57E
Peebles 11 55.39N 3.12W
Peel r. 38 68.13N135.00W
Peel 8 54.14N 4.42W
Peene r. 16 53.53N 13.49E
Pegasus B. 29 43.15S173.00E
Pegu 27 17.20N 96.36E
Pehuajó 49 35.50S 61.50W
Peking see Beijing 26
Peleng i. 27 1.30S123.10E
Pelly r. 38 62.50N137.35W
Pelotas 45 31.45S 52.20W
Pematangsiantar 27 2.59N 99.01E
Pemba I. 53 5.10S 39.45E
Pembroke 9 51.41N 4.57W
Peñaranda de Bracamonte 13 40.54N 5.13W
Penarth 9 51.26N 3.11W
Peñas, Cabo de c. 13 43.42N 5.52W
Pendine 9 51.44N 4.33W
Penge 52 5.31S 24.37E
Penicuik 11 55.49N 3.13W
Pennsylvania d. 44 40.45N 77.30W
Penny Highland mtn. 39 67.10N 66.50W
Penola 36 37.23S140.21E
Penonomé 43 8.30N 80.20W
Penrith 8 54.40N 2.45W
Penryn 9 50.10N 5.07W
Pensacola 41 30.30N 87.12W
Penticton 38 49.29N119.38W
Pentland Firth str. 11 58.40N 3.00W
Pentland Hills 11 55.50N 3.20W
Penzance 9 50.07N 5.32W
Pereira 46 4.47N 75.46W
Pergamino 49 33.53S 60.35W
Péribonca r. 44 48.45N 72.05W
Périgueux 12 45.12N 0.44E
Perm 20 58.01N 56.10E
Péronne 12 49.56N 2.57E
Perpignan 12 42.42N 2.54E
Perranporth 9 50.21N 5.09W
Perth Australia 33 31.58S115.49E
Perth U.K. 11 56.24N 3.28W
Peru 46 10.00S 75.00W
Perugia 14 43.06N 12.24E
Pervouralsk 20 56.59N 59.58E
Pesaro 14 43.54N 12.54E
Pescara 14 42.27N 14.13E
Pescara r. 14 42.28N 14.13E
Peshāwar 25 34.01N 71.33E
Petatlán 42 17.31N101.16W
Petauke 53 14.16S 31.21E
Peterborough 9 52.35N 0.14W
Peterhead 11 57.30N 1.46W
Peterlee 8 54.45N 1.18W
Petersfield 9 51.00N 0.56W
Petropavlovsk 22 54.53N 69.13E
Petropavlovsk Kamchatskiy 23 53.03N158.43E
Petrópolis 45 22.30S 43.06W
Petrovsk 20 52.20N 45.24E

Troy N.Y. 44 42.43N 73.40W
Troyes 12 48.18N 4.05E
Trujillo 46 8.06S 79.00W
Truk is. 30 7.23N151.46E
Truro 9 50.17N 5.02W
Trust Territory of the Pacific Is. 30
10.00N155.00E
Trysil r. 19 61.03N 12.30E
Tselinograd 22 51.10N 71.28E
Tshane 54 24.02S 21.54E
Tshela 52 4.57S 12.57E
Tshikapa 52 6.28S 20.48E
Tshofa 52 5.13S 25.20E
Tshopo r. 52 0.30N 25.07E
Tshuapa r. 52 0.14S 20.45E
Tskhinvali 21 42.14N 43.58E
Tsu 28 34.43N136.31E
Tsuchiura 28 36.05N140.12E
Tsumeb 54 19.12S 17.43E
Tsushima 28 35.10N136.43E
Tuam 50 53.32N 8.52W
Tuamotu, Îles is. 31 17,00S142.00W
Tuapse 21 44.06N 39.05E
Tubarão 45 28.30S 49.01W
Tubbercurry 10 54.03N 8.45W
Tübingen 16 48.32N 9.04E
Tubruq 51 32.06N 23.58E
Tucson 40 32.15N110.57W
Tucumcari 40 35.11N103.44W
Tudela 13 42.04N 1.37W
Tukums 19 57.00N 23.10E
Tukuyu 53 9.20S 33.37E
Tula 20 54.11N 37.38E
Tulcea 15 45.10N 28.50E
Tuli 54 21.50S 29.15E
Tuli r. 54 21.50S 29.15E
Tullamore 10 53.17N 7.31W
Tulle 12 45.16N 1.46E
Tullins 12 45.18N 5.29E
Tullow 10 52.49N 6.45W
Tully 34 17.55S145.59E
Tuloma r. 20 68.56N 33.00E
Tulsa 41 36.07N 95.58W
Tulun 23 54.32N100.35E
Tumaco 46 1.51N 78.46W
Tumba, L. 52 0.45S 18.00E
Tummel, Loch 11 56.43N 3.55W
Tump 24 26.07N 62.22E
Tunceli 21 39.07N 39.34E
Tunduma 53 9.19S 32.47E
Tunduru 53 11.06S 37.21E
Tundzha r. 15 41.40N 26.34E
Tunis 50 36.47N 10.10E
Tunisia 50 34.00N 9.00E
Tunja 46 5.33N 73.23W
Tupelo 41 34.15N 88.43W
Tura 53 5.30S 33.50E
Tura 23 64.05N100.00E
Turangi 29 38.59S175.48E
Turgutlu 15 38.30N 27.43E
Türi 19 58.48N 25.26E
Turia r. 13 39.27N 0.19W
Turin see Torino 14
Turkana, L. 53 4.00N 36.00E
Turkestan f. 25 40.00N 79.00E
Turkestan 25 43.17N 68.16E
Turkey 24 39.00N 35.00E
Turks Is. 43 21.30N 71.10W
Turku 19 60.27N 22.17E
Turneffe Is. 43 17.30N 87.45W
Turnu Măgurele 15 43.43N 24.53E
Turnu-Severin 15 44.37N 22.39E
Turpan Pendi f. 26 43.40N 89.00E
Turquino mtn. 43 20.00N 76.50W
Turriff 11 57.32N 2.28W
Tuscaloosa 41 33.12N 87.33W
Tuticorin 25 8.48N 78.10E
Tuttlingen 16 47.59N 8.49E
Tutubu 53 5.28S 32.43E
Tuvalu 30 8.00S178.00E
Tuxpan 42 21.00N 97.23W
Tuxtla Gutiérrez 42 16.45N 93.09W
Tuz Gölü l. 21 38.45N 33.24E
Tuzla 15 44.33N 18.41E
Tweed r. 11 55.46N 2.00W
Twizel 29 44.15S170.06E
Twyford 9 51.01N 1.19W
Tyler Tex. 41 32.22N 95.18W
Tyne r. 8 55.00N 1.25W
Tyne and Wear d. 8 54.57N 1.35W
Tynemouth 8 55.01N 1.24W
Tyrone d. 10 54.35N 7.15W
Tyrrell, L. 36 35.22S142.50E
Tyrrhenian Sea 14 40.00N 12.00E
Tyumen 22 57.11N 65.29E
Tywi r. 9 51.46N 4.22W
Tzaneen 54 23.49S 30.10E

U

Uanda 34 21.34S144.54E
Ubangi r. 52 0.25S 17.40E
Ubeda 13 38.01N 3.22W
Uberaba 45 19.47S 47.57W
Überlândia 45 18.57S 48.17W
Ubombo 54 27.35S 32.05E
Ubundu 52 0.24S 25.28E
Ucayali r. 46 4.40S 73.20W
Udaipur 25 24.35N 73.41E
Uddevalla 19 58.21N 11.55E
Uddjaur l. 18 65.55N 17.49E
Udine 14 46.03N 13.15E
Udon Thani 27 17.25N102.45E
Uele r. 51 4.08N 22.25E
Uelzen 16 52.58N 10.34E
Ufa 20 54.45N 55.58E
Uffculme 9 50.45N 3.19W
Ugab r. 54 21.12S 13.37E
Ugalla r. 53 5.43S 31.10E
Uganda 53 2.00N 33.00E
Uglegorsk 23 49.01N142.04E
Ugra r. 20 54.30N 36.10E
Uig 11 57.35N 6.22W
Uíge 52 7.40S 15.09E
Uinta Mts. 40 40.45N110.30W
Uitenhage 54 33.46S 25.23E
Ujiji 53 4.55S 29.39E
Ujjain 25 23.11N 75.46E
Ujpest 17 47.33N 19.05E
Ujung Pandang 27 5.09S119.28E
Uka 23 57.50N162.02E
Ukerewe I. 53 2.00S 33.00E
Ukiah 40 39.09N123.12W
Ulaanbaatar 26 47.54N106.52E

Ulaangom 26 49.59N 92.00E
Ulan Bator see Ulaanbaatar 26
Ulan-Ude 23 51.55N107.40E
Uliastay 26 47.42N 96.52E
Ulla r. 13 42.38N 8.45W
Ulladulla 37 35.21S150.25E
Ullapool 11 57.54N 5.10W
Ullswater l. 8 54.34N 2.52W
Ulm 16 48.24N 10.00E
Ulongwé 53 14.34S 34.21E
Ulsberg 18 62.45N 9.59E
Ulúa r. 43 15.50N 87.38W
Uluguru Mts. 53 7.05S 37.40E
Ulverston 8 54.13N 3.07W
Ul'yanovsk 20 54.19N 48.22E
Uman 17 48.45N 30.10E
Umeå 18 63.45N 20.20E
Umfuli r. 54 17.32S 29.23E
Umiat 38 69.25N152.20W
Umm Durmân 51 15.37N 32.59E
Umm Lajj 24 25.03N 37.17E
Umtata 54 31.35S 28.47E
Una r. 15 45.16N 16.55E
Uncompahgre Peak 40
38.04N107.28W
Underberg 54 29.46S 29.26E
Ungarie 37 33.38S147.00E
Ungava B. 39 59.00N 67.30W
União da Vitória 45 26.13S 51.05W
Uniondale 54 33.39S 23.07E
Union of Soviet Socialist Republics
17 50.00N 28.00E
United Arab Emirates 24 24.00N
54.00E
United Kingdom 7 54.00N 2.00W
United States of America 40
39.00N100.00W
Unst i. 11 60.45N 0.55W
Ünye 21 41.09N 37.15E
Upemba, L. 52 8.35S 26.28E
Upernavik 39 72.50N 56.00W
Upington 54 28.26S 21.12E
Upper Hutt 29 41.07S175.04E
Upper Tean 8 52.57N 1.59W
Uppsala 19 59.52N 17.38E
Ural r. 21 47.00N 52.00E
Uralla 37 30.40S151.31E
Ural Mts. see Uralskiy Khrebet mts. 20
Ural'sk 21 51.19N 51.20E
Uralskiy Khrebet mts. 20 60.00N
59.00E
Urana, L. 37 35.21S146.19E
Uranium City 38 59.32N108.43W
Urbino 14 43.43N 12.38E
Urda 21 48.44N 47.30E
Urdzhar 22 47.06N 81.33E
Ure r. 8 54.05N 1.20W
Uren 20 57.30N 45.50E
Urfa 21 37.08N 38.45E
Urgüp 21 38.39N 34.55E
Urlingford 10 52.44N 7.35W
Uruaçu 47 14.30S 49.10W
Uruapan 42 19.26N102.04W
Uruguaiana 49 29.45S 57.05W
Uruguay r. 49 34.00S 58.30W
Uruguay 49 33.15S 56.00W
Ürümqi 26 43.43N 87.38E
Urunga 37 30.30S152.28E
Usa r. 20 65.58N 56.35E
Uşak 21 38.42N 29.25E
Usambara Mts. 53 4.45S 38.25E
Ushant i. see Ouessant, Île d' i. 12
Usk r. 9 51.34N 2.59W
Üsküdar 15 41.00N 29.03E
Ussuriysk 23 43.48N131.59E
Ustica i. 14 38.42N 13.11E
Ustí nad Labem 16 50.41N 14.00E
Ustinov 20 56.49N 53.11E
Ust'kamchatsk 23 56.14N162.28E
Ust-Kamenogorsk 22 50.00N 82.40E
Ust'Maya 23 60.25N134.28E
Ust Olenëk 23 72.59N120.00E
Ust'Tsilma 20 65.28N 53.09E
U.S. Virgin Is. 43 18.30N 65.00W
Utah d. 40 39.00N112.00W
Utembo r. 52 17.03S 22.00E
Utete 53 8.00S 38.49E
Utiariti 46 13.02S 58.17W
Utica N.Y. 44 43.06N 75.14W
Utiel 13 39.33N 1.13W
Utrera 13 37.10N 5.47W
Utrecht 16 52.04N 5.07E
Uttar Pradesh d. 25 26.30N 81.30E
Uttaradit 27 17.38N100.05E
Uusikaupunki 19 60.48N 21.25E
Uvinza 53 5.08S 30.23E
Uvira 53 3.22S 29.06E
Uyuni 48 20.28S 66.50W
Uzhgorod 17 48.38N 22.15E

V

Vaagö i. 18 62.03N 7.14W
Vaal r. 54 29.04S 23.37E
Vaal Dam 54 26.51S 28.08E
Vaasa 18 63.06N 21.36E
Vadodara 25 22.19N 73.14E
Vaduz 16 47.40N 9.31E
Vaggeryd 19 57.30N 14.07E
Váh r. 17 47.40N 17.50E
Valday 37 50.59N 33.10E
Valdemarsvik 19 58.12N 16.36E
Valdepeñas 13 38.46N 3.24W
Valdez 61.07N146.17W
Valdivia 49 39.46S 73.15W
Valence 12 44.56N 4.54E
Valencia r. 13 39.29N 0.24W
Valencia d. 13 39.20N 0.40W
Valencia de Don Juan 13 42.18N
5.31W
Vale of Evesham f. 9 52.05N 1.55W
Vale of Pewsey f. 9 51.21N 1.45W
Vale of York f. 8 54.12N 1.25W
Valga 20 57.44N 26.00E
Valjevo 17 44.16N 19.56E
Valkeakoski 19 61.16N 24.02E
Valladolid 13 41.39N 4.45W
Valledupar 46 10.31N 73.16W
Valletta 14 35.53N 14.31E
Valleyfield 44 45.15N 74.08W
Valmiera 20 57.32N 25.29E
Valnera mtn. 13 43.10N 3.40W
Valognes 12 49.31N 1.28W
Valparaíso 49 33.02S 71.38W

Vals, Tanjung c. 27 8.30S137.30E
Valverde 43 19.37N 71.04W
Valverde del Camino 13 37.35N
6.45W
Van 21 38.28N 43.20E
Vancouver 38 49.13N123.06W
Vancouver I. 38 50.00N126.00W
Van Diemen G. 34 11.50S132.00E
Vänern l. 19 59.00N 13.15E
Vänersborg 19 58.22N 12.19E
Vanga 53 4.37S 39.13E
Vännäs 18 63.58N 19.48E
Vannes 12 47.40N 2.44W
Van Rees, Pegunungan mts. 27
2.35S138.15E
Vanrhynsdorp 54 31.37S 18.42E
Vanuatu 30 16.00S167.00E
Var r. 16 43.39N 7.11E
Várānasi 25 25.20N 83.00E
Varazdin 14 46.18N 16.20E
Varberg 19 57.06N 12.15E
Vardar r. Yugo. see Axiós r. 15
Varel 16 53.22N 8.10E
Varennes 12 46.19N 3.24E
Varna 17 43.13N 27.57E
Värnamo 19 57.11N 14.02E
Vasa see Vaasa 18
Vasilkov 17 50.12N 30.15E
Västerås 19 59.37N 16.33E
Västervik 19 57.45N 16.38E
Vatnajökull ice. 18 64.20N 17.00W
Vättern l. 19 58.30N 14.30E
Vaughn N.Mex. 40 34.35N105.14W
Växjö 19 56.52N 14.49E
Vaygach 22 70.28N 58.59E
Vega i. 18 65.39N 11.50E
Vejle 19 55.42N 9.32E
Velhas r. 45 17.20S 44.55W
Velikiye-Luki 20 56.19N 30.31E
Velletri 14 41.41N 12.47E
Vellore 25 12.56N 79.09E
Venado Tuerto 49 33.45S 61.56W
Vendas Novas 13 38.41N 8.27W
Vendôme 12 47.48N 1.04E
Venezia 14 45.26N 12.20E
Venezuela 46 7.00N 65.20W
Veniaminof Mtn. 38 56.05N159.20W
Venice see Venezia 14
Vera 13 37.15N 1.51W
Veracruz 42 19.11N 96.10W
Vercelli 14 45.19N 8.26E
Verdon r. 12 43.42N 5.39E
Verdun Meuse 12 49.10N 5.24E
Vereeniging 54 26.40S 27.55E
Verín 13 41.55N 7.26W
Verkhoyanskiy Khrebet mts. 23
66.00N130.00E
Vermont d. 44 43.50N 72.45W
Verona 14 45.27N 10.59E
Versailles 12 48.48N 2.08E
Vert, Cap c. 50 14.45N 17.25W
Verviers 7 50.36N 5.52E
Vesoul 16 47.38N 6.09E
Vesuvio mtn. 14 40.48N 14.25E
Vetlanda 19 57.26N 15.04E
Vettore, Monte mtn. 14 42.50N
13.18E
Vézère r. 12 44.53N 0.55E
Viana do Castelo s. 13 41.41N 8.50W
Viangchan 27 17.59N102.38E
Viborg 19 56.26N 9.24E
Vic 13 41.56N 2.16E
Vicenza 14 45.33N 11.32E
Vichuga 20 57.12N 41.50E
Vichy 12 46.07N 3.25E
Victor Harbour 36 35.36S138.35E
Victoria r. 37 37.20S145.00E
Victoria r. 32 15.12S129.43E
Victoria Canada 38 48.26N123.20W
Victoria Hong Kong 26
22.16N114.13E
Victoria, L. 53 1.00S 33.00E
Victoria, Mt. 34 8.55S147.35E
Victoria de las Tunas 43 20.58N
76.59W
Victoria Falls f. 54 17.58S 25.45E
Victoria I. 38 71.00N110.00W
Victoria Nile r. 53 2.14N 31.20E
Victoria West 54 31.24S 23.07E
Vidin 17 43.58N 22.51E
Viedma 49 40.45S 63.00W
Vienna see Wien 16
Vienne 12 45.32N 4.54E
Vienne r. 12 47.13N 0.05W
Vientiane see Viangchan 27
Vieques i. 43 18.08N 65.30W
Vierwaldstätter See l. 16 47.10N
8.50E
Vierzon 12 47.14N 2.03E
Vietnam 27 15.00N108.30E
Vigan 27 17.35N120.23E
Vigo 13 42.15N 8.44W
Vijayawāda 25 16.34N 80.40E
Vijosë r. 15 40.39N 19.20E
Vikna i. 18 64.52N 10.57E
Vila 30 17.45S168.19E
Vila da Maganja 53 17.25S 37.32E
Vila Nova do Seles 52 11.24S 14.15E
Vila Real 13 41.17N 7.45W
Vila Velha 45 20.20S 40.17W
Vila Veríssimo Sarmento 52 8.08S
20.38E
Vilhelmina 18 64.37N 16.39E
Vilhena 46 12.40S 60.08W
Viliya r. 17 54.40N 25.30E
Viljandi 20 58.22N 25.30E
Villa Ångela 48 27.34S 60.45W
Villach 16 46.37N 13.51E
Villagarcía 13 42.35N 8.45W
Villahermosa 42 18.00N 92.53W
Villajoyosa 13 38.31N 0.14W
Villa María 48 32.25S 63.15W
Villa Montes 48 21.15S 63.30W
Villanueva de la Serena 13 38.58N
5.48W
Villarrobledo 13 39.16N 2.36W
Villefranche 12 46.00N 4.43E
Villena 13 38.39N 0.52W
Villeneuve 12 44.25N 0.43E
Villeurbanne 16 45.46N 4.54E
Vilnius 17 54.40N 25.19E
Vilyuy r. 23 64.20N126.55E
Viña del Mar 49 33.02S 71.34W
Vincennes 44 38.41N 87.30W
Vindel r. 18 63.54N 19.52E

Vinnitsa 17 49.11N 28.30E
Vire 12 48.50N 0.53W
Vire r. 12 49.20N 0.53W
Virginia 41 47.30N 92.28W
Virginia d. 41 37.30N 79.00W
Virovitica 17 45.51N 17.23E
Vis i. 14 43.03N 16.10E
Visby 19 57.38N 18.18E
Viscount Melville Sd. 38
74.30N104.00W
Viségrad 15 43.47N 19.20E
Viseu 13 40.40N 7.55W
Vishākhapatnam 25 17.42N 83.24E
Viso, Monte mtn. 14 44.38N 7.05E
Vistula r. see Wisla r. 17
Vitebsk 20 55.10N 30.14E
Viterbo 14 42.26N 12.07E
Viti Levu i. 30 18.00S178.00E
Vitim r. 23 59.30N112.36E
Vitoria 13 42.51N 2.40W
Vittoria 14 36.57N 14.21E
Vladimir 20 56.08N 40.25E
Vladivostok 23 43.09N131.53E
Vlorë 15 40.28N 19.27E
Vltava r. 16 50.20N 14.28E
Voghera 14 44.59N 9.01E
Voi 53 3.23S 38.35E
Voiron 12 45.22N 5.35E
Volga r. 21 45.45N 47.50E
Volgograd 21 48.45N 44.30E
Volkhov r. 20 60.15N 32.15E
Vologda 20 59.10N 39.55E
Vólos 15 39.22N 22.57E
Volsk 20 52.04N 47.22E
Volta, L. 50 7.00N 0.00
Volta Redonda 45 22.31S 44.05W
Volterra 14 43.24N 10.51E
Volturno r. 14 41.02N 13.56E
Volzhskiy 21 48.48N 44.45E
Vopnafjördhur town 18 65.46N
14.50W
Vordingborg 19 55.01N 11.55E
Voriai Sporádhes is. 15 39.00N
24.00E
Vorkuta 20 67.27N 64.00E
Voronezh 21 51.40N 39.13E
Voroshilovgrad 21 48.35N 39.20E
Vosges mts. 16 48.10N 7.00E
Voss 19 60.39N 6.26E
Votuporanga 45 20.26S 49.53W
Vouga r. 13 40.41N 8.38W
Voves 12 48.16N 1.37E
Voznesensk 21 47.34N 31.21E
Vranje 52 42.34N 21.52E
Vratsa 15 43.12N 23.33E
Vrbas r. 15 45.06N 17.29E
Vrede 54 27.24S 29.09E
Vršac 17 45.08N 21.18E
Vryburg 54 26.57S 24.42E
Vyazma 20 55.12N 34.17E
Vyazniki 20 56.14N 42.08E
Vyborg 20 60.45N 28.41E
Vyrnwy, L. 8 52.46N 3.30W
Vyshniy-Volochek 20 57.34N 34.23E

W

Wabash r. 41 38.25N 87.45W
Waco 41 31.33N 97.10W
Wad 25 27.21N 66.22E
Waddeneilanden is. 16 53.20N 5.00E
Waddenzee b. 16 53.15N 5.15E
Waddington, Mt. 38 51.30N125.00W
Wadhurst 9 51.03N 0.21E
Wādī Halfā' 51 21.55N 31.20E
Wad Madani 51 14.24N 33.30E
Wager Bay town 39 65.55N 90.40W
Wagga Wagga 37 35.07S147.24E
Wahpeton 41 46.16N 96.36W
Waigeo i. 27 0.55S130.30E
Waihi 29 37.24S175.50E
Waikato r. 29 37.19S174.50E
Waimakariri r. 29 43.23S172.40E
Waimate 29 44.45S171.03E
Waingapu 32 9.30S120.10E
Wainwright 38 70.39N160.00W
Waiouru 29 39.29S175.40E
Waipukurau 29 40.00S176.33E
Wairau r. 29 41.32S174.07E
Wairoa r. 29 39.03S177.25E
Waitaki r. 29 44.56S171.09E
Waitara 29 38.59S174.13E
Waiuku 29 37.15S174.44E
Wajir 53 1.46N 40.05E
Wakatipu, L. 29 45.10S168.30E
Wakayama 28 34.13N135.11E
Wakefield 8 53.41N 1.31W
Wakkanai 26 45.26N141.43E
Walbrzych 16 50.48N 16.19E
Walcha 37 31.00S151.36E
Wales d. 9 52.30N 3.45W
Walgett 37 30.03S148.10E
Walsall 9 52.36N 1.59W
Walton on the Naze 9 51.52N 1.17E
Walvis B. 54 22.55S 14.30E
Walvisbaai 54 22.57S 14.30E
Walvis Bay town see Walvisbaai 54
Wamba r. 52 3.57S 17.15E
Wami r. 53 6.10S 38.50E
Wanaaring 36 29.42S144.14E
Wanaka, L. 29 44.30S169.10E
Wanganella 37 35.13S144.53E
Wanganui 29 39.56S175.00E
Wangaratta 37 36.22S146.20E
Wantage 9 51.35N 1.25W
Wanxian 26 30.52N108.20E
Warangal 25 18.00N 79.35E
Waratah B. 37 38.55S146.04E
Warden 54 27.49S 28.57E
Warialda 37 29.33S150.36E
Wark Forest hills 8 55.06N 2.24W
Warkworth 29 36.24S174.40E
Warley 9 52.29N 2.02W
Warmbad 54 28.26S 18.41E
Warminster 9 51.12N 2.11W
Warracknabeal 36 36.15S142.28E
Warragul 37 38.11S145.55E
Warrego r. 37 30.25S145.18E
Warren Mich. 44 42.31N 83.01W
Warrenpoint 10 54.06N 6.15W
Warri 50 5.36N 5.46E
Warrington 8 53.25N 2.38W
Warrnambool 36 38.23S142.03E

Warsaw see Warszawa 17
Warszawa 17 52.15N 21.00E
Warta r. 16 52.45N 15.09E
Warwick 9 52.17N 1.36W
Warwickshire d. 9 52.13N 1.30W
Washington U.K. 8 54.55N 1.30W
Washington d. 40 47.00N120.00W
Washington D.C. 44 38.55N 77 00W
Wasian 27 1.51S133.21E
Wasior 27 2.38S134.27E
Waswanipi Lac l. 44 49.36N 76.39W
Watchet 9 51.10N 3.20W
Waterbury 44 41.33N 73.03W
Waterford 10 52.16N 7.08W
Waterford d. 10 52.10N 7.40W
Waterloo Iowa 41 42.30N 92.20W
Waterville 10 51.50N 10.11W
Watford 9 51.40N 0.25W
Watson Lake town 38
60.07N128.49W
Wauchope 37 31.27S152.43E
Wausau 41 44.58N 89.40W
Waveney r. 9 52.29N 1.46E
Wâw 51 7.40N 28.04E
Wear r. 8 54.55N 1.21W
Wedmore 9 51.14N 2.50W
Weiden in der Oberpfalz 16 49.40N
12.10E
Weimar 16 50.59N 11.20E
Weissenfels 16 51.12N 11.58E
Welkom 54 27.59S 26.42E
Welland 44 42.59N 79.14W
Welland r. 8 52.53N 0.00
Wellingborough 8 52.18N 0.41W
Wellington N.Z. 29 41.17S174.47E
Wellington d. 29 40.00S175.30E
Wellington Shrops. 9 52.42N 2.31W
Wells 9 51.12N 2.39W
Wells-next-the-Sea 8 52.57N 0.51E
Welshpool 9 52.40N 3.09W
Welwyn Garden City 9 51.48N 0.13W
Wem 8 52.52N 2.45W
Wembere r. 53 4.07S 34.15E
Wenatchee 40 47.26N120.20W
Wensleydale f. 8 54.19N 2.04W
Wentworth 36 34.06S141.56E
Wenzhou 26 28.02N120.40E
Werris Creek town 37 31.20S150.41E
Weser r. 16 53.15N 8.30E
Wessel, C. 34 10.59S136.46E
West Bengal d. 25 23.00N 88.00E
West-Berlin d. 16 52.30N 13.20E
West Bromwich 9 52.32N 2.01W
Western Australia d. 32
24.20S122.30E
Western Isles d. 11 57.40N 7.10W
Western Sahara 50 25.00N 13.30W
Western Samoa 30 13.55S172.00W
West Felton 9 52.49N 2.58W
West Frisian Is. see Waddeneilanden
16
West Germany 16 51.00N 8.00E
West Glamorgan d. 9 51.42N 3.47W
West Linton 11 55.45N 3.21W
Westmeath d. 10 53.30N 7.30W
West Midlands d. 9 52.28N 1.50W
West Nicholson 54 21.06S 29.25E
Weston 27 5.14N115.35E
Weston-Super-Mare 9 51.20N 2.59W
West Palm Beach town 41 26.42N
80.05W
Westport 10 53.48N 9.32W
Westray i. 11 59.18N 2.58W
West Sussex d. 9 50.58N 0.30W
West Virginia d. 41 38.45N 80.30W
West Wyalong 37 33.54S147.12E
West Yorkshire d. 8 53.45N 1.40W
Wetar i. 27 7.45S126.00E
Wetzlar 16 50.33N 8.30E
Wexford 10 52.20N 6.28W
Wexford d. 10 52.20N 6.25W
Weymouth 9 50.36N 2.28W
Whakatane 29 37.56S177.00E
Whangarei 29 35.43S174.20E
Wharfe r. 8 53.50N 1.07W
Wharfedale f. 8 54.00N 1.55W
Wheeling 44 40.05N 80.43W
Whernside mtn. 8 54.14N 2.25W
Whitburn 11 55.52N 3.41W
Whitby 8 54.29N 0.37W
Whitchurch Shrops. 8 52.58N 2.42W
White r. Ark. 41 33.53N 91.10W
White r. Ind. 44 38.29N 87.45W
White r. S.Dak. 40 43.40N 99.30W
Whitehaven 8 54.33N 3.35W
Whitehorse 38 60.41N135.08W
White Nile r. see Abyad, Al Bahr al r.
24
White Sea see Beloye More sea 20
White Volta r. 50 9.13N 1.15W
Whithorn 11 54.44N 4.25W
Whitley Bay 8 55.03N 1.25W
Whitney, Mt. 40 36.35N118.17W
Whitstable 9 51.21N 1.02E
Whitton 8 53.42N 0.39W
Whyalla 36 33.02S137.35E
Wichita 41 37.43N 97.20W
Wichita Falls town 40 33.55N 98.30W
Wick 11 58.26N 3.06W
Wicklow 10 52.59N 6.03W
Wicklow d. 10 52.59N 6.25W
Wicklow Mts. 10 53.06N 6.20W
Widnes 8 53.22N 2.44W
Wien 16 48.13N 16.22E
Wiener Neustadt 16 47.49N 16.15E
Wiesbaden 16 50.05N 8.15E
Wigan 8 53.33N 2.38W
Wight, Isle of 7 50.40N 1.17W
Wigston 9 52.35N 1.06W
Wigton 8 54.50N 3.09W
Wilcannia 36 31.33S143.24E
Wildhorn mtn. 12 46.22N 7.22E
Wildspitze mtn. 16 46.55N 10.55E
Wildwood 44 38.59N 74.49W
Wilhelmshaven 16 53.32N 8.07E
Wilkes-Barre 44 41.15N 75.50W
Willemstad 46 12.12N 68.56W
Williamsport Penn. 44 41.14N 77.00W
Williston L. 38 55.00N126.00W
Willmar 41 45.06N 95.03W
Willmore 54 33.18S 23.28E
Willunga 36 35.18S138.33E

Wilmington Del. 44 39.44N 75.33W
Wilmington N.C. 41 34.14N 77.55W
Wilmslow 8 53.19N 2.14W
Wilson's Promontory c. 37
39.06S146.23E
Wilton 9 51.05N 1.52W
Wiltshire d. 9 51.20N 0.34W
Winam b. 53 0.15S 34.30E
Wincanton 9 51.03N 2.24W
Winchester 9 51.04N 1.19W
Windermere l. 8 54.20N 2.56W
Windhoek 54 22.34S 17.06E
Windsor Ont. 44 42.18N 83.01W
Windsor U.K. 9 51.29N 0.38W
Windward Is. 43 13.00N 60.00W
Windward Passage str. 43 20.00N
74.00W
Winisk r. 39 55.20N 85.20W
Winnebago, L. 44 44.00N 88.25W
Winnipeg 39 49.53N 97.10W
Winnipeg, L. 39 52.45N 98.00W
Winnipegosis, L. 39 52.00N100.00W
Winona Minn. 41 44.02N 91.37W
Winschoten 16 53.07N 7.02E
Winsford 8 53.12N 2.31W
Winslow Ariz. 40 35.01N110.43W
Winston-Salem 41 36.05N 80.05W
Winton 34 22.22S143.00E
Wisbech 9 52.39N 0.10E
Wisconsin d. 41 45.00N 90.00W
Wisconsin Rapids town 41 44.24N
89.55W
Wisla r. 17 54.23N 18.52E
Wismar 16 53.54N 11.28E
Witham r. 8 52.56N 0.04E
Withernsea 8 53.43N 0.02E
Witten 16 51.53N 12.39E
Wittenberge 16 52.59N 11.45E
Witu 52 2.22S 40.20E
Wiveliscombe 9 51.02N 3.20W
Wodonga 37 36.08S146.09E
Woking 9 51.20N 0.34W
Wolfenbüttel 16 52.10N 10.33E
Wolfsburg 16 52.27N 10.49E
Wolin 16 53.51N 14.38E
Wollaston L. 38 58.15N103.30W
Wollongong 37 34.25S150.52E
Wolmaransstad 54 27.11S 25.58E
Wolseley 36 36.21S140.55E
Wolverhampton 9 52.35N 2.06W
Wönsan 26 39.07N127.26E
Wonthaggi 37 38.38S145.37E
Woodbridge 9 52.06N 1.19E
Woodside 37 38.31S146.52E
Wooler 8 55.33N 2.01W
Woomera 36 31.11S136.54E
Woonsocket 44 42.00N 71.31W
Wooroorooka 37 28.59S145.40E
Worcester 9 52.12N 2.12W
Worcester U.S.A. 44 42.16N 71.48W
Workington 8 54.39N 3.34W
Worksop 8 53.19N 1.09W
Worland 40 44.01N107.58W
Worms 16 49.38N 8.23E
Worthing 9 50.49N 0.21W
Worthington Minn. 41 43.37N 95.36W
Wragby 8 53.17N 0.18E
Wrangell 38 56.28N132.23W
Wrangle 8 53.03N 0.09E
Wrath, C. 11 58.37N 5.01W
Wrexham 8 53.05N 3.00W
Wrigley 38 63.16N123.39W
Wroclaw 17 51.05N 17.00E
Wuhan 26 30.37N114.19E
Wuhu 26 31.25N118.25E
Wulian Shan mts. 26 24.27N100.43E
Wuppertal 16 51.15N 7.10E
Würzburg 16 49.48N 9.57E
Wuwei 26 38.00N102.59E
Wuxi 26 31.34N120.20E
Wuzhou 26 23.28N111.21E
Wyandotte 44 42.11N 83.10W
Wyangala Resr. 37 33.58S148.55E
Wye 9 51.11N 0.56E
Wye r. 9 51.37N 2.40W
Wymondham 9 52.34N 1.07E
Wyndham 32 15.29S128.05E
Wyoming d. 40 43.00N108.00W

X

Xai-Xai 54 25.05S 33.38E
Xangongo 52 16.31S 15.00E
Xánthi 15 41.07N 24.55E
Xau, L. 54 21.15S 24.50E
Xiaguan 26 25.33N100.09E
Xiamen 26 24.30N118.08E
Xi'an 26 34.16N108.54E
Xiangfan 26 32.04N112.05E
Xi Jiang r. 26 23.23N113.20E
Xingtai 26 37.04N114.26E
Xingu r. 47 1.40S 52.15W
Xining 26 36.35N101.55E
Xugou 26 34.30N119.26E
Xuzhou 26 34.14N117.20E

Y

Yablonovyy Khrebet mts. 23
53.20N115.00E
Yahuma 52 1.06N 23.10E
Yakima 40 46.37N120.30W
Yakutsk 23 62.10N129.20E
Yallourn 37 38.09S146.22E
Yalong Jiang r. 25 26.35N101.44E
Yaman Tau mtn. 20 54.20N 58.10E
Yamuna r. 25 25.25N 81.50E
Yana r. 23 71.30N136.00E
Yanchuan 26 36.51N110.05E
Yangtze r. see Chang Jiang r. 26
Yanqi 25 42.00N 86.30E
Yantabulla 37 29.33S150.36E
Yantai 26 37.27N121.26E
Yao 28 34.35N135.56E
Yaoundé 52 3.51N 11.31E
Yap i. 30 9.30N138.09E
Yapehe 52 0.10S 24.20E
Yaqui r. 42 27.40N110.30W
Yare r. 9 52.34N 1.45E
Yarkant He r. 25 40.30N 80.55E
Yarlung Zangbo Jiang r. China see
Brahmaputr. r. 25

Yaroslavl 20 57.34N 39.52E
Yarrow r. 11 55.32N 2.51W
Yass 37 34.51S148.55E
Yatakala 50 14.52N 0.22E
Ya Xian 27 18.19N109.32E
Yegorlyk r. 21 46.30N 41.52E
Yegoryevsk 20 55.21N 39.01E
Yegros 45 26.24S 56.25W
Yell i. 11 60.35N 1.05W
Yellowknife 38 62.30N114.29W
Yellow Sea 26 35.00N123.00E
Yellowstone r. 40 47.55N103.45W
Yellowstone L. 40 44.30N110.20W
Yell Sd. 11 60.30N 1.11W
Yelwa 50 10.51N 4.46E
Yemen 24 15.15N 44.30E
Yeovil 9 50.57N 2.38W
Yerbent 22 39.23N 58.35E
Yerevan 21 40.10N 44.31E
Yershov 21 51.22N 48.16E
Yerushalayim 24 31.47N 35.13E
Yeu, Île d' i. 12 46.43N 2.20W
Yeysk 21 46.43N 38.17E
Yibin 26 28.42N104.34E
Yichang 26 30.43N111.21E
Yinchuan 26 38.27N106.18E
Yingtan 26 28.11N116.55E
Yogyakarta 27 7.48S110.24E
Yokadouma 52 3.26N 15.06E
Yokkaichi 28 34.55N136.37E
Yokohama 28 35.27N139.39E
Yokosuka 28 35.18N139.40E
Yola 50 9.14N 12.32E
Yonne r. 12 48.22N 2.57E
York U.K. 8 53.58N 1.07W
York Penn. 44 39.58N 76.44W
Yorkshire Wolds hills 8 54.00N 0.39W
Yorkton 38 51.12N102.29W
Yoshkar Ola 20 56.38N 47.52E
Youghal 10 51.58N 7.51W
Young 37 34.19S148.20E
Youngstown 44 41.05N 80.40W
Yoxford 9 52.16N 1.30E
Yozgat 21 39.50N 34.48E
Ystad 19 55.25N 13.49E
Ythan r. 11 57.21N 2.01W
Yuan Jiang r. Yunnan China see Hong
Hà r. 26
Yucatan Pen. 42 19.00N 90.00W
Yugoslavia 15 44.00N 20.00E
Yukon r. 38 62.35N164.20W
Yukon Territory d. 38
65.00N135.00W
Yuma Ariz. 40 32.40N114.39W
Yumen 26 40.19N 97.12E
Yungera 36 34.48S143.10E
Yvetot 12 49.37N 0.45E

Z

Zaandam 16 52.27N 4.49E
Zacapa 43 15.00N 89.30W
Zacatecas 42 22.48N102.33W
Zadar 14 44.08N 15.14E
Zafra 13 38.25N 6.25W
Zagorsk 20 56.20N 38.10E
Zagreb 14 45.49N 15.58E
Zāgros, Kühhā-ye mts. 24 32.00N
51.00E
Zagros Mts. see Zāgros, Kühhā-ye
mts. 24
Zāhedan 24 29.32N 60.54E
Zaïre 52 2.00S 23.00E
Zaïre r. 52 6.00S 12.30E
Zaječar 15 43.55N 22.15E
Zákinthos i. 15 37.46N 20.46E
Zambezi r. 53 18.15S 35.55E
Zambezi 52 13.30S 23.12E
Zambia 53 14.00S 28.00E
Zamboanga 27 6.55N122.05E
Zamora 13 41.30N 5.45W
Zamość 17 50.43N 23.15E
Záncara r. 13 38.55N 4.07W
Zanzibar 53 6.10S 39.16E
Zanzibar I. 53 6.00S 39.20E
Zapala 49 38.55S 70.05W
Zaporozhye 21 47.50N 35.10E
Zara 21 39.55N 37.44E
Zaragoza 13 41.39N 0.54W
Zárate 49 34.05S 59.02W
Zaraza 46 9.23N 65.20W
Zave 53 17.14S 30.02E
Zaysan, Ozero l. 22 48.00N 83.30E
Zebediela 54 24.19S 29.17E
Zeebrugge 16 51.20N 3.13E
Zeehan 35 41.55S145.21E
Zeerust 54 25.32S 26.04E
Zeila 51 11.21N 43.30E
Zemio 51 5.00N 25.09E
Zeya r. 23 50.20N127.30E
Zêzere r. 13 39.28N 8.20W
Zhangjiakou 26 40.47N114.56E
Zhangzhou 26 24.57N118.32E
Zhanjiang 26 21.10N110.33E
Zhdanov 21 47.05N 37.34E
Zhengzhou 26 34.40N113.38E
Zhitomir 17 50.18N 28.40E
Zhlobin 17 52.50N 30.00E
Zibo 26 36.50N118.00E
Zielona Góra 16 51.57N 15.30E
Zile 20 41.18N 35.52E
Zimatlán 42 16.52N 96.45W
Zimbabwe 54 18.55S 30.00E
Zimnicea 17 43.38N 25.22E
Zinder 50 13.46N 8.58E
Znamenka 21 48.42N 32.40E
Znojmo 16 48.52N 16.05E
Zomba 53 15.22S 35.22E
Zonguldak 21 41.26N 31.47E
Zrenjanin 15 45.22N 20.23E
Zug 16 47.10N 8.31E
Zújar r. 13 38.58N 5.40W
Zumbo 53 15.36S 30.30E
Zunyi 26 27.39N106.48E
Zürich 16 47.23N 8.33E
Zwickau 16 50.43N 12.30E
Zwolle 16 52.31N 6.06E
Zyryanovsk 22 49.45N 84.16E